CHINA
CEO II

CHINA
CEO II

Voices of Experience

FROM

25 TOP EXECUTIVES
LEADING MNCs IN CHINA

JUAN ANTONIO FERNANDEZ

LAURIE ANN UNDERWOOD

WILEY

Cover design: Alicia Beebe and Wiley
Cover images: Portrait and design by Alicia Beebe

Research interns: James Warren, Nikki Pinder

ISBN 978-1-119-58343-1 (paper)
ISBN 978-1-119-58339-4 (ePDF)
ISBN 978-1-119-58321-9 (ePub)

Printed and bound in Singapore by Markono Print Media Pte Ltd
10 9 8 7 6 5 4 3 2 1

I dedicate this book to the China Europe International Business School (CEIBS) on the 25th anniversary of its founding. I also dedicate this book to the wonderful people at CEIBS who helped us during the work on this book. Finally, to my wife, Hanning, and my three sons, Simon, Oscar, and Daniel, who give meaning to my life.

—Dr. Juan Antonio Fernandez

China CEO II *is dedicated to my family—Sydney and Schafer Wilson; Dorothy and Glenn Staley; Matthew, Larry and Sally Underwood—and to my beloved and excellent partner, Eric Desvallees. Their love provided me the power to complete this book. I am also grateful to CEIBS, my alma mater, as well as to Xi'an Jiaotong Liverpool University (International Business School Suzhou) and Sino Associates for the support of my colleagues.*

—Dr. Laurie Ann Underwood

Contents

Foreword

It is my pleasure to endorse *China CEO II*, the latest China business book produced by Professors Juan A. Fernandez and Laurie A. Underwood. Both have worked and lived in China for more than 20 years, which has given them a first-hand, front-row view of the enormous changes that have transformed this county over the past two decades. In the space of time since our year 2000 MBA and EMBA graduates entered the working world, China has moved forward to become a leading global player across many fronts at once—as the world's largest exporter (and most populous nation), with the largest consumer base and the fastest growing one in terms of spending power, and now as a global leader of the digital revolution. Although rapid, China's economic progress has been steady as the nation shifted from serving as the factory of the world to an innovation powerhouse. MNCs in today's China face highly sophisticated consumers, fiercely competitive local players across nearly all industries, and a new population of local digital heroes who are changing the world order and giving China's younger generation a new set of life goals and priorities, as well as a new sense of home-grown pride. Taken together, China's multifaceted economic and social transformation is unique in the history of the world.

This book attempts to give readers a first-hand view into this multifaceted transformation through the lens of in-depth interviews with China CEOs and various experts on China. The 25 interviewees with China CEOs share their personal insights into succeeding in the new China. As a foretaste of what you will learn from of this book, some of the key qualities that the China CEOs deemed essential to success in China include passion and energy, speed of decision-making, clear vision, a shared framework, the ability to empower local teams, and the ability to make tough judgment calls in an environment of constant change and uncertainty.

Before closing, I would like to note two important trends that can be seen when comparing *China CEO II* with the original book published in 2006: the new book includes an increased number of Chinese CEOs and an increased number of women CEOs. Both trends are intensely positive not only for China but for the global business arena. The rise of more Chinese nationals into the top executive positions at MNCs is a positive trend that closely matches the goals of CEIBS. Likewise, the rise of more women into top executive spots in international companies in China is another trend to which CEIBS is deeply committed.

Let me conclude by reminding readers that China's importance in the world is growing—and will continue to grow for decades to come. It is our hope that this book will serve as a bridge, closing the gap between China and the rest of the world by promoting better understanding, deeper collaboration, and more beneficial interactions with multinational companies. The goal of this book is to assist both foreigners working in China and Chinese executives working internationally to better communicate and better cooperate, to the benefit of all.

Dipak Jain, President (European)
and Professor of Marketing, CEIBS

Chapter 1
Why *China CEO II?*

Introduction

Why did we decide to write *China CEO II*? Following the success of our first book—*China CEO*—released in 2006, we have been asked why we wanted to repeat the whole exercise again 14 years later. Why again seek interviews with top executives running large-scale operations for high-profile multinational companies (MNCs) in China? Was there really a need to write a new edition of the same book?

The short answer to this question is: yes. By 2020, the time was right to embark on *China CEO II* for one main reason: China has changed—dramatically. And meanwhile, interest in working in or with China from the rest of the world remains as strong and vibrant as it was in 2006. Thus, the advice given by our interviewees in 2006—detailing how to lead large teams and complex operations for MNCs in China—needed updating.

What we didn't know until we began conducting interviews is whether another China CEO book was needed. Given China's high-profile and rising global presence in both the international business and political arenas during the country's 40 years of reform and opening, perhaps most non-Chinese executives working in or with China already knew how to succeed here. Maybe enough information was available—online and digitally—to offer the resources needed to close cultural gaps and to prevent business mistakes from being made.

"…[M]ultinational companies still grapple with significant challenges when operating in China."

—Authors of
China CEO II

But as soon as we conducted the first interviews for *China CEO II*, we confirmed another compelling reason to write this book: multinational companies still grapple with significant challenges when operating in China. Namely, foreign companies—and the executives running them—continue to face difficulties, including cultural differences between an MNC's home country and China, misunderstandings caused by geographical distance or psychological separation from a company's top executives, and problems caused by variations in standards or misalignments in business communications norms, negotiating styles, or operating procedures. After the first two interviews for the potential new book, we felt affirmed in the value of our endeavor to again gather first-hand information and advice through in-depth interviews with those holding top executive positions at selected high-profile multinational companies with large-scale operations in China. As with the first book, we interviewed only those holding the position of China CEO or the equivalent position in the language of their company. Each of our interviewees had been in his or her position for at least one year at the time of our interview. This time period was essential for us to feel that the challenges detailed and advice given had survived the test of time and that the CEOs' advice will therefore be fully useful to our readers. (Most had been in the role of leading China operations for their company for at least five years.)

China's Boom Since 2006

To help readers to grasp the extremely fast pace of change underway in China today, we offer a snapshot of the giant strides the nation has made in terms of both economic and societal development between the publishing of *China CEO* (in 2006) and *China CEO II* (in 2020). Consider these changes:

In 2006, China was the world's fourth largest economy (after the US, Japan and Germany).[1] In 2018, China was the world's second largest economy[2] (surpassing Japan as of 2010).[3] Some analysts project China to surpass the US as the world's largest economy by 2030 (HSBC).[4] When purchasing power parity is factored in, China has been the world's leading economy since 2016.[5]

---

[1] http://www.aei.org/publication/dynamic-graph-of-the-day-top-ten-countries-by-gdp-1961-to-2017/.
[2] https://www.weforum.org/agenda/2018/04/the-worlds-biggest-economies-in-2018/.
[3] http://www.aei.org/publication/dynamic-graph-of-the-day-top-ten-countries-by-gdp-1961-to-2017/.
[4] https://www.gbm.hsbc.com/insights/growth/the-world-in-2030.
[5] https://www.weforum.org/agenda/2016/12/the-world-s-top-economy-the-us-vs-china-in-five-charts/.

In 2006, China was the world's third-largest exporting nation (after the EU and the US) with exports of US$968 billion.[6] By 2018, China was the globe's leading exporter, with US$2.49 trillion[7] in exports.

Per capita GDP for Chinese citizens went from US$2,099 in 2006[8] to US$10,099 in 2019.[9] This places China above both Mexico (US$9,866) and Bulgaria (US$9,504) in terms of per capita GDP, and close to Russia (US$11,461).[10] And in China's first-tier cities, incomes are far higher. In Shanghai, for example, per capita GDP was over US$20,000 in 2018.[11]

China's cell phone subscriptions went from 34 per 100 Chinese citizens in 2006[12] to 115 per 100 citizens in 2018,[13] reflecting that some users have more than one phone.

China's internet users jumped from 10.5% of the population (2006)[14] to 59.6% by late 2019,[15] 98% of which access the internet by mobile phone.

Economic development tells only part of the story of China's transformation during the years between the writing of our first and second books. Those 14 years also saw the

---

[6] https://wits.worldbank.org/CountryProfile/en/Country/CHN/Year/2006/Summarytext.

[7] CIA. http://www.worldstopexports.com/worlds-top-export-countries/.

[8] World Bank. http://datatopics.worldbank.org/world-development-indicators/.

[9] IMF. http://statisticstimes.com/economy/countries-by-projected-gdp-capita.php.

[10] IMF. http://statisticstimes.com/economy/countries-by-projected-gdp-capita.php.

[11] Shanghai City Government. http://www.china.org.cn/business/2019-01/28/content_74416303.htm.

[12] World Bank. https://data.worldbank.org/indicator/IT.CEL.SETS.P2?locations=CN.

[13] World Bank. https://data.worldbank.org/indicator/IT.CEL.SETS.P2?locations=CN.

[14] https://data.worldbank.org/indicator/IT.NET.USER.ZS?locations=CN.

[15] China Internet Network Information Center (CNNIC) https://www.chinainternetwatch.com/29010/china-internet-users-snapshot/.

country gain significant clout in the international business and diplomatic circles as it changed from a developing to a developed nation.

In terms of political recognition, China also measurably gained stature on the world diplomatic stage since 2006. For example, the country moved from being invited as a Guest Developing Nation to G8 summits in 2008 to hosting the G20 summit in the city of Hangzhou in 2016. In addition, the central government's Belt and Road Initiative, launched in 2013, has caught the world's attention as an ambitious campaign for China to strengthen its diplomatic and trade ties with 64 countries located along the former Silk Road. Another example is the central government's high-profile China International Import Expo (CIIE), first held in 2018 to improve the nation's international image regarding trade practices and to promote the China market globally. Hosted by Chinese President Xi Jinping, the event featured Microsoft's Bill Gates alongside Alibaba's Jack Ma as guests and attracted more than a million attendees from 172 countries, regions, and organizations.[16] And in the global arena of environmental protection, China has, in recent years, emerged as a proactive international participant. For example, immediately after President Donald Trump removed the US from the Paris Agreement in 2017, China strengthened its commitment to the accord. In the months and years that followed, China has been widely seen as stepping into the void created after the exit of the US to become the new world leader in climate change.

In all the ways mentioned above, we as authors recognize that we now live and work in a vastly different China than the one in which we published *China CEO* in 2006. Thus, it was high time to start a new book from scratch, interviewing a new set of current top executives of MNCs in China. Our goal, and our wish for our readers, is to present detailed, relevant, and useful advice gleaned directly from today's China CEOs regarding the most commonly experienced challenges faced by all who lead teams and manage complex operations in China today.

"...[W]e now live and work in a vastly different China than the one in which we published China CEO in 2006. Thus, it was high time to start a new book from scratch."

—**Authors of** *China CEO II*

---

[16] Devan Shira & Associates. Retrieved from https://www.china-briefing.com/news.

Who's in *China CEO II*?

When the interviews conducted for the first and second editions of this book are compared, several very clear differences emerge. First, all 20 of the China CEOs we originally interviewed were male. Additionally, all 20 held citizenship outside China. In fact, only one of the original CEOs had been born a citizen of the PRC but had later received a US passport.

Not so for *China CEO II*. This time, among the 25 China CEOs included in the book—including 7 working for the same companies as the original *China CEO* book—8 were born in China (including the Hong Kong Special Administrative Region), although 3 of these later changed their citizenship. Meanwhile, 4 are women (all of them ethnically Chinese, and three PRC nationals).

The new set of CEO interviewees show more subtle but also important differences from their predecessors: Many of the 20 China CEOs interviewed in 2006 were senior executives nearing the end of their careers. They were very experienced, having worked in many countries, and China was their last step. And many were sent to China to open their company's operations or to expand them significantly. The CEO of L'Oréal China in 2006 described arriving in China with one assistant and a suitcase full of cosmetic samples. The CEO of Siemens in 2006 told us of working out of a Friendship Hotel in Beijing with one secretary. Others told of the extreme pace of expansion many MNCs experienced during the early 2000s. The former China heads of both Carrefour and Coca-Cola, for example, described to us very fast expansion throughout China during that earlier time.

Another clearly visible change is the increase in average working time in China among the new group of CEOs, illustrating the increased recognition among MNCs of the benefits of promoting an executive with extensive prior China experience into the top domestic role. While the initial group of 20 China CEOs had worked in China for an average of five years, the new batch of 25 top executives for China had worked domestically for an average of nearly 15 years (an average of 19 years for Chinese citizens, 10 years for non-Chinese).

> "This time, among the 25 China CEOs included in the book... 8 were born in China... [and] 4 are women"
> —Authors of *China CEO II*

> "While the initial group of 20 China CEOs had worked in China for an average of five years, the new batch of 25 top executives for China had worked domestically for an average of nearly 15 years."
> —Authors of *China CEO II*

And finally, the new set of 25 China CEOs interviewed in 2019 were generally younger than the first set, and most were thus still building their careers. In fact, after meeting with us for this book, interviewee Stéphane Rinderknech, China CEO for L'Oréal, went on to be promoted to a global role within his firm. Shortly before our publishing date, Mr. Rinderknech was named as president and CEO of L'Oréal USA, executive vice president North America, and a member of the group's executive committee. Many of our interviewees commented that, today, the top executive role for China is not generally seen by MNCs as a final career stop for senior executives but more often as a necessary position for an executive to hold before joining a company's top global echelons. This change provides more evidence of the rising importance of China as a key market for MNCs worldwide.

As an expert in the executive recruitment field, Korn Ferry's top China executive, Charles Tseng, acknowledges this trend: "China is clearly becoming a 'must posting' for up-and-coming CEOs. . . . Executives who go to China are on an inside track to take on bigger positions—because of the size of China market, because of the complexity and the recognition that companies and businesses have of the importance of the unique China market to their future business, and because of the tough conditions in China. Tough means that it's not a traditional classic economy. Executives who come here gain a great deal in living through this very different environment."

L'Oréal's Rinderknech describes the new importance a posting in China holds for many MNCs: "For all top talents of L'Oréal, China is a must for their career-building, because this is where you learn so much." After spending "eight fascinating years in this country," Rinderknech leaves these words of wisdom to his successor and other incoming executives taking positions here: "You have to know China from the inside. It's not something that you can theorize. You have to live it; you have to make it work. You have to connect with the Chinese, and you have to understand the way they think. It's an absolute must. You have to go and survive this battle. China is very exciting, and it's very unforgiving."

"China is clearly becoming a 'must posting' for up-and-coming CEOs.... Executives who go to China are on an inside track to take on bigger positions."

—Charles Tseng,
Chairman, Asia Pacific, China, Korn Ferry

"For all top talents of L'Oréal, China is a must for their career-building, because this is where you learn so much.... You have to go and survive this battle. China is very exciting, and it's very unforgiving."

— Stéphane Rinderknech,
CEO, China, L'Oréal

China CEOs Interviewed

Company	HQ	Name	Title	Gender	Nationality
ABB	Switzerland	Chunyuan Gu	Chairman and CEO, China	M	China
AB InBev	Belgium	Frederico Freire	BU President, China	M	Brazil
Bayer	Germany	Celina Chew	President, Greater China	F	Australia (born in Singapore)
Bosch	Germany	Chen Yudong	President, China	M	US (born in China)
Carrefour	France	Thierry Garnier	President/CEO, China; CEO, Asia; Group Vice President	M	France
Coca-Cola	US	Curt Ferguson	President, Greater China and Korea	M	US
IKEA	Sweden	Freda Zhang	Country Commercial VP, China	F	China
Korn Ferry	US	Charles Tseng	Chairman, Asia Pacific	M	Malaysia (born in Singapore)
LEGO	Denmark	Jacob Kragh	General Manager, China	M	Denmark
L'Oréal	France	Stéphane Rinderknech	CEO, China	M	France
Mango	Spain	David Sancho	CEO East Asia and India	M	Spain
Manulife-Sinochem	Canada	Kai Zhang	President and CEO, China	F	US (born in China)
Marriott International	US	Rainer Burkle	Area Vice President, Luxury, Greater China	M	Germany
Maserati	Italy	Alberto Cavaggioni	Managing Director, China	M	Italy
Microsoft	US	Alain Crozier	CEO, Greater China Region	M	France (born in Canada)
NIIT	India	Kamal Dhuper	President, China	M	India
Philips	Holland	Andy Ho	Leader, Greater China	M	Canadian (born in Hong Kong SAR, China)
SAP	Germany	Clas Neumann	Head of Global SAP Labs; Sr. Vice President, Head of Fast-Growth Market Strategy Group	M	Germany

Company	HQ	Name	Title	Gender	Nationality
Scania	Sweden	Mats Harborn	Executive Director, China (also President, European Chamber of Commerce in China)	M	Sweden
Sony	Japan	Hiroshi Takahashi	Chairman and President, China (also Sr. Vice President Sony Corp)	M	Japan
Standard Chartered	UK	Jerry Zhang	Executive Vice Chairman and CEO, China	F	China
Tata Sons*	India	James Zhan	President, China	M	Hong Kong, SAR (born in mainland China)
Udacity	US	Robert Hsiung	Managing Director, China	M	Canada
Victoria's Secret / Lbrands Int'l	US	Arun Bhardwaj	President, Greater China	M	New Zealand (born in India)
Volvo Cars	Sweden	Xiaolin Yuan	President and CEO, Asia Pacific (also Sr. Vice President Volvo Cars Group)	M	China

Holding company of Tata Group

China Experts and Consultants Interviewed

Company	HQ	Name	Title	Gender	Nationality
American Chamber of Commerce, Shanghai	US	Kenneth Jarrett	President	M	US
China Cooperation Fund (underwritten by Goldman Sachs), MTS Systems Corp, Nottingham University Business School, Ningbo	US (UK for NUBS)	Kenneth Yu	Advisor, Board Member, Advisor (respectively) (also: former President, 3M Greater China)	M	Singapore (born in Hong Kong, SAR, China)
Community Center Shanghai	China	Zhen Zeng	Executive Director	F	China
Economist Corporate Network	UK	Mary Boyd	Director, Shanghai	F	Canadian
McKinsey & Company	Global	Jonathan Woetzel	Senior Partner (also Director, McKinsey Global Institute)	M	US

Note: In some cases, the China CEOs and experts listed in the two charts changed job positions or companies after the interviews were completed. The comments and quotations in this book reflect the views they held at the time of the interview.

Infrastructure Improvement, China Style

When asked to share an example that illustrates the speed of change that is now the new normal in China, Kenneth Yu likes to describe how Beijing's Sanyuan Bridge was rebuilt in 43 hours in 2015. He explains: "Imagine a 200-meter-long overpass built along a six-lane highway over the ring road leading to the international airport. When the original overpass became too old, the government faced a problem: The ring road is so busy, you cannot stop it for half year to fix it." The problem was solved with China-style speed. "You know how they did it? Go on YouTube and type in 'Sanyuan Bridge replacement' to see it."[17] Yu promises that what readers will find will shock them. "The government replaced that whole section of bridge in less than 43 hours." The method, Yu says, went like this: "On Friday evening, they stopped traffic. Then, they quickly dismantled the old bridge. Then they slid the new bridge in. I am talking about something that is 150 meters long, six lanes. This is humungous. What do you mean, 'slide it in'? Actually, they built the new bridge on the road parallel to the old bridge. There were about 1,500 people working there. They dismantled the old bridge, slid in the new one, put asphalt on top, and Monday morning they started using it. Now, that's what I call speed."

Front-Line CEO Analysis: China Then and Now

From the preceding list, one interviewee was included in both editions of the books. We were extremely pleased to include Kenneth Yu in both editions. In 2006, Yu was China CEO of 3M; in 2020, he was a board chairman and academic, business, and financial advisor to several business funds and organizations (see the chart on page 8). Given his previous and present professional roles, we chose him as an excellent source to comment on the key changes in China pertaining to successful MNCs. In the rest of Chapter 1, we recap Yu's six keys to success for executives running international companies in today's China.

The first key to success from Yu was to recognize that "*both Chinese businessmen and consumers are getting much more sophisticated.*"

[17] https://www.businessinsider.com/time-lapse-bridge-gets-built-in-43-hours-2015-11.

MINI-CASE 2

Air Quality Improvement, China Style

For a second example of China-style city planning that he likes to share, Kenneth Yu gives insight into the recent transformation of air quality in Beijing. Back in 2015, the city suddenly became infamous worldwide for serious air pollution levels. International news media reported on the city's "off-the-charts" levels of PM2.5 (exceeding the 600 level at times), creating "air-pocolypse" conditions that appalled the public inside and outside China.

Fast-forward to 2019, and a different scenario is seen. In March 2019, the United Nations Environment Program (UNEP) chose Beijing as a model city for other developing nations, mainly because the metropolis had reduced a range of different air pollutants by 25% to 83%. One UNEP report praises the city with these words: "In just five years, from 2013 to 2017, fine particle levels in Beijing and the surrounding region fell by 35% and 25% respectively. No other city or region on the planet has achieved such a feat."[18] The UNEP went on to recognize the city for initiatives that included industrial restructuring, restrictions on coal-fired boilers, and a shift toward cleaner domestic fuels.

For those living and working in Beijing, the change has been extremely welcomed. Says Yu: "Lately, in Beijing, the sky is blue, and traffic is not as heavy. It is hard to believe, but it's true." To explain this remarkably speedy improvement, Yu points to ambitious government projects, such as the ongoing relocation of many industries outside Beijing. He clarifies: "In order to solve the issue of traffic jams and the pollution, the government is in the process of moving virtually all the major SOEs formerly in Beijing to the city of Xiong'An in Hebei Province—a move of 200 kilometers." He continues: "They also moved much of the government for the city of Beijing to the city of Tongzhou, outside of Beijing." And finally, Beijing also relocated most of the steel mills and heavy industry formerly within the city limits to outside—mainly to Henan Province and the outskirts of Hebei Province. Yu concludes: "That's the type of change that takes place in China. You cannot do this in other countries, that's for sure. In China, it's not just about speed; it's about real change."

He clarifies: "I am talking about customers, about suppliers, about competitors. Chinese people are not just getting smarter but also getting a lot more sophisticated. This is one of the major changes."

For MNCs, this shift in mindset creates both advantages and disadvantages. "This means more sophisticated, high-technology products can find their customers. That's nice. But

[18] UN Environmental Program. https://wedocs.unep.org/bitstream/handle/20.500.11822/27645/airPolCh_EN.pdf?sequence=1&isAllowed=y.

don't forget that Chinese customers are no longer just buying 'good enough' products or accepting whatever is available. They can afford to pay, but they also want to have value for the money they spend. The bottom line, my fellow MNC CEOs, is: When you come to China, don't assume there are gold nuggets waiting for you to pick them up. You gotta be good, because your competitors are good. You gotta be good to earn your bread!"

"When you come to China, don't assume there are gold nuggets waiting for you to pick them up. You gotta be good, because your competitors are good."

—Kenneth Yu,
advisor, CCF & MTS

The second critical key to success is to recognize that the main driver transforming China's business environment over the past 13 years has been *the rapid rise of domestic Chinese competitors*. To MNCs in China, he says: "Today, Chinese competitors are more challenging than non-Chinese competitors. In fact, they are actually creating more pressure on foreign enterprises."He reminds MNCs that this development, in which local competitors gain ground, has previously occurred elsewhere in Asia. "This is not new. Look at Japan; look at Korea. In the 1950s and 60s, who were the tech providers in these countries? MNCs. But in Japan today, it's all Japanese. In Korea today, it's all Korean. So what we see in China is not something very new. History is repeating itself." The challenge, he emphasizes, is that for many MNCs, China remains a key market for the company's future growth. Success, then, increasingly depends on beating newly powerful local competitors in their own home courts.

Third, Yu notes that *local employees have also become "much more effective and sophisticated."* He explains the change: "They know more, they learn fast. And over these past two decades, there are many well-educated Chinese students coming from overseas and from domestic Chinese universities." And today, Yu cautions, Chinese graduates of top domestic schools are not necessarily interested in working for MNCs. "Graduates from China's 'Ivy League' universities are now supporting not just the MNCs but also the state-owned enterprises. And these graduates are good; they are not like 15 years ago, when the last book was written. Things have changed." What does that mean for China CEOs of foreign companies? "MNC leadership: you have to recognize that on the positive side, there are a lot more resources for you to deploy. But on the negative side, your competitors are also getting these talents."

Fourth, *the pace of China's evolution has picked up speed* over the past 13 years. Yu notes: "This one is obvious—everyone sees it but sometimes we forget it. That is, the speed of change." He advises incoming foreign managers to observe the rampant growth and success of WeChat, of Alipay, and of China's high-speed trains, as well as studying the rapid expansion of electric vehicles. "Look at the building of highways and infrastructure in China. The country is making changes so fast and doing things so quickly that the speed often scares people."

Yu also points to *a new entrepreneurial spirit* that has taken root in China since 2006. Yu calls this new mindset "the new culture of risk-taking throughout the populace." He explains: "What do I mean by that? This is really a cultural change." He uses himself as an example to explain the shift in thinking: "Although I was born and grew up in Hong Kong, I am ethnically Chinese. My parents and grandparents were born in mainland China. I was brought up with that influence. We were taught to be careful, to take our time." Today, as an ethnic Chinese, he feels a new mindset taking root. "In today's world, you have to be fast. In China, the environment has created this new culture of 'You gotta do it!' And: 'Don't wait until everything is proven or approved. Just do it!' And: 'If you have to make changes along the way, we'll do it later.'"

Fifth, Yu says that *China's new technology companies*—including Alibaba, Tencent, and Baidu—*follow this "just do it" mindset.* "These are fantastic companies that have grown at breakneck speed because they are willing to roll the dice. They are willing to take the risk." And following the rise of the domestic tech companies, Yu says, other private companies and even SOEs are following suit today. "It's not just them." In fact, the culture of entrepreneurialism has roots in China's changing political environment, he says. "This culture of risk-taking probably originated from the leadership in Beijing." Yu mentions that, under Premier Zhu Rongji, China invested heavily in expanding its infrastructure—an investment that has now paid off. Under Zhu, Yu says, the Chinese leadership had the "foresight" to fund ambitious infrastructure projects, such as Shanghai's second ring road, and expansions to the high-speed rail and maglev transportation systems. He adds: "I don't think Zhu Rongji or the central

"In today's world, you have to be fast. In China, the environment has created this new culture of 'You gotta do it!' And: 'Don't wait until everything is proven or approved. Just do it!' And: 'If you have to make changes along the way, we'll do it later.'"

—**Kenneth Yu,**
advisor, CCF & MTS

government leadership expected that Shanghai would grow to what it is now. But they were willing to take the risk." Today, an adventurous new mindset now permeates Chinese society. He adds: "This is the 'new normal' among Chinese entrepreneurs: they are willing to take the risk. Some fail, some collapse—no question. But if you look, there are winners all over the place."

In his final key message to MNCs, Yu emphasizes his confidence in the continuing importance of China going forward. "The Chinese economy is growing way beyond the point of no return; there's no going back," he comments. "As the GDP grows bigger, it would be naive to expect that the country can keep on growing at 6 or 7%. It just won't happen. But on a PPP basis, China is already the world's biggest economy. At current prices, it's number two after the US and—depending on whose prediction you look at—it's only a matter of years until the Chinese economy, even at current prices, will catch up with the US."

His advice? Go with the flow. "Quite frankly, I don't think this is such a big deal. The US has 330 millions people; China has 1.4 billion—four times the population. Plus a track record of building the economy at a break-neck rate. So what's the big surprise? It should happen." He advocates growing with China rather than competing against it. "I would not worry about it. On the other hand, I would think about this: What are the opportunities for MNCs?" He ends with a word of optimism for those MNC executives who do their homework, integrate well, and follow the right strategies in China: "The Chinese economy is so big—it's big enough for everyone. I am not sure whether we have enough big companies in the world to come and share with China's future economic growth."

In this book, our goal is to present the opportunities for MNCs to share in China's future economic growth, as described to us by our China CEO interviewees. It is our deepest hope that the information we share in this book—the hard-won advice, the front-line strategies, and the detailed insights collected directly from experienced top executives for MNCs in China as well as from veteran consultants and advisors—will serve our readers well. We wish you all a fruitful read and the very best of luck in your own China adventures.

Chapter 2
Prerequisites for China CEOs

One of my biggest learnings when I came to China was to understand that I had to relearn what I knew. I had to relearn the way I was managing because culturally, China, as compared to Europe, has plenty of nuances and differences that you need to really understand. And this takes time.

—**David Sancho,** CEO, East Asia & India, Mango

You need an open personality—a personality which is willing to learn. Because you will have to unlearn a lot of things and learn a lot of things in China, to be able to succeed here.

—**Kamal Dhuper,** President, China, NIIT

INSIDE CHAPTER 2

Must-Have Qualities for Foreign CEOs in China

Foreign Managers' Top Mistakes in China

Shifting from Foreign to Local CEOs

Qualities Needed for Today's China CEOs (Either Foreign or Chinese Nationals)

Summary of Tips

Introduction

What qualities do the current executives leading MNCs in to-day's China need to be successful? This was among the first questions we posed to each of our interviewees in collecting data for *China CEO II*. For a glimpse into the complexity of taking a top executive post for MNCs in China, Jonathan Woetzel, senior partner at McKinsey & Company, offers this summary: "Operations are still often quite profitable [for MNCs in China]. Generally speaking, multinationals are seeing the same margins in China as they do globally. But the bar to achieve that performance continues to go up." He names several specific challenges that China CEOs tend to face, including "the high level of investment that's required, the level of localization of management needed, and the capacity to address regulatory challenges that are China-specific—whether it's data sovereignty or food safety." Other CEOs mentioned the following key challenges: grappling with the overall speed of change in China, the size and complexity of the domestic market, and the impact of disruptive technologies. To manage in such a difficult operating environment, the China CEO needs several qualities. The rest of this chapter summarizes the qualities identified by our interviewees.

When we asked interviewees to name which characteristics are most needed to run large-scale operations for high-profile MNCs in China, significant differences emerged between the answers received earlier (for *China CEO* in 2006) and now (for *China CEO II*). There are two reasons for the difference. First, market conditions in China have evolved. Second, the characteristics of the CEOs leading MNCs in China have also changed. Consider that (as mentioned in Chapter 1) all 20 of the original "China CEOs" interviewed in 2006 were foreigners—they did not hold Chinese passports (only one among these was originally born in China but had later changed nationality). Thus, the qualities required to run large operations for MNCs in China were, by default, a mindset and skillset needed by foreigners. Among the 25 China CEOs interviewed this time, 5 are PRC nationals, and another 3 were originally PRC citizens who later changed their citizenship. Thus, the discussion has expanded to cover the skills needed by two groups of China CEOs—native Chinese and foreigners—each requiring a different skillset and mindset in order to lead large-scale MNCs in China.

Thus, Chapter 2 addresses the qualities needed by both non-Chinese and Chinese CEOs of MNCs in China, with some interesting differences identified. We start with advice for foreign top executives. The following section discusses the qualities China CEOs identified as must haves for non-Chinese business executives to be successful in leading large-scale operations for MNCs in today's China.

Must-Have Qualities for Foreign CEOs in China

Quality 1: Humility and Cultural Sensitivity

Being humble and also being culturally respectful were two of the qualities most frequently named as necessary for foreign CEOs in China. Non-Chinese interviewees for this book commented that although humility is not necessarily a quality widely exhibited by top-tier business leaders, such a mindset is needed by those running China-based operations.

David Sancho, Mango's top executive for China, voices a viewpoint represented among many China CEOs: "One of my biggest learnings when I came to China was to understand that I had to relearn what I knew. I had to relearn the way I was managing because, culturally, China as compared to Europe has plenty of nuances and differences that you need to really understand. And this takes time." How long? "It took me more than two years to understand how things were done in China," says Sancho.

Sancho describes his initial mindset in this way: "I came here as a young manager. I was 35 years old—pretty young, fresh, and very impatient. I was used to the European style of managing, which was: 'I tell [you] things and you execute.'" Eventually, Sancho realized that this approach was failing in China. "At

"At the beginning, I was thinking that they [the local team] needed to follow what I knew. This was a totally wrong approach."

—**David Sancho,**
CEO, East Asia & India,
Mango

"Chinese people know their country now is much better than it was. The result: we [Chinese] now have the world's fastest high-speed trains, and more electric vehicles than the US. Chinese are proud. They don't like to be looked down on."

—**Kenneth Yu,**
advisor, CCS & MTS

the beginning, I was thinking that they [the local team] needed to follow what I knew. This was a totally wrong approach. The best learning was to understand that I had to learn myself how the things were done in China and to adapt myself to the culture and to the country to make my managerial style successful."

Kenneth Yu, former China CEO of 3M, agrees that the right strategy for incoming foreign managers is humbly acknowledging one's initial lack of first-hand knowledge of China, along with showing respect for and interest in Chinese culture. He advises: "For non-Chinese, another important attribute is [to] show genuine respect for diverse cultures, regardless of your own beliefs." He warns Western executives not to show insensitivity even when values clash. "Don't insult the Chinese—not about IPR, or the one-party system. And especially not in front of their peers." He advises Westerners to be mindful of the new—and in many ways justified—national pride that many Chinese feel today. Yu notes: "Chinese people know their country now is much better than it was. The result: we [Chinese] now have the world's fastest high-speed trains, and more electric vehicles than the US. Chinese are proud. They don't like to be looked down on." One aspect of culture that Yu says continues to confuse Westerners is the Chinese tendency to avoid expressing disagreement or dissatisfaction directly. As he notes: "No one will tell you, but they feel it [if you insult China]." They may show their unhappiness indirectly and express unhappiness long after the original incident—leading Western managers to misunderstand.

Another aspect of humility, as Frederico Freire of AB InBev stresses, is the importance of listening. He notes: "Listen and understand the context before you make final decisions. This, for me, was key." He adds: "Someone who is not really open to learn—to listen, to understand—is not going to work well in China. They will fail." But for some top executives, this advice is not easy to take. Freire states: "It's something so simple, but it is not necessarily true that leaders listen." Listening, he clarifies, does not indicate weak decision-making, but instead wise decision-making. "Of course, at the end of the day, we need to make the tough calls. I'm here to make the calls. But I never make the call without understanding first."

Foreign CEO Profile: Thierry Garnier (Carrefour) on Professional Commitment to China

In this book, the foreign China CEOs interviewed agreed that leaders need to make a tremendous personal and professional investment to educate themselves on China in order to succeed in China. Regarding the amount of commitment needed to learn Mandarin, Thierry Garnier, Carrefour's top executive in China, offers an inspiring role model. He shares the sacrifice he made in order to achieve a high level of Chinese language ability: "I took four to five hours per week of Chinese class for seven years. Not for one year—for seven years." Today, he has passed the Chinese education system's official HSK exam at level 5 and was planning (at the time of our interview) to take the level 6 exam—the most rigorous test, for which Chinese university students must prepare well in order to pass. At this level of ability, Garnier is able to deliver professional speeches and attend government negotiations held entirely in Chinese. Garnier says: "I continue to take lessons because I want to continue improving my [Chinese] characters." He describes the level of sacrifice needed to gain a working knowledge of Mandarin as "a physical engagement."

Garnier says mastering Mandarin has been a critical success factor in his career in China: "This is a key factor if you want to succeed as a foreigner." Many professional opportunities have opened to him because of his Chinese skills, he says. "By speaking Chinese, I have developed a professional network. I don't spend my time only with foreigners; I try to spend a larger part of my time with Chinese." He explains that he has developed a broad social network of Chinese friends and contacts in both his professional and personal spheres. In this way, he has made impressive connections, including developing a friendship with top executives at Alibaba and Tencent. Garnier says: "I know every retail CEO. We send each other our vacation pictures on WeChat. It's a personal relationship. It's a huge value. And this comes from speaking Chinese, from being integrated into the Chinese community."

Kamal Dhuper, the top executive of NIIT for China, advises foreign managers coming to China to prepare to spend time and energy educating themselves on important aspects of Chinese culture. He says: "There are certain nuances of Chinese culture which most foreigners don't know. So, understanding of culture is an important first step." And learning about Chinese culture requires an open, humble, and willing mindset. "You need an open personality—a personality which is willing to learn. Because you will have to unlearn a lot of things and learn a lot of things in China to be able to succeed here."

"You need an open personality—a personality which is willing to learn. Because you will have to unlearn a lot of things and learn a lot of things in China to be able to succeed here."

—Kamal Dhuper,
President, China, NIIT

Kenneth Jarrett, president of the American Chamber of Commerce in Shanghai, identifies the "ability to lead cross-cultural teams" as a critical skill for non-Chinese CEOs. "Whoever is leading the operation here would have to understand what's different about the Chinese workforce, what's different about China." One of the biggest and most challenging differences, he adds, is that norms regarding "face" can make it difficult for top executives to solicit the views of Chinese staff members during meetings. Jarrett has noted this issue in his own organization: "I see it here: if we have a staff meeting, at the senior level, we have now expats and locals, and the expats tend to be the most talkative. Then, after the meeting, we have to go around to all of the local staff and ask them what they really think because they did not say much during the meeting." He says not finding a way to hear from the local team is a mistake. "For an executive, it would be a mistake to overlook those informed views. You have to spend a bit extra time to hear from the local side."

To ensure that foreign top management team members can quickly start working effectively in China, Kenneth Yu advises MNCs to choose people with prior overseas experience. This strategy goes a long way toward guaranteeing cultural sensitivity and humility: "If you are sending someone to China to be a CEO, previous experience in other international subsidiaries for international assignment—whether it is in Western Europe or South America or in other part of Asia—will help. This ensures that the person has exposure to a non-home culture—the person has already been baptized on how to adapt to a different culture."

Quality 2: Respect "Face" and *Guanxi*

Among specific cultural elements to be aware of, most China CEOs mentioned the well-known but still impactful societal norms related to *guanxi* and "face." NIIT's Kamal Dhuper names "face" as the most important cultural aspect for incoming foreign managers to understand. According to Dhuper: "To Chinese, losing face is very embarrassing. So, how you give feedback, how you ensure that he doesn't lose face in front of people or in front of you, is important." While the concept of face exists in nearly all cultures, Dhuper explains that many Westerners or Asian outside China misunderstand the level of importance awarded to face in China. He advises that respecting and protecting "face" "makes a lot of difference in the motivation and morale" of Chinese team members—which can directly impact behavior. "Understanding cultural nuances is important."

Charles Tseng, Korn Ferry's top executive for China, argues that the most important differences between Chinese and Western managers and teams today stem from basic cultural differences. He explains: "In Greek Socratic culture, it was considered a good thing to come together to argue. And the more logical, stronger argument held sway." Tseng says this tradition runs counter to traditional Chinese societal norms. "Chinese don't have this tradition; for us, conflict is not a very good thing." The reason has to do with protecting "face." "We like to start with agreement and from the agreement point, we approach the areas where we disagree—to feel each other out. For a Western Judeo-Christian context, that way is too slow, too indirect, not practical. But in a Chinese environment, starting immediately with the point of disagreement and deciding that whoever can hammer it out, will win—this doesn't work." Thus, modern business discussions are still impacted by long-standing traditional social norms. One of the biggest misunderstandings, he says, comes when Chinese remain silent during a business meeting, in order to save the face for the speaker or themselves. "Westerners will then take silence as agreement, but in a Chinese context, silence doesn't necessarily mean agreement. Chinese silence might mean: 'I respect you, but I still have my own view.'" Mango's David Sancho is one foreign top executive who has learned the importance of face when leading his local team: "It's really important how you empower people, how you take care of your managers in China, and how you give face. In Europe, the face issue is not so common."

Frederico Freire, AB InBev's head of China, has worked to diminish one aspect of face within his China-based team by

"Westerners will then take silence as agreement, but in a Chinese context, silence doesn't necessarily mean agreement. Chinese silence might mean: 'I respect you, but I still have my own view.'"

—Charles Tseng,
Chairman, Asia Pacific, Korn Ferry

encouraging team members to voice disagreement. "It's difficult for Chinese to say no. But I have seen, in our company in the last ten years, a big transformation. What I saw ten years ago is not what I see nowadays." As a result, he says, his discussions with his team are richer and more informative than they were when he first arrived in China. "When I first came here, everybody agreed with me. But that did not necessarily mean they would do what they said." As a result, many misunderstandings occurred. Today, Freire has convinced his team to speak out, especially the younger employees. "I see the young talents; they are much more open to say no. . . . I see within our organization an environment in which we have debates, we have some disagreements. The Chinese employees, I do see that they are changing. This is pretty much aligned with our 'DPC initiative'—Dream, People, and Culture principles—where we incentivize a culture of openness and informality."

The other important cultural aspect non-Chinese should understand and respect, China CEOs said, is *guanxi*. As NIIT's Dhuper explains: "The second most important cultural aspect, after face, is *guanxi*—personal relationships. That is true at every level of a society. Interaction with your immediate team, your business partners, your customers, the government, or academics. Relationships are important." Dhuper adds: "It takes a lot of time to develop. First you have to be genuine, you have to open up, and you have to show interest in the other side—whether it's your customer or a prospect. You have to understand what's important to them. You have to be genuine and open." How can someone build *guanxi*? Dhuper recommends socializing over meals. "In Chinese culture, eating and drinking together goes a long way. If you do that more with your people, with your partners, with your customers, bonding happens, relationships get built." He sums up by explaining that, in China, relationships can be more important than contracts because it is understood that the relationship forms a foundation for cooperation. "China is all about relationships. In business, the spirit beyond the contract is important. And that spirit behind the contract depends on how well you are able to build relationships."

Freire agrees that building relations after hours, especially while eating and drinking, is a useful method of building *guanxi*. "If I could mention one big difference, it is that relationships are key in China. Relationships build the trust." He says the way trust is strengthened in China requires more time and effort than is needed in his home country of Brazil. In China, the best method, Freire says, is to spend after work time with team members—especially over meals: "I see in China that the ways of building the relationship is different. Everything in China is at a table—over a meal, over a few beers. You need to create your connections, create your bonds, not only in the meeting room or in the work environment, but also outside the work environment. And Chinese do that with food, with beer." He adds: "There are beer-lovers in China!" In fact, he says that part of a CEO's duties includes spending one's after-hours time with the team, building rapport and trust. "That means a lot of talks and conversations."

David Sancho of Mango agrees that *guanxi* remains an important factor for leaders, both in leading internal teams and in managing external relations: "In China, what I learned is that you need to understand how things are done and that relationships matter—the famous *guanxi*. Not only with government, with other institutions, but also across the teams." Advisor Kenneth Yu also stresses that *guanxi* extends to creating close bonds within your team. He advises: "Treat your people nicely. This shows respect and makes it more fun. Speaking of fun: Take them for karaoke sometimes. People in the office won't look at you badly. It's OK to have a bit of fun sometimes."

Charles Tseng of Korn Ferry emphasizes that for Western business leaders, taking time and expending the effort to understand Chinese culture is the main critical success factor. In English-speaking areas of Asia, such as Hong Kong and Singapore, newly arrived foreigners can jump immediately into their work. He says. "They can actually land and, on day one and day two, can be effective because they speak English." But while these Western hubs are attuned to international managers for linguistic and historical reasons, this is not the case

"If I could mention one big difference, it is that relationships are key in China. Relationships build the trust."

—Frederico Freire,
BU President, China,
AB InBev

"In China... relationships matter—the famous guanxi. Not only with government, with other institutions, but also across teams."

—David Sancho,
CEO, East Asia & India,
Mango

in mainland China. Tseng warns foreigners coming to China that, "Shanghai is a Chinese hub. That means the cultural context is Chinese. We go back to the strong Confucian related principles of trustworthiness, loyalty, filial piety, respect, reliability, trust. In the Chinese framework, these values bring people together."

Quality 3: Flexibility with Firmness

Another aspect that non-Chinese CEOs—especially Westerners—need in China is a degree of flexibility, but wisely coupled with firmness, at times. This requirement not only stems from Chinese culture but is also required by the status of China's economic development. Kai Zhang, Manulife's top executive for China, explains: "One difference in the operating environment in China is that, in the US and Canada, there are more stable operating procedures. While in China, as well as some of the emerging markets, operational standards are not that well established. So, you need to establish standards and actually build the company culture from the basics. That's the difference in the operating environment: one is more mature and the other is still developing."

"We see some [foreign] CEOs who are stubborn and locked in their mindset.... A lot of times, rigidity happens at a multinational level. Then, they miss some opportunities [in China]."

— Alain Crozier,
CEO, Greater China Region, Microsoft

Alain Crozier, Microsoft's head of China, echoes this sentiment, explaining: "We see some [foreign] CEOs who are stubborn and locked in their mindset. . . . We need people who have a very open mindset and can make sure that if there is a good idea somewhere, you can take it in and make it happen. A lot of times, rigidity happens at a multinational level. Then, they miss some opportunities [in China]." The best attitude, he advises, is an open mind along with open eyes and open ears. He explains: "Others, on the other hand, are looking at what's coming out of China and are ready to take those ideas and bring them home in a heartbeat. In MNCs, you still have a group of stubborn people, but you also have some very agile and flexible people who are learning—because a lot of things are happening in China."

One area where adaptation to Chinese norms is recommended, according to China CEOs, is recognizing the Chinese norm of blurring work and on-work life. AB InBev's Freire says that the division between work and non-work is "not so clear in China," producing a lifestyle that "is a difference for those of us coming from the West." He clarifies: "In the West, we really have this work-life balance. . . . The idea that 'I need time for my family.' But in China, it's tough to see these boundaries between work and family." He adds: "Chinese are workaholics. They are very diligent with their work ethic. They work very hard, so you need to adapt yourself to this culture."

Alternatively, some China CEOs mentioned that establishing a flat corporate culture was one area where they could bring global norms to China to gain efficiencies and foster collaboration. Jacob Kragh, LEGO's top China executive, explains how he has instilled his company's non-hierarchical culture into local offices: "When we are in the office, we have an open space. Nobody has an office—not even me, as the CEO. I sit along the rows like everybody else." For many Chinese employees, he says, this lack of hierarchy is "just completely ground-breaking." Kragh explains: "We all have this activity-based work in which you come in the morning and you find where to sit. For a lot of people in China, that's a very radical approach to work. It is a Nordic culture we're bringing from LEGO. It is a breath of fresh air for a lot of Chinese colleagues." Despite the respect for hierarchy in China's underlying culture, some domestic employees do quickly adjust to the flat structure. "There are Chinese talent who would not want to work with LEGO because they prefer a more traditional hierarchy. But we definitely feel that there [are] a lot of Chinese who find [it] a quite appealing way of working as well."

Frederico Freire brought a similar transformation to the corporate culture when he took the top China post at AB InBev. "The first time I came to China, [the Chinese team] was not used to crossing the halls with your CEO or having your president talk to you or shake hands with you. So, breaking this hierarchy was interesting for me." Initially, because hierarchy was important to his Chinese team members, he found that it was difficult for managers to ask for assistance or collaboration from colleagues who did not directly report to them. "This, for me, was a big difference. Because we, as a company, work in an open environment. We don't have walls; we have everybody in a big, big room with tables attached to each other. Communication goes very easily." Thus, in this area, Freire adapted the working culture in China to his company's global culture.

In addition to ensuring that certain key aspects of the company's global culture are continued in the MNCs' China operations, foreign CEOs also emphasized the importance of maintaining unbending adherence to certain important international standards and ethical guidelines. The China CEOs we interviewed emphasized that part of their role as leaders is to clarify which aspects of their organizations can and should be adapted to China and which should not. One key responsibility is establishing and rigidly maintaining codes of conduct, ethics, standards, and even certain practices and policies.

One such China CEO is Mango's David Sancho, who explains that one of his first duties upon taking his position in 2011 was to instill the values and standards of his company into operations in China. In some ways, he says his company originally localized its operations in China too quickly. "It was a mistake, back then. We didn't really train our own people to understand 'What is Mango?'"

Quality 4: Long-Term Commitment to China

Advisor Kenneth Yu says the attitude of a foreign manager toward China is also critically important to his or her success as a business leader. As a newcomer, a foreign manager will be analyzed by local team members in terms of the sincerity of their attitudes toward working in or with China. Yu says Chinese colleagues will wonder: "What is he looking for? Is this assignment a stepping-stone for [moving] up the hierarchy in the organization? Or is he really serious about coming to China and doing a good job, [understanding] the people, and [fulfilling] his fiduciary responsibility?" Yu says even big MNCs make mistakes in this regard. "Some of the people sent over are clearly not the right people. The trouble is, once they are here, you have to put up with them for a certain period of time."

Carrefour's top executive in China, Thierry Garnier, also feels strongly that a long-term commitment to working in China is a key prerequisite for a successful career here: "There are different kinds of foreigners in China. There are foreigners who stay longer in order to learn and to invest part of their lives in China. You need to say: 'I agree to consider China as part of my life.'" He adds: "A foreign manager must be physically integrated in Chinese society."

Microsoft's Alain Crozier agrees, advising foreign CEOs of large operations in China not only to adapt to China but also to find a way to enjoy the environment of change and constant uncertainty. He says: "You need to adapt—adaptability is important. And there is no recipe for China. You just need, at some point, to be able to say: 'I can feel good here.' You better very quickly understand it and really like it. You can't force yourself to like it; that's not the way it works."

Quality 5: Language Skills

Regarding the question of Chinese language skills, foreign CEOs without Chinese language skills (perhaps not surprisingly) tended to consider learning Mandarin to be "optional," while those foreigners who had made the significant effort to gain fluency in Mandarin deemed it far more important. Frederico Freire of AB InBev expresses a common viewpoint among those not speaking fluently: "Speaking Chinese is not a must, but it's of course a barrier. If I would choose between the language and the culture, the most important would be understanding the culture." He does describe hardships caused by the language gap: "Of course, I have had the situation, a few times, of meeting someone who works for the company and doesn't speak any English. And I myself do not have a good conversation level in Chinese. So, we sit in front of each other and we cannot talk. This is frustrating." Still, he maintains that cultural understanding is more significant. "More [important] than the language barrier is the cultural understanding. The cultural barrier is much bigger than that. And if you don't get to understand their culture—what triggers their emotions, what triggers their engagement—even if you have the language, you don't get things done."

When asked if language is important for foreign managers in China, Kenneth Yu, former 3M China CEO, answers: "Yes and no. We have to accept reality: most MNCs don't have enough Chinese speakers at the top level—people who the head office can trust. So, Chinese language is a plus but not a requirement." He clarifies that, at 3M, "all three of my successors [as CEO for China] did not speak Chinese. You don't have to, in order to show your appreciation for China. The people reporting to the China CEO—his N-1 and N-2—all speak English."

Other foreign China CEOs, however, did emphasize the importance of learning Mandarin. One such international top executive is Carrefour's Thierry Garnier: "One good piece of advice—which has changed my life, because it's not only for business [but] for personal life—is to dedicate time to learn Chinese." At the time of our interview, Garnier was preparing to take the Chinese government's HSK 6 level Chinese language exam—the test's top level, which is considered challenging to pass even for Chinese university graduates. "You have a lot of positive consequences coming from learning Chinese." (See "Foreign CEO Profile: Thierry Garnier [Carrefour] on Professional Commitment to China" later in chapter.) Fellow foreign CEO Arun Bhardwaj of Victoria's Secret comments: "For me to be more effective, I felt that it's very important to have a decent working knowledge of Chinese. It certainly improves efficiency and communications. It improves engagement and brings you closer to the people you're working with. So you're not seen as an outsider. It's a critical skill."

Our CEO interviewees also shared the top mistakes that foreign (non-Chinese) top managers made while running operations in China.

"One good piece of advice—which has changed my life, because it's not only for business [but] for personal life—is to dedicate time to learn Chinese."

—Thierry Garnier, President & CEO, China, Carrefour

MINI-CASE 1

"We Need to Work Like a SOE" (Bosch Group)

Bosch's Chen Yudong shares an example from a time when he advised his multinational company to react to an issue in a traditional Chinese way, both as a matter of conscience and also to let the company show goodwill toward domestic employees. The case involves a young employee who was gravely injured in a sports accident after hours and needed financial and social support. Chen retells the real-life case in this way:

"When I was working in my former company, one young fresh graduate had a serious accident. He played snow-boarding and flipped over. He was in intensive care." Chen explains that, in such cases in China, the patient's family members typically must provide food, clothing, and basic assistance such as bathing during the hospital stay.

"He was living in Shanghai alone. He had no family here and he did not have money to hire an ayi [housemaid]. Because he had just graduated, he did not even have money to pay the hospital deposit." When Chen learned of the case, he decided to push his company to react in a traditionally Chinese manner even though the company was foreign owned.

"I said, 'We need to work like a state-owned company in this case.' That young man was three levels below me. So I told the engineers: 'We will form a ten-person team to take care of him in the hospital.' That's how a SOE would operate. Also, I collected the hospital money from the company and gave it to him." He adds, "At first, the company was not happy. But I said: 'This is the way Chinese people handle things.'"

Chen maintains that his response was correct in this case and is pleased to report that the young man recovered after several months. "I grew up in the environment of SOEs. When I was young, I knew the advantage of SOEs—they take care of their people. That's a part of the humanity which I hope to keep. That's why I organized people to take care of this guy. We still did good work in the daytime, but every evening, we rotated at the hospital. For me, the people touch is very important."

Foreign Managers' Top Mistakes in China

Mistake 1: Not Adapting to China

Kenneth Yu says one of the most serious, but still most commonly made, mistakes among foreign top executives is to bring international practices into this market without adapting them to domestic norms. He says: "Another mistake is forced-fitting of China into the business model. People come to China who had success back in, let's say, the UK. They bring that success model and they want to apply it in China. It happens all the time—if the guy was successful before, he wants to clone it in China. That's a mistake."

Yu says this mistake is most often linked to a larger, more serious issue: cultural arrogance. "Underlying that mistake is the inability to learn and adapt to the Chinese environment. They don't know China. And if they don't know China, then they do what they know best. . . . The root cause is an inherent belief that 'We are smarter than you are' and 'You cannot grow without me' or 'The China company cannot grow without the home office.' That's arrogance." Yu says at the worst stage, foreigners believe: "We will teach you how to do things, and you should be grateful." Instead, adapting global operations to China is most often a matter of two-way collaboration, in which Chinese input is also needed. A one-way approach, Yu warns, is likely not only to fail operationally but also to alienate the local team. Instead, he advises: "Be humble. When you are humble, people are willing to share with you what they know."

Microsoft's Crozier adds this comment: "What I have seen, with the multinationals in China—the big US, German, Japanese companies—is that before five years ago, most had just one business model. So in China, their core model was coming from the US, from Germany, et cetera. And many of them failed, for many reasons. So today, a lot of them now have a different way of operating in China. They had to adapt their business model."

Alberto Cavaggioni, Maserati's top executive for China, says he learned this lesson the hard way: "I struggled at the beginning [of his China posting] on certain aspects." Initially, he says, he assumed that the methods and strategies deployed by his company elsewhere would be best for China as well. He says: "Sometimes, I thought, 'Why don't you do this in the way I was used to [doing] it?' But then, you realize very quickly that you need to keep these comments to yourself. You need to understand first. Probably your approach was not the right one. You need to find another way to do those things [in China]—in line with local habits—to achieve the same results or even better."

"You need to understand first. ...You need to find another way to do those things [in China]—in line with local habits—to achieve the same results or even better."

—Alberto Cavaggioni, Managing Director, China, Maserati

Mistake 2: Keeping a Distance

Another mistake some foreign CEOs make is to remain distant—from their teams, the market, and customers. Kenneth Yu advises: "Get to know your people—not by sitting in the office. This is one of the common mistakes: Companies send good people, but when they rise to the top, they distance themselves from their employees and their customers." He says this continues to hinder top-tier executives. "I know of cases where those rising to the top levels start to mingle only with other [foreigners], having lunch only with their peers from Hong Kong or [the] US." Yu continues: "How can you lead an organization without connecting with the employees and customers? This mistake is still being made, big time" He adds: "Don't forget: you need your China team *more* than they need you. The company will change the China leader, but not change the China team."

Yu clarifies that this advice also implies that top executives need to stay in contact with customers: "You can't learn about China by sitting in your office, with a team of people who worship you, thinking, 'If I want to see someone, I [will] summon them.' This becomes a vicious cycle. You need to be side-by-side with your customers—you must go to the customer, at their site."

Thierry Garnier of Carrefour describes the type of international hire he seeks for his China team: "We don't need colonial guys—we need foreigners with a Chinese mindset." He says he expects foreigners at Carrefour China to be fully integrated with the local culture.

"Get to know your people—not by sitting in the office."

—**Kenneth Yu,** advisor, CCF & MTS

"We don't need colonial guys—we need foreigners with a Chinese mindset."

—**Thierry Garnier,** President & CEO, China, Carrefour

Mistake 3: Under-Estimating the Complexity of China

A third mistake mentioned by CEO interviewees is that of misjudging the level of complexity of the Chinese market. Mango's David Sancho explains: "My first mistake was to believe that China was only one country. Before, I thought there were 32 provinces forming one great nation, which is China. But actually, every province has a different situation and needs different approaches. You really need to tackle China in different ways." The solution, he shares, was eventually to divide China into three regions—north, central, and south. Sancho notes: "The regions are so different in terms of weather, languages, and food, even culture. This approach was much more successful, and [it was important] to really have dedicated teams for each region [that] are understanding their local complexities."

One of Ikea's top executives for China, Freda Zhang, adds that one area of complexity for foreign managers is understanding China's economic evolution. "In my view, for those successful executives working in foreign companies—both inside and outside IKEA—it is important that they really understand that China has a unique economic structure." She elaborates: "When doing business in China, you need to understand that in the Chinese economy, we never distinguish between economy and politics. This is very, very important. The Chinese government plays a very strong role in the country's economic development—and so far, it has proven successful." Zhang also points out that the government, while still influential, has evolved in its methods and means. "Nowadays the Chinese government is becoming more professional; they are more and more market driven." She also adds that officials from the younger generation—those born after 1990—are "at a different level of internationalization."

Shifting from Foreign to Local CEOs

One urgent question which must be asked of today's top executives leading MNCs in China is: In the long term, is there still a need or a role for foreign CEOs in China? Certainly, their numbers have shrunk since *China CEO* was published in 2006. In fact, at the American Chamber of Commerce in Shanghai, fully half of all members are now Chinese. Says Kenneth Jarrett, the chamber's president: "There are lots of big US companies here which are now led by ethnic Chinese. That's a big change."

Jarrett says this group also includes professionals originally hailing from Hong Kong, Taiwan, Singapore and other parts of Southeast Asia, as well as American-born Chinese. Another new trend, he says, is a growing number of returnees—citizens of the PRC who studied and lived abroad before returning to work in China. This option can provide MNCs with an ideal cross-cultural background, he says: "Then the person at the top has a very natural understanding of China as well as the West."

Other interviewees also commented that the overall reception and perception of foreign managers in China has changed in recent years. Chunyuan Gu, ABB's China CEO, explains the shift in attitude among Chinese business and government leaders: "Ten years, twenty years ago, people were delighted to see a foreign face. But this [has] changed completely." Today, he says, it is "absolutely" a good idea to hire local Chinese management to run China operations. "For a multinational company, you need to find people who can understand the culture and are well connected to the customers and the market that you are serving."

And while the value of international top managers has grown less clear, China CEOs noted that the skillset and abilities of China's domestic talent pool has improved. One CEO emphasizing the latter trend is Bosch's top executive for China, Chen Yudong. He says Chinese middle managers have, as a demographic group, matured and internationalized. "For the past 20 years, China's globalization pushed the [Chinese] leadership teams at many companies to grow. You can see it more and more." Within Bosch China, Chen says, more Chinese nationals have recently been promoted to higher management positions. "If they joined the business 20 years ago, by now they must be mature. For sure, if they did not have the chance to go abroad as students, then we have to train them through different assignments in different regions globally." He says this is a natural and beneficial progression. "We have to let the Chinese grow up."

Are Foreigners Still Needed?

Most CEOs interviewed did not advocate a fully Chinese management team for the MNCs they run in China. Bosch's

Chen Yudong expresses a representative view: "I always say we should not strive for zero [foreigners]. We need a healthy portion of [foreigners] to bring new technology and bring cultural exchange." The question is, what quantity of foreigners is optimal. In Chen's view, 1% is the right mix—a level that also encourages sending a similar percentage of high-potential Chinese abroad for international assignment. "One percent is healthy because it also allows us to exchange international assignments—because we also send our Chinese people to take overseas assignment. We have to globalize the team."

Another point Chen emphasized is that, when dealing with the Chinese government, foreign managers are sometimes preferred. "If it's a foreigner, for example, some local government [officials] like it." He emphasizes that the foreigner must show a certain mindset. "If the foreigner has very quick learning and also likes Chinese [culture], then there is no issue." In fact, bringing a foreign face can help to solidify government negotiations by representing an international aspect. Chen notes: "I have seen many, many cases in which local government [officials] politely . . . say: 'Can you send a foreigner?' [laughs] Because they want to show this is a foreign company—in ceremonies, et cetera. That's why I always say I do not strive for 100% localization. We need some foreigners."

AB InBev's Freire also advocates a certain level of diversity as part of his company's global culture: "We like to blend: the cultural differences, the diversity is important for a company. If everybody comes from the same background, same country, same school, or same province, they think like each other. We like to have people who think differently. If you have people who oppose your ideas in a constructive way, you build solutions with them. So, we believe that diversity has a big role in our organization."

Giving the perspective of an executive recruiter in China, Charles Tseng of Korn Ferry agrees that there is a continuing need for foreign managers in China. "It's very important to have non-Chinese in an organization here in China. Diversity enriches the workplace environment, enables the staff to communicate, to discuss, to interface in an international environment. . . . It's very advantageous."

David Sancho, Mango's top China executive, says that although he has seen his company reduce the number of foreign managers from 50% to around 1% during the eight years he has been in China, his company will not localize to 100%. "We still need to make sure the DNA of the company and culture from headquarters is maintained. But the number [of foreigners] is less and less."

In fact, many MNCs are rapidly localizing. Carrefour's Thierry Garnier explains the process at his company: "If I look at the number of [foreigners] in China in 2011 versus today, they are divided by four." During that time, the company went from around 80 European management-level employees to 15 as of 2019. And those remaining face stricter requirements regarding language ability and cultural assimilation. Says Garnier: "The [foreigners] who stay have to speak Chinese and to be fully integrated, as in a Chinese company." In the past two years, he comments that he has hired "many more Chinese below 40 years of age" than he has foreigners. Why this shift? His first reason is to create the right impression among employees regarding the priorities of management. "You have to show, tangibly, that you like this country and you are physically committed to China."

Manulife's Kai Zhang explains a similar evolution; while her predecessors at Manulife were Caucasian males from the US and UK, she was born and raised in China. Today, she says, only a few gaps remain between local and foreign talent at the senior management levels. "The only differences right now probably are language and international exposure," she says, while emphasizing that Chinese executives are advancing rapidly in both regards. Zhang says her own study and work pattern are becoming more common among Chinese: "I had an advantage because I went to the United States at a young age, and my major in college was English literature. So I had no problem with bilingual communication. . . . Today, there are more and more people with my background. More local managers speak English very well; they have studied or worked in the US." She muses that: "There may be a day when foreign companies in China are run completely by local people."

AB InBev has witnessed a similar shift. Frederico Freire notes: "Back in 2010, when I arrived, we had a lot of [foreigners] coming to China. There was a move to create our global company culture within ABI China. But now, we have [fewer foreigners] in our organization in China. We have people from within coming to top management positions." Chunyuan Gu, ABB's China CEO, makes a similar observation: "If you compare 10 years ago, the number of foreigners [in ABB China] is declining. And their positions are very different. Ten years ago, most of them were general managers. Now they are coming from different levels and functional specialties." Among his team, Gu's CFO is German, his supply chain manager is American, and his account manager is from the UK. For such MNCs, diversity and internationalization are reasons to retain a certain percentage of internationals among the management team.

For other MNCs, however, the main role of non-Chinese professionals is simply to transfer knowledge to the local team. Volvo Car's top executive for China, Xiaolin Yuan, explains that foreign hires have taken roles within his company mainly for "a specific reason." He explains: "Usually, the assignment is for two to three years, with the option to extend one more term. The purpose is to play a specific role and to grow the successor. The goal is to grow the capacity of the organization instead of moving the capacity around. We need to build up the capability of the organization as our global operation requires." Over the years, Yuan says, this strategy has served Volvo Cars well in China: "Our successful track record demonstrates that we have built up the organization. As one example, in China alone, we grew from selling around 30,000 units per year back in 2010 to more than 130,000 units in 2018." He adds that knowledge transfer from non-Chinese has played a role in this expansion: "Particularly in the initial phase, quite a number of [foreigners] came in to establish the system and to grow the people and train the people. And the system that we built—in manufacturing, procurement, and all the other functions, as well as the processes—contributed to the results I just showed you, the commercial success. That shows how powerful this method is."

"If you compare 10 years ago, the number of foreigners [in ABB China] is declining. And their positions are very different. Ten years ago, most of them were general managers. Now they are coming from different levels and functional specialties."

—Chunyuan Gu,
Chairman & CEO,
China, ABB

Other top executives in China state that foreign managers are not important to their business success. Udacity is one such MNC. Robert Hsiung, the company's top China executive, says: "For us, the value of foreigners in China is less. For those on my team, unless they are absolutely fluent in Chinese, it's difficult to take on a marketing role, it's difficult to take on a product role, it's difficult to take on a business development role—because of the importance of being able to read and write fluently. The importance of being able to go through a document—like a legal agreement—in Chinese, or the importance of building relationships at a local level is just so high."

In fact, several foreign China CEOs interviewed expect that their successors will be Chinese nationals. Says AB InBev's Freire: "It will be my desire to have a successor who is Chinese." Mango's David Sancho also expressed that one of the key characteristics needed by future top executives in China is "local knowledge." Sancho explains: "I do believe the next leader [of Mango China] should be Chinese. I think the company is ready for it; they're already prepared."

At Victoria's Secret, China CEO Arun Bhardwaj says his team is already very localized: "Besides my director of merchandise planning, everybody else is Chinese [on] my team. So, I get it—and if I don't understand something, they will tell me." He describes his entire China team as "localized but with international expectations."

Prerequisite for Chinese CEOs: Understanding the MNC's Home-Country Culture

Among the foreign China CEOs who are preparing for a Chinese successor or heavily localizing their China teams, several mentioned that the incomer would need the reverse quality compared against their own adaptation to China. In other words, the Chinese national top executive would need to show a deep understanding of the company's home-country culture and close, positive communications with headquarters.

Mango's David Sancho explains the need for future Chinese top executives to integrate with and fully relate to those in corporate headquarters. Sancho predicts that the new leader may need "coaching or training to really understand the culture back in Spain—to make sure the communication from China to Spain [takes place]." The challenge, he says, will be in ensuring that understanding among those in HQ "is not lost." Sancho says his successor will need to "explain well" to be sure their messages regarding China are received and understood in Spain and that headquarters "really follow their advice." Says Sancho: "I myself had this situation. Sometimes it's still really complicated to pass the message to headquarters." He adds: "Being used to talking with people from Europe—that will help to really enhance the communication. In this kind of regional position, communication is a key for success."

Tata's China head, James Zhan, also expects that his successor, like him, will hail from China. He gives this advice in such a case: "You have to be very international, because our business is very international. You cannot just focus on China." In addition to deeply understanding all aspects of the China market—especially working with the local governments and managing customers—Zhan says his successor will also need to be a master of international-style communications. "You must communicate with our stakeholders—and our stakeholders in headquarters may not necessarily be Indian. You have to have an international mindset plus communications skills."

A similar comment came from Andy Ho, Philips' head of China, who commented that China CEOs for MNCs need to bridge two cultures, bringing two skillsets to the role. "My successor will have to be able to get into two dimensions. One is to understand the management system and operating model of the MNC. . . . As the leader in an MNC, you need to leverage the global resources and provide value to the local market. You also have to understand how the company works—how group global decisions are made, how to work with different department heads. There is a certain 'MNC operating model'

"You have to be very international, because our business is very international. You cannot just focus on China."

—**James Zhan,**
President, China, Tata Sons

"My successor will have to be able to get into two dimensions. One is to understand the management system and operation model of the MNC.... [S]econdly,...you have to be able to drive the local business."

— **Andy Ho,**
Leader, Greater China, Philips

which you have to know. And secondly, particularly in a country like China which is a highly regulated, you have to be able to drive the local business. You need to adapt your business to local needs."

Given the challenge inherent in deeply understanding both of these dimensions, several China CEOs mentioned the strong appeal of hiring returnees to fill top executive positions for MNCs in China. These Chinese nationals who have spent significant time working or studying abroad can offer a best of both worlds solution for international companies.

Allure of Returnees

Given the challenge of finding a China CEO who seamlessly bridges the cultures of both China and the MNC's home country, Charles Tseng of Korn Ferry explains the important role of returnees—Chinese nationals who studied and worked abroad before returning to China. In the 1990s, he remembers, MNCs initially hired many Taiwanese because they spoke Mandarin, or citizens of Hong Kong or Singapore "because [they] also came from a modern market economy." But by the 2000s, he says, companies also began hiring a new group called "returnees." He explains: "What is a returnee? No other country has this term. A returnee is somebody who came from China, went overseas, learned English, and came back. If you're from England and you go to America and then come back after ten years, you're not a returnee, because there was no drastic change. But in China, because of the significant change, they became returnees." During the time abroad, Chinese typically transformed themselves professionally by learning English, working for international firms, and gaining a first-hand understanding of a free market economy. Thus, in the 2000s, he says such returnees were sought after by companies and offered high compensation. In the years since, Tseng says, MNCs have become more discerning about the returnees they hire, ensuring that they not only speak English and understand a market economy but also have proven professional experience and expertise.

Returnee Profile 1: ABB's Chunyuan Gu

Chunyuan Gu, ABB's top China executive, began college at Shanghai Jiaotong University after the Cultural Revolution. When he graduated, China was just beginning to open to the outside world. Seizing this opportunity, Gu was among the first batch of Chinese to study abroad following the nation's reopening. After receiving both a master's degree and PhD in Sweden, Gu worked for several years in a Swedish university. In 1989, he joined ABB's corporate research center in Sweden, then took a research and development posting in China in 2005. Once back in China, he moved from R&D to the business side, becoming Head of Robotics, then Head of Discrete Automation and Motion. Gu was named Chairman and President of North Asia and China for ABB in 2014 and became a member of the company's Executive Committee in 2017.

Returnee Profile 2: Tata's James Zhan

James Zhan graduated from Shanghai Jiaotong University with a bachelor's in science, then began his professional career at the state-owned China Trust and Investment Corporation in Beijing. After three years in CITIC's investment department, he had the chance to study in the US, receiving an MS from Stanford. After graduating, he first worked for a power company on the US East Coast, then joined Bechtel Corporation in San Francisco. He returned to Asia after Bechtel promoted him to a position in Hong Kong, then to Beijing. There, a professional recruiter headhunted him for a position at Tata Group. He joined Tata in 2006 and has now risen to President of Tata Group, China.

Today, Tseng says returnees can help to bridge the gaps between Chinese and Western cultures—gaps with deep historical roots: "Chinese people come from a more Confucian DNA, where cohesiveness and collaboration are more important than contention." He says this leads non-Chinese leaders to find their domestic teams to be "less prepared to argue out loud than those coming from a Judeo-Christian Socratic context" where employees are encouraged to debate. The cultural gap, he says, can lead to misunderstandings: "Many head office people like the Chinese to be more vocal and vociferous. But they don't get that behavior from the Chinese because it's not their nature." These misaligned expectations can trigger conflicts.

Returnee Profile 3: Volvo Cars' Xiaolin Yuan

After receiving both a BA and BL from China Foreign Affairs University, Xiaolin Yuan began his career in China's Foreign Affairs Ministry. After a stint in the home office, he spent four years on assignment in the Philippines. He then moved to the private sector by joining BP, first in business development, then joining the mergers and acquisitions team in London. It was his expertise in M&A that triggered an approach from the owner of Geeley, Li Shufu, who eventually offered Yuan a position after the global acquisition of Volvo Cars by Geeley. Yuan then spent four years in Gothenburg, Sweden, working as Board Secretary and head of the Chairman's Office. In 2014, he returned to his home country as President of Volvo Cars China. He was promoted in 2017 to his current role as Sr. Vice President of Volvo Cars Group as well as President and CEO of Volvo Cars Asia Pacific (a region extending from Australia to India, including China).

Returnee Profile 4: Bosch's Yudong Chen

One returnee whose career path has included stints in both the US and Europe is Yudong Chen. After several years of both working and studying in the US, Chen returned to China in December of 1998 to take a position with Delphi. After beginning with a role in the engineering team, nine years later he was overseeing three divisions with combined yearly revenues of US$400 million. But after a restructuring closed two of the divisions he had managed, Chen found a new opportunity with Bosch in early 2007. He could not work directly for Bosch, because it was a competitor to Delphi, so he began work with his new employer by taking a position overseas. After 15 months in Germany, he returned to China in 2008 to oversee the company's automotive sales. He was promoted to serve as China President in 2011.

"One of the big challenges of Western companies is to persuade the Chinese executive to be more like a Westerner. But that's not easy to do. But just as it's not easy for a Westerner to become like a Chinese, it is likewise not easy for Chinese to become like Westerners." All this adds to the suitability of returnees for top executive roles for MNCs in China: "One reason why returnees are very attractive to many companies is because they've lived there [in the West]; they understand the culture."

One such returnee CEO, Volvo Car's Xiaolin Yuan, explains that today's China business leaders must create operating styles that leverage the best of both Western and Chinese norms. Thus, the best top executives are able to draw from the strengths of either system to benefit the company. Yuan explains: "Either extreme is not ideal. Either the company becomes too rigid, and the management team would not be able to respond to the fast-changing market. Or the other extreme is that the company becomes too chaotic and loses its identity. Then it won't have a sustainable way of development." He says finding the right mix of both operating norms is a necessity among those leading operations in China: "The trick is how you strike this balance." (See mini-profiles of returnees later in this chapter.)

Qualities Needed for Today's China CEOs (Either Foreign or Chinese Nationals)

When China CEOs discussed leading large-scale operations in China, many gave similar advice regardless of their nationality. The following key strategies were most often mentioned by our interviewees, regardless of nationality or ethnicity.

China CEO Quality 1: Passion and Energy

"The energy level needed to operate in China is a lot higher than what is needed in the US....The amount of pressure on the leader is a lot more than in the West because it's not only professional standards and professional behavior which are different; it's also the level of personal impact that you make on the company."

—**Kai Zhang,**
President & CEO, China,
Manulife-Sinochem

Many CEOs used the words "passion" and "energy" or related terms such as "stamina" when describing the qualities top executives need to succeed in China. Kai Zhang of Manulife expressed this opinion: "The energy level needed to operate in China is a lot higher than what is needed in the US. I definitely think that, for the same level of job responsibility, the amount of detailed work one has to go through [in China] is a lot more." She continues: "To be a good CEO here and grow your company in this market as a global company . . . takes a tremendous amount of passion and devotion. The amount of pressure on the leader is a lot more than in the West because it's not only professional standards and professional behavior which are different; it's also the level of personal impact that you make on the company. Because of the market environment, because of the experience level of the people, and because of cultural differences, I work a lot harder in China than I might need to in the US." Zhang concludes by warning China CEOs that the high expectations from employees covers not only one's professional life but also one's after-work life. She explains: "Culturally, employees expect a lot more from a leader in China—not only on the professional side, but also as a role model in all aspects."

Bayer's head of China, Celina Chew, expresses a similar view, emphasizing that in her role, she is "leading people who have a lot of technical skills and professional skills already." Therefore her own role, she says, is to bring to the organization "clarity of communication, direction, empathy, and passion." Jacob Kragh, LEGO's top China executive, voices a matching opinion on leading operations in China. "You have to be passionate. You have to truly believe in what you are doing. You have to be truly people-centric. You may not have any trace of arrogance. . . . You need to be sincere, or you will not bring people with you."

China CEO Quality 2: Speed in Decision-Making

One reason why China CEOs need passion and energy, top executives explain, is to manage the speed of change in today's China. Mary Boyd, Economist Corporate Network director (Shanghai), says: "One of the key challenges that CEOs would face in China, as compared to other markets they may have worked in, is the speed with which everything changes in China." In particular, she names as challenging "the new possibilities that are opened up whenever policy changes." These changes require CEOs to adapt to "new market opportunities which are opened, or a new target or particular objectives set by the government." As an example, she points to the central government's 2017 directive requiring automotive manufacturers selling vehicles in China to suddenly meet new quotas: by 2019, 10% of cars sold in China would be new energy cars; and by 2020, the percentage would be 12%. This announcement, Boyd says, marked a "radical change" that triggered many MNCs to totally recreate their business strategy in China.

"One of the key challenges that CEOs would face in China, as compared to other markets they may have worked in, is the speed with which everything changes in China."

—Mary Boyd,
Director, Shanghai, Economist Corporate Network

"Focusing Is Key" (Microsoft)

Microsoft's top China executive Alain Crozier gives a telling example of the type of difficult judgement calls that CEOs must make in China's fast-changing, chaotic business environment. He describes the situation when five different bike-sharing companies approached his company simultaneously—each looking to form a partnership—when the nation was suddenly flooded by the new transportation mode in 2018. Crozier notes: "You have so many startups who come to you and say: 'I'm planning to do this.' You have to, at some point, be very good at making a choice and focusing. Because when the choices are too many, you may become confused. Or you may say: 'I want to do everything. I want to work with everybody.' But, no, you can't."

Remembering the height of the 2017–2018 bike-sharing boom in China, he explains the dilemma he faced: "When you have five bike-sharing companies coming to you within six months to partner with you, you say, 'Which one do we want to partner with?'" The problem, he remembers, was complex, because each of the five bike-sharing companies had an aggressive growth plan and strategy but it was likely that only a few would survive. "You can build very sophisticated models. You can ask external companies to do valuations. You can do due diligence. It's not going to work. At the end, the CEO has to decide: 'I'm going to go with this one or that one.' Or 'I can do two, but I can't do five.' Focusing is key." Crozier emphasizes that this example illustrates the booming atmosphere for Chinese startups today, and the resulting tough calls that China CEOs must make. "You have to try to focus on the right thing in order to develop something big. And if you fail, you have to know how to rebound quickly. This is very important because the choices are just crazy."

As a final example, he points to the Caohejing Industrial Park in Shanghai, where Microsoft opened new offices in mid-2019: "You take this industrial park. I made a list of 70 startups I want to talk to in this park alone. Then I need to go from 70 to 20 to maybe 10 to really have a conversation with. But this is just one industrial park out of 20 in Shanghai; and Shanghai is only one small part of China. So, focus is definitely a key challenge."

Carrefour's Thierry Garnier offers a similar view: "Another key challenge in China is speed." He says his company missed some opportunities during the 2000s by not matching the domestic pace of change. In his view, speed is critical—even though it will come with a cost. He clarifies with this comment: "When we move faster, what is the consequence? You need to accept mistakes from day one. You need to agree that mistakes will happen. Everybody agrees about speed—but the consequence of speed is that, sometimes, when you go so fast, it may be disorganized. You have to accept that."

Stéphane Rinderknech, L'Oréal's top executive for China, also emphasizes the importance of trusting the local team in order to maintain speed: "Trust is very important. Trust is the most important thing to gain speed. Trust, delegation, involvement, engagement—and collective achievement. We win together; we lose together." Another necessary component to achieving speed, Rinderknech adds, is that the team must feel safe and empowered in case of project failure. "At every step of the chain, if we lose, that means we are all wrong. And we just take it as such—we are all wrong. It's not a question of blaming one person."

> *"Trust is the most important thing to gain speed. Trust, delegation, involvement, engagement—and collective achievement."*
>
> **—Stéphane Rinderknech,** CEO, China, L'Oréal

China CEO Quality 3: Clear Vision, Shared Framework

Kai Zhang of Manulife explains how the role of a top executive in China is expanded by the need to provide a clear and inspiring central vision and detailed steps to achieving it: "For the qualities of a leader in China, it is not only providing the strategic vision but also providing the roadmap and then overcoming challenges together with the team. Because in China, the team will likely hit a wall at some point."

Robert Hsiung, Udacity's head of China, expresses a similar opinion on the CEO's role in motivating and aligning the team: "The number one most important thing is the ability to come up with a clear vision and a strategy and to communicate that strategy to your team. Then to get everyone to move together."

L'Oréal's Rinderknech explains how he and his leadership team create motivating central guidelines for China that cover more than 10,000 employees: "We create a frame and then we make sure that framework is shared with everyone. Then, we make sure that everything we ask of the team fits into that frame. And then, we leave freedom within the frame for people to do their jobs. We do not tell them what to do." He emphasizes that this framework tells the team where they are headed.

> *"The number one most important thing is the ability to come up with a clear vision and a strategy and to communicate that strategy to your team. Then to get everyone to move together."*
>
> **—Robert Hsiung,** CEO, China, Udacity

Rinderknech notes: "My role is to kick off, to explain the vision, to send the big message and make people understand what's expected of them. Once that is clear, we [top executives] do something else. Our job is done. We know the employees will deliver because they are the most committed people on earth. Once they feel trust—once they feel that the contribute to the vision, that it's an objective which is collective, that we will shine together—once you have achieved that, you can just go sleep! In our role, we have nothing left to do! [laughs]."

Advisor Kenneth Yu also emphasizes that one of the most important qualities for a China CEO is the ability to create a clear, compelling vision. As a final point, Yu urges China-based CEOs to give encouraging feedback that acknowledges the challenges of this market: "Stick your thumb up for jobs well done and show your understanding for honest mistakes or failures when people have tried their best."

"Stick your thumb up for jobs well done and show your understanding for honest mistakes or failures when people have tried their best."

—Kenneth Yu,
advisor, CCF & MTS

China CEO Quality 4: Empower the Local Team

Given the complexity of China as well as the scope, scale, and speed of change, China CEOs expressed that one of the chief success factors was the ability to empower local teams. Kenneth Yu sums up his advice to top executives in China: "The key objectives (as CEO) are: First, find the right people. Second, make sure your objectives are well communicated—specific, clear, observable, quantifiable, and obtainable with stretch. Third, make sure the team has enough resources and time. Last, as a leader, you give them empowerment but with access to your knowledge."

IKEA's China head, Freda Zhang, agrees that growing and empowering the local team is a critical success factor for MNCs in China now—and a winning strategy for China CEOs. "What I see in the successful leaders is that they dare to utilize Chinese for the strategic part of their operations." She stresses that IKEA has created a nurturing and supportive environment for advancing not only her career but also that of many Chinese employees. "I was one of those fast-growing, first generation of the local leaders in the region. I still cannot understand how they dared to promote me into the management team at the age 24! [laughs] I knew nothing." She says foresight, support, and nurturing are critical to building the next generation and thus keeping an MNC healthy. "This kind of daring in the leadership is crucial: put the Chinese into strategic positions. Because, nowadays, with the market dominated by competition from Chinese local brands, you need local China leaders who understands the logic from their hearts."

By contrast, she says, what "does not work" is for CEOs (especially foreigners) to rely on the local team only for implementation. Zhang notes: "I see a lot of foreign leaders who are still focusing on Chinese as being good at implementation. Chinese [are] super good at doing that. Because of our education background, we are used to: 'The teacher tells me what to do—first step, second step.' Then when I come to the company, I take instructions from my boss exactly like I took them from my teacher. I expect you to give me all the instructions.'" Zhang adds: "Some foreign leaders enjoy this part: 'I tell you what you should do.' Or even, 'The head office tells us what you should do.' In that case, the strategy probably doesn't really involve the Chinese intelligence and then, the company can take a totally wrong direction in China."

At L'Oréal, Stéphane Rinderknech says empowering local team members is a necessity for his role: "We cannot tell a 25-year-old product manager what to do, because we don't know what to do. . . . I don't know which KOL [key opinion leader], which influencer, which sportsman in China is resonating with young Chinese. We don't know that—*they* know that. They watch the dramas; they know the channels; they are super smart." He adds that delegation is "a must" in today's China: "You have no choice because you have no time."

For this reason, he describes L'Oréal China as "extremely horizontal." He himself directly manages 17 direct reports—a system that works only because he creates "a strategic frame" for his large team to work within. "I'm not doing micromanagement—if we micromanage, we're gonna do things wrong." Instead, Rinderknech views his own role as setting the guide-

"Nowadays, with the market dominated by competition from Chinese local brands, you need local China leaders who understands the logic from their hearts."

—**Freda Zhang,** Country Commercial VP, China, IKEA

lines, then monitoring the overall progress. Of his China-based team, he says: "They know what their role is in the frame. Then it's delegation, empowerment, engagement. It's *their* thing." His role is one of referee and coach. "I bring the cherry on the cake—which is to decide 'We're on track,' or 'We're not on track.' And I need to make all the 17 [direct reports] fit together. Really, it's the strategic vision and direction and checking whether we are all aligned—that's my job."

Carrefour's Thierry Garnier, agrees that trusting and empowering the local team is a critical success factor: "The key thing is: you have to trust Chinese management at every level—including young people." And part of trusting locally is delegating authority to China, he adds: "In retail, 95% of the decisions are made here [in China]. We don't have worldwide products; the staff are local; the products are local. Some decisions are made in Paris, sure, but the large majority of decisions are made locally. For other companies which are more matrix organizations, this can be very painful because the delay of the decisions."

At Maserati, the company's top executive for China describes the benefits he has discovered from delegating more to his local team. Alberto Cavaggioni recounts: "As soon as you give your team the opportunity to contribute to the business, rather than being just an executer—contributing in terms of ideas, in terms of views—then they are completely different. It's as if you had polished something and now it is shining. This for me has also been amazing."

The fact that the quality of local talent is improving was another point expressed by China CEOs. Andy Ho, Philips' top China executive, expressed this idea with these words: "Local talent is better educated now, with degrees from the best universities in the world. They are aggressive, mobile." Overall, Ho describes China's talent pool as "increasingly competitive."

"Local talent is better educated now, with degrees from the best universities in the world. They are aggressive, mobile."

— **Andy Ho,**
Leader, Greater China, Philips

But empowering the local team is often challenging for cultural reasons. Curt Ferguson, Coca-Cola's head of China, advises that, empowering the local team to take risks and make mistakes in the course of growing the business can be difficult. He describes a recent encounter with one of his senior Chinese team members:

"The other day, somebody came to me and said: 'Here are five options. What should I do?' And I said, 'Yes.' [laughs] Then I said, 'You know better than I do. You know the problems.'" But Ferguson remembers that the Chinese manager continued to push back. "He said: 'So, you want me to make the decision?' I said: 'Yes.' 'But what if I'm wrong?' 'Well, then we were wrong and we both learned something.'" Ferguson realizes that, given the norms of Chinese culture, it is "very hard" for more junior team members to take a risk that may not succeed. Thus, he works to ensure that his team members see him as a coach. "I develop the team to do the best they can on the field. And to let them know that mistakes happen when you are playing the game. That is part of the development process."

China CEO Quality 5: Ability to Make Tough Judgment Calls

One area that CEOs in China must grapple with is determining which parts of global operations and policies to maintain strictly and which to adapt to China. Kenneth Jarrett, president of the American Chamber of Commerce in Shanghai, explains that this requires thoughtful judgment, because reacting too strictly or too loosely both have disadvantages for MNCs. Jarrett indicates that a key challenge for CEOs is determining "where to draw the lines either regarding governance or legal concerns." He explains: "Corporations have very established internal practices. They must pay attention to compliance and process. It's a strength in terms of compliance. But in terms of process, sometimes too much attention to process can actually be a disadvantage as it slows down the speed of decision-making."

Kai Zhang of Manulife adds: "Working in an emerging market requires more leadership in terms of the educational aspect, the motivation aspect, and the oversight—and also the creativity." She explains the difference between leadership styles in the US and China. "Operating in the US, you have a well-established corporate culture, governance processes, strategic vision, and well-established business practices. But here, while you're part

"Corporations have very established internal practices. ...But in terms of process, sometimes too much attention to process can actually be a disadvantage as it slows down the speed of decision-making.

—**Kenneth Jarrett,** President, American Chamber of Commerce, Shanghai of a global organization or a local organization, you are competing day to day with the local players—and so, you must change at a faster pace. Also, the standards, the culture, and governance are not as established." For that reason, she advises CEOs: "You may need to actively exert more influence."

Bayer's Celina Chew also names "dealing with ambiguity" and "being flexible" as necessary skills, while also emphasizing that CEOs also must show the ability to "come to a decision." She explains: "It is not helpful to have endless discussions. You must keep the process moving forward. And part of that is the ability to assess which information is most relevant and needed, then analyze the situation, and come to a decision. Often this is done without every single detail having been clarified. Then you must get everyone—or at least the main stakeholders—to buy into the decision. This is a helpful characteristic." (See "Mini-Case 2: 'Focusing Is Key' [Microsoft]" earlier in this chapter.)

Interviewees also emphasized that China CEOs will need to make difficult calls in one particular area: the possible growth directions to pursue. L'Oréal's Rinderknech explains how he chooses between possible new initiatives introduced by his team: "In every meeting you run, in every decision that you make, you need to ask the question: Is it scalable? Because the danger of this country is that it's so big and there are so many opportunities that you can really get lost in the noise."

Rinderknech clarifies that the top executive in China must ultimately use his or her experience and expertise to set priorities on those projects and initiatives with the highest potential. "You need to do one important thing very, very well instead of trying to do ten things not well enough. So what is that one thing that you're going to choose? In all the decisions [you make] and meetings you have, the number one question is: 'In what was proposed, is it scalable?' Are we going to mobilize the team energy, workload, financial resources for something that we can really scale later? Are we really building some foundations?"

"In every meeting you run, in every decision that you make, you need to ask the question: Is it scalable? Because the danger of this country is that it's so big and there are so many opportunities that you can really get lost in the noise."

—**Stéphane Rinderknech,** CEO, China, L'Oréal

Summary of Tips

1. **Passion and energy**
   The China CEO role requires a tremendous amount of passion and energy, more so than in the West, because of the immaturity of the market and the amount of influence the top executive has on the success of local operations. The sheer workload is greater, according to China CEOs.

2. **Speed of decision-making**
   Because the China market changes frequently and sometimes dramatically, China CEOs must be adept at responding quickly—whether the new circumstances are evolving market conditions or new government regulations. You have to accept that, with speed, mistakes may also occur.

3. **Clear vision, shared frameworks**
   Explain your vision in the form of a roadmap or a framework, then communicate it clearly to all employees. Employees understand the overall direction and goals well but enjoy an appropriate level of freedom in meeting individual targets within the framework.

4. **Empowerment of local teams**
   Place your Chinese team in strategic positions. They understand the local competitors and the market better than you. Hire the best and then trust them. Make sure they understand and share your vision. Create a positive work culture in which successes are recognized and honest failures are accepted when lessons were learned.

5. **Ability to make tough judgment calls**
   As a China CEO, you must manage ambiguity by being flexible but at the same time decisive. You are competing with local players and must change and adapt at a faster pace than you would in other markets. Part of your success in China will depend on setting priorities and not trying to do all projects at once. Choose those projects that have the potential to reach an attractive scale.

Chapter 3
China's Changing Talent Pool

No matter that, as a country, China is big. We don't have enough talent. There is a big war for talent.

—**Alain Crozier,** CEO, Greater China Region, Microsoft

Keeping employees is absolutely essential. If you lose the people every six months, you just lose traction. You waste your investment. That's one big piece of the environment in China.

—**Arun Bhardwaj,** President, Greater China, LBrands International (Victoria's Secret)

INSIDE CHAPTER 3

Chinese Professional Women: Holding Up Half the C-Suite

Meet China's Millennials

Strengths and Weaknesses of China's Talent Pool

HR Strategies

Summary of Tips

Introduction: China's War for Talent Continues

Of the few themes voiced by the top executives interviewed for both *China CEO II* and *China CEO*, one is the continuing shortage of qualified human resources at MNCs in China. Our China CEOs consistently remarked on this difficulty during interviews, and recent large-scale surveys have shown similar results. In fact, when the 2019 *China Business Survey* (created by CEIBS, the *China Business Survey* has been polling more than 1,000 executives in China annually since 2011) asked "Which are the major human resources issues facing your company in China?," the most common response from wholly foreign-owned enterprises (WFOEs) was "finding and hiring talent" (84% vs. 81% for Chinese private companies), followed by "rising labor costs" (70% vs. 75% of Chinese private companies).[1]

Alain Crozier, Microsoft's top executive for China, sums up the difficulty faced by many foreign companies in today's China regarding HR: "No matter that, as a country, China is big. We don't have enough talent. There is a big war for talent." He clarifies the central problem in this way: "The biggest challenge is: since you live in a very dynamic and aggressive market, talent makes a difference." Companies in booming sectors, such as technology, know that success is driven by the quality of its staff—a recipe for heightened competition with local players. Crozier notes: "We don't have machines. We don't have big infrastructure. It's all about people; it starts and ends with people." For MNCs, a growing challenge is direct competition from domestic tech for attracting top talent. "Today, when you look at the market, because the number of startups in the tech industry rises every day—that is putting a lot of pressure on talent." The result, says Crozier: "It is a real war for talent."

What changed between the writing of our first and second books (between 2006 and 2020)? According to our China

---

[1] CEIBS. *China Business Survey*, 2019.

CEO interviewees, MNCs now generally face more difficult challenges in attracting top talent. Microsoft's Crozier offers a representative view: "What would make Chinese people go to Microsoft, when today China has very large domestic companies that offer them what we offer?" He says while this situation was "not the case five years ago," today Microsoft goes head-to-head with China's home-grown tech heroes. "Today, if a Chinese person wants to represent a national champion, there are such national champion companies. Before, it was not the case." The result is fierce competition for the best talent. (See the mini-profiles on Alibaba and Tencent in Chapter 4.)

In the arena of fashion, Arun Bhardwaj, head of China for Victoria's Secret, expresses similar concerns about the new pressures on MNCs seeking to hire top performers: "There's intense competition for talent. Employees expect a high degree of investment in their learning and development and their growth. They expect companies to invest in them, in their training and their skill development and in their learning." MNCs are expected, Bhardwaj says, to address "the human aspects which help to engage and inspire employees." He advises MNCs that "keeping employees is absolutely essential. If you lose the people every six months, you just lose traction. You waste your investment. That's one big piece of the environment in China."

At AB InBev, retention of employees in China is a serious challenge, especially for younger domestic employees. Frederico Freire, the company's top executive for China, says: "They have less attachment to the company. This is true." Part of the problem, he says, is that the China market is "quite warm" with job opportunities. "We find high turnover today, even in our organization. . . . But the turnover is mostly from young people—people with less time in our company rather than more time." He explains that Chinese youth are generally "not as attached to the company as the old generation used to be" and are more likely to job-hop.

A related issue is rising labor costs. In terms of professional salaries, Jonathan Woetzel, Senior Partner at McKinsey & Company, says wages have risen rapidly in recent years, eliminating China's cost advantage for professional staff—especially in

"There's intense competition for talent. Employees expect a high degree of investment in their learning and development and their growth."

—**Arun Bhardwaj,** President, Greater China, LBrands International (Victoria's Secret)

"Employing middle-level Chinese professionals in Shanghai today will cost you the same as in Singapore or Tokyo."

—**Jonathan Woetzel,**
Senior Partner, McKinsey & Company

the nation's first-tier cities. Woetzel notes: "Employing middle-level Chinese professionals in Shanghai today will cost you the same as in Singapore or Tokyo."

Kenneth Jarrett, President of the American Chamber of Commerce in Shanghai, makes similar comments regarding rising wages: "For example, if you're looking for a senior government relations hire here, you definitely pay more than you would in the United States for someone in that position. Those new to the China market might be surprised by the relative shortage of the right people with that skillset." He adds that wages have risen especially fast for some highly specialized positions, such as government relations specialist.

Another outcome of the war for talent, Woetzel explains, is that many MNCs end up hiring younger management team members in China—or advancing their careers faster—than in other countries: "In general, you may not find the level of experience and talent that you would find outside of China. As a result, the Chinese management team is typically a bit younger—up to ten years younger than they would be elsewhere—and without the benefit of all of that experience." He says that the younger demographic of management teams in China is a double-edged sword, offering some benefits along with drawbacks. "If you're in a fast-changing environment, having a younger team might actually not be so bad, because you would have some willingness to experiment. But in most cases, it will also lead you to a higher probability that something will go wrong at some point."

"The talent-development process needs to reflect the relatively young age of the team. Emphasis shouldn't necessarily be placed on whether what was done was correct—but instead [on] whether something was learned from it."

—**Jonathan Woetzel,**
Senior Partner, McKinsey & Company

Woetzel advises China CEOs to adjust their leadership style to take into account the relative youth and inexperience of the team: "The talent-development process needs to reflect the relatively young age of the team. Emphasis shouldn't necessarily be placed on whether what was done was correct—but instead [on] whether something was learned from it. In other words: 'It's OK to make a mistake, but don't make the same one twice.' That has real implications for employers and how they think through their internal performance measures, their accountabilities, as well as their trainings and their rotation philosophy."

Waning Appeal of MNCs in China

One key challenge noted by China CEOs in this version of the book was a marked drop in the appeal of MNCs among Chinese employees over the past 15 years. Chen Yudong, the top executive for China at Bosch, explains the viewpoint of today's Chinese 20- and 30-somethings: "First, they do not care too much regarding the branding and foreign company name. Twenty years ago, 15 years, the feeling was [that] foreign companies were best. First was wholly owned, then joint venture. SOEs or Chinese private enterprises were last." Today, he says, the thinking has changed: "The heritage of [the] international company and brand within the young generation is lower. For our generation, we usually think that foreign brands are better. But the young generation, they don't have that view."

Instead, Chen says, members of the young generation are driven by other motives besides international brand image. "They have the passion to work in a good environment. Hierarchy and rank do not match the young generation much. They put happiness above everything else; they want to work for a company with a purpose and a future vision. . . . The new generation, they go to wherever the best environment is, and the best offer."

For MNCs, this new mindset can create high turnover. Chen says: "That's why, for the young generation, if they are not happy in a company, they jump very quickly. Unlike old guys. No matter what, we wanted to stay longer. But for the young generation, it is easier for them to jump." Another reason younger employees might change companies quickly, Chen says, is dissatisfaction with their supervisor. "They jump quickly if they do not feel they have a good boss." Thus, he advises MNCs to pay attention to middle managers and their rapport with team members.

Freda Zhang, IKEA's head of China, offers a similar assessment about the transformation of attitudes toward MNCs between her generation (i.e., those born in the 1970s) and today's post-90s generation. During the 1990s and 2000s (the early part of her career), she remembers the respect that she and others of

"Hierarchy and rank do not match the young generation much. They put happiness above everything else; they want to work for a company with a purpose and a future vision."

—Chen Yudong,
CEO, China, Bosch

her generation held for multinational firms in this way: "In the past, while working for a European company, every time [the management] spoke with me about something, I considered it to be a global truth." She gives this example: "I still remember the first time I listened to a European professor talk about 'think outside of the box.' I said 'Oh my God! I never heard about this in my whole life!' I never questioned it; I just believed it. I just fell in love. That's how I fell in love with IKEA's values very quickly, after only one year."

However, Zhang says that today members of China's young generation are less likely to blindly admire an MNC's corporate culture. Instead, they are more skeptical, questioning the company's business values, norms, and procedures. "Nowadays, Chinese born in the 1990s who join IKEA, they don't really believe, to be honest. When we talk about 'down to earth,' or when we talk about 'lead by example,' they need to understand 'why.' They need to understand: 'How does that connect with my daily work?'"

Not all MNCs reported waning appeal with potential Chinese employees. Alberto Cavaggioni, Maserati's top China executive, says his brand attracts a specific segment of the domestic population as employees: "There are still some very talented Chinese—mainly female—who want to join a brand such as Maserati because it's Italian, because it's a luxury brand, because we are manufacturing 'super cars,' amazing cars." But Cavaggioni adds that the appeal is not so much based on working for a foreign brand but more on developing, growing, and attaining self-actualization through work. He says: "Today, the Chinese people who are coming over to us are very, very interested in discovering new things. They bring fresh air, because they don't just come to do the job—they come to contribute to the growth of the business with their own creativity, their own passion, their own views." Cavaggioni says he encourages employees to share their viewpoints as "they are probably more willing to have the type of new thoughts or confrontation that I'm looking for" to gain insight into the complex China market.

Jacob Kragh, LEGO's head of China, also feels that his company's brand attracts Chinese talent: "We have a brand that, in

China, is certainly well known in the geographies where we operate. We have our offices in the tier-one cities, notably in Shanghai. We have a very strong brand. And that also means that, from the employer branding point of view, we have a relatively strong presence—and strong ability to attract talent."

Direct Competition from Domestic Tech Companies

Other MNCs, such as Philips, find themselves competing directly with domestic tech companies for top-tier talent. Andy Ho, the company's top executive for China, says: "Talent retention is very tough for a couple of reasons. Number one: there are a lot of local internet companies and technology companies. They're growing very fast and they all offer quite attractive stock plans. For the younger generation it's easier for them to work with those companies than for MNCs." (For more on the generation gap, see "Meet China's Millennials" later in this chapter.)

"Talent retention is very tough for a couple of reasons. Number one: there are a lot of local internet companies and technology companies."

—**Andy Ho,** Leader, Greater China, Philips

Ho counters the appeal of domestic competition by emphasizing Philip's strong track record in innovation: "We promote the company's image and the fact that Philips is a technology and innovation company. We continuously say that we are a very aggressive, open, and innovative company. So if you like innovation and technology, then come to Philips."

At Coca-Cola, Curt Ferguson, the company's top executive for China, echoes this sentiment. He advises that, due to the high-profile rise of China's domestic tech firms, MNCs can follow suit—attracting local employees by emphasizing a nonhierarchical corporate culture: "You can't operate in the classic American [hierarchical] system in China." He clarifies that he himself started his career in a US-based consumer company with a traditional structure: "You have that hierarchy. You have that ladder to climb. But I don't see that when I'm dealing with the digital people in China—with Alibaba and Tencent. That hierarchy thing, it doesn't work anymore. It has to be a circular, flat organization."

"That hierarchy thing, it doesn't work anymore. It has to be a circular, flat organization."

—**Curt Ferguson,** President, Greater China & Korea, Coca-Cola

Freda Zhang of IKEA describes the current assessment of MNCs by Chinese employees in this way: "By working in a

European company—especially in a Swedish company which has a company's culture and values of 'engage everybody'—there's always good part and negative part." The positive aspect, she says, is her company's long-proven value system, which is not dependent upon any individual corporate leaders—a phenomenon she describes as limiting in traditionally hierarchical, boss-led Chinese companies in the past. Zhang notes: "The good part is that the system itself will work with you or without you. So, basically, it will not be possible to have a one-man-show." The negative aspect, in terms of attracting Chinese employees, is the difference in pace. "The negative part is that because we try to engage everybody in Swedish culture, the decision-making process is very slow." The difficulty IKEA and other Western MNCs face in China now, Zhang says, is that the company culture may ring hollow with members of younger generations. She explains by referring to an actual case in which her company experienced multiple starts and stops that slowed the development of one particular bath product. Says Zhang: "When my son was a one-year-old, we were developing that bath toy. Now he's eight years old, and we are still developing that bath toy. Because in between people change, and then you need to have a product development workshop again, and the process restarts again." Zhang cautions MNCs that such delays can hinder morale among Chinese teams, given the general quickness of domestic private companies. By contrast, Zhang says China's domestic tech firms offer a more exciting culture with short reaction times and constant change to match market demand. She says: "For Alibaba and Tencent, what is good about them is that when they talk about their values, they are using the most 'local' words. They make their values very local. They connect with the changing daily life."

"For Alibaba and Tencent, what is good about them is that ...[t]hey make their values very local. They connect with the changing daily life."

—Freda Zhang,
Country Commercial VP, China, IKEA

Chinese Professional Women: Holding Up Half the C-Suite

One significant change "in the years between the publication of *China CEO* and *China CEO II* is some clear gains in the status of women. For one thing, while none of the 20 China CEOs interviewed for the original book were women, among the new interviewee group, four of the 25 top executives featured are women. While this is a small example of change, the top China executives interviewed consistently assessed the quality of China's female talent pool positively, especially as measured against their peers worldwide.

As an expert in executive recruitment, Charles Tseng, Korn Ferry's head of China, says part of the reason for the relative strength of the female professional talent in China is historical and cultural. He explains: "In terms of population, the number of highly qualified, capable women executives in China today outranks other countries on a proportionate basis because modern China was free of feudal and traditional practices. So, women were able to reach new heights career-wise. At the same time, China's fast growth increased the demand for high-quality talent. Therefore, people didn't restrict themselves to hiring only males or people from their region; they just looked at who was the best. So, in some respects, China grew from that type of model." The result, he says, is that "the quality of professional women in China is very high. This speaks to the new business environment, a new era. And the opportunity ahead is actually very, very attractive because what we have in China is an economy and an environment that are not tethered to or held back by traditional practices which limit a woman's career advancement." He points out that women now account for more than 60% of partners in China's professional firms.

One China CEO agreeing with this assessment is Victoria's Secret's Arun Bhardwaj. He states: "During the time of Chairman Mao, Chinese women were liberated in many ways." The Communist Revolution, he says, "got rid of some of the old societal norms" as well as "liberating women to make them a productive economic force for the development of China." He adds: "From that, came a greater degree of independence and confidence in women. Today, this is expressed in workplace gender balance and the ability of Chinese women to

"the quality of professional women in China is very high.... What we have in China is an economy and an environment that are not tethered to or held back by traditional practices which limit a woman's career advancement."

—Charles Tseng, Chairman, Asia Pacific, Korn Ferry

Female China CEOs Mini-Profile 1: Freda Zhang (IKEA)

Born in the northern Chinese city of Qingdao in the 1970s, Freda Zhang says she had a "typical" childhood among her generation; her parents worked in a state-run plastics factory. As a teenager during the 1990s, she witnessed China's economic transition first-hand. "The Chinese economy changed a lot—from a demand-driven economy to the market-driven. And that changed my life a lot."

During that decade, many Chinese SOEs began going bankrupt—including her father's factory. That left her father essentially jobless at age 45. Zhang remembers this time period as one of upheaval. "After that, the Chinese economy started booming. Many people started to invest in their own businesses. Some of these big brands—like Huawei and Wahaha and others—their owners are the same age as my father. They are the first generation of new entrepreneurs." Unfortunately, when her father tried launching a company, the result was, in Zhang's words "more debt for the family."

For Zhang, this meant self-reliance at an early age. "I needed to finance myself in order to finish my studies," she says. "From 18, I was working in different companies to manage my income and balance my self-study." As soon as she finished college in manufacturing accounting, she began working in a range of jobs from shipping to customer clearance while teaching herself English at night. "I studied at night and worked in the daytime."

Around this time, Zhang noted a sudden influx of foreign manufacturers into China. Thus, when a Taiwanese manufacturer opened a factory in Qingdao, she rushed to apply. "I was the second employee hired by the company. My job was to help the owner to establish the whole set-up of the factory from zero." As a startup, the company offered Zhang opportunities to expand her professional skills. "Within this Taiwanese company, although I was hired as an accountant, I was actually handling almost all the roles—from sales to manufacturing, even quality control issues regarding workers on the production floor."

After two years in the factory, she began pursuing her career dream of working in a Big Four accounting firm. But she faced a challenge: "Because I didn't have a very good educational background, I needed another way to advance my career." Her strategy? To land a job in a real international company.

When Zhang discovered that IKEA was hiring in Qingdao, she says she decided to apply for only one reason: "When I looked at the newspaper, IKEA's was the only ad in English. So I said: 'This is a real foreign company. It doesn't matter what kind of company.'"

Since no one in Qingdao had heard of IKEA at that time (2001), she describes preparing for the interview in this way: "My oral English was still not good because I was studying by night. And the Chinese way of studying English is that you know a lot of grammar, but you don't know how to speak." In this case, how would she to pass the interview? Zhang explains her solution: "I practiced by myself several nights. I memorized from the internet the entire website of IKEA. I memorized the whole story of IKEA in English so I could tell the 'IKEA story' during the interview." The result? "The interviewer was super impressed by me because I was the only candidate who could tell the entire IKEA story by heart." [laughs]

The strategy worked. After Zhang was hired as an accountant, her career within IKEA has progressed fast. After just one year in her initial role, at the age of 23, she was hired as finance manager for north China. "I was the first Chinese promoted into the management team."

Since then, her role has expanded as China has become an increasingly important market for IKEA. She went on to become Purchasing and Logistics Area Manager for East Asia, then Country Commercial Manager for IKEA China in December 2018.

Today, Zhang sees part of her role as educating her company's top executives and headquarters staff about a new shift in China's business environment, triggered by the rise of domestic tech companies and the new entrepreneurial mindset they represent.

speak for themselves and to do things which would probably not be so common in other countries." Summing up, Bhardwaj states: "Here in China specifically, the quality of the talent that exists among women employees is absolutely outstanding. . . . Most of my leadership team is comprised of women. I find them to be very good at detail, very good at understanding our products and our consumers—excellent managers, excellent leaders."

Jonathan Woetzel of McKinsey & Co. adds that, although gender balance "still has a long way to go across Asia," ongoing developments in high tech and new industries are offering new opportunities to women. "Essentially, these are sectors which allow low barriers to entry, have low capital requirements, are meritocracy based, and benefit from the highly educated pool of women in Chinese society. So, tech in China has been very good for women. There has definitely been progress."

As a female China CEO, IKEA's Freda Zhang notes differences in the status of professional women in China versus the other countries with which she regularly works. She says: "I have

Female China CEOs Mini-Profile 2: Kai Zhang (Manulife)

As a college student, Kai Zhang secured the chance to study abroad in the US as a result of her advanced English-language skills. When she left her hometown of Nanjing for the US to attend Mount Holyoke College (in Massachusetts) in 1992, she did not know she would end up staying abroad for 12 years.

After receiving a BA in mathematics and economics in 1994, she went on to spend four years at Watson Wyatt in Washington, DC, before seeking an MBA from Columbia University. Upon graduating, she spent four years as a management consultant at McKinsey & Company in New York. She then joined Citibank's Strategy and Mergers and Acquisitions team at the company's global headquarters in 2004.

In 2006, Citibank began urging Zhang to return to Asia. She remembers the company's reasoning back then: "The market was growing very quickly. . . .There were very few local talents who could run the whole business. So [Citi] encouraged me to move back to Asia."

After Zhang relocated to Shanghai as Citibank's Managing Director for China in 2008, one of the first things she realized was the "difference [in] the operating environment." She clarifies: "In the US and Canada, there were a lot more stable, established operating procedures than existed in China. That was the difference—a more mature market versus one that was still developing."

As a result, her new role in China required a broader skillset. She remembers: "Working in an emerging market requires more leadership in terms of the educational aspect, the motivation aspect, the oversight, and the creativity."

Back then, she recalls that bringing Western best practices to China also comprised a significant proportion of her new role. "At that time, foreign companies were held in very high regard, and local companies all wanted to learn from foreign companies. It was natural for foreign companies to bring their experts to China. Back then, foreign companies could not find people who knew the local market and also knew international operations."

Zhang describes herself as part of the "third wave" of managers sent by MNCs to leading roles in China. "The first generation of leaders for foreign companies [in China] were mostly expats[foreigners]. The second wave typically are from Hong Kong or Taiwan. And then came local-locals, like myself. It was a natural, gradual progression." With her impressive academic and professional background, she was approached by Manulife-Sinochem Life Insurance Company in 2015 and became the company's CEO and General Manager in December that year.

to say that Chinese women are super strong." Compared with women in South Korea, Japan, and India, she adds, Chinese females tend to exhibit a richer professional skillset. The reason, Zhang says, has to do with Chinese familial norms. "Chinese families are more open—investing more in their girls." She tells that some of her contemporaries with female children place high expectations on them. "I know some [Chinese] families with girls who even invest more in them than the boys, to give them a better education and to encourage to be independent in their careers."

Another aspect leading to the rise of Chinese women within MNCs today, according to Zhang, is that "we females have more persistence." She points out that the length of her 17-year career at IKEA is fairly usual among women colleagues, but less so among men. "A lot of Chinese men at IKEA are also very intelligent, but they check out of the company." She says Chinese men can be more attracted by the country's fast-growing tech companies. "In China, so many IT companies and new businesses started after 2005. Many of the Chinese men who had been working at international companies 'checked out' of MNCs to join domestic startups."

Echoing the sentiment that Chinese women enjoy a stronger status nowadays, Marriott International's top executive for luxury hotels in China, Rainer Burkle, says that Chinese society has a "mindset and commitment" that supports the professional development and advancement of women. The company offers several specific initiatives to promote women's development, including a program to encourage female employees to design their own local "Women in Leadership" initiatives to advance the presence of women in management. The company also promotes mentoring and role-modeling" in which women employees are interviewed in order to inspire others. As part of a global company, Burkle says he has insights to share in terms of gender diversity within the hotels in his scope. "Marriott International's talented women associates are guided into senior leadership positions from early in their careers—by both men and women. This results in a critical mass of women in leadership roles across corporate teams as well as our hotel functions. So, yes, we have the intrinsic interest to move on this issue."

Female China CEOs Mini-Profile 3: Celina Chew (Bayer)

Celina Chew was born into an ethnically Chinese family in Malaysia. She received her BL at the University of Western Australia in Perth in 1989, then her ML at the University of Hong Kong in 1992.

In describing her professional career, Chew explains that the first 18 years were spent as a lawyer, first for Clifford Chance in Hong Kong, then for Bayer in Shanghai. "I was a lawyer for a long time, starting in Australia with general corporate work and then focusing on China investment advice since 1993."

She describes the moment her career path changed from continuing as a legal expert toward a general management role. "One Saturday, my boss, who was then China CEO of Bayer, told me there was a proposal from the global board for me to move to Thailand as the country head and head of Bayer's Material Science Business for North ASEAN." She remembers her surprise. "I had not asked for this role, and it was also not part of my development dialogue. In addition, I only had two days to decide as he needed my answer by Monday."

Over that weekend, Chew's thought process evolved dramatically. "Originally, I didn't want to take up the role because I really liked working in China. I found China very interesting and there were many things I still wanted to accomplish here. So by Sunday morning, I thought I would not take on the role."

But that was not her final decision. "Later, I started to consider why I would not take on this role. I wondered if it was due to personal fear, to not being brave enough to take on something new and unknown. It was an unusual opportunity especially because I lacked direct experience in running a business." Chew says the tipping point that weekend was a conversation with a friend who pointed out that "the role involved many things that I had not tried and maybe felt reluctant to try." The friend stressed that the new role was "a good opportunity to try new things, take on a very different experience, face some fears, and gain new skills." Chew remembers: "I found this to be the most persuasive reason to accept the role. To refer to one of my favorite quotes from an Australian movie: 'A life lived in fear is a life half-lived.' So by Monday morning, I had accepted."

Chew then spent three years as CEO for Thailand and North ASEAN, a role that also covered the company's operations in Vietnam, Myanmar, Laos, and Cambodia, as well as managing the Material Science business. She remembers the feeling of being out of her comfort zone: "It was a big change from law to leadership of a big operation in an organization and within several cultures that I was not familiar with, and in business and political environments that I did not know. It was a very good learning experience."

In the end, Chew succeeded so well that in 2014 she was promoted to President of Bayer Group, Greater China. She describes her feelings as she took her current position, relocating from Thailand back to China: "It was challenging because China is ten times bigger than North ASEAN in terms of sales, turnover, and staff, and it has its own complexity. China is also much more visible in terms of the Bayer Group—being the third biggest market in the world for Bayer." In the end, she says the experience she gained overseeing the North ASEAN region prepared her as a seasoned leader, and she accepted the promotion in China.

Meet China's Millennials

As China CEOs discussed the challenges related to attracting, retaining, and developing employees in today's China, one word came up again and again: "millennials." In China, the generation born after 1990 (known in Mandarin as *jiu-ling-ho*) hold values, life priorities, and interests that are vastly different from those of their parents and grandparents. In fact, in today's China, many companies experience significant generation gaps between employees in their 20s to 30s versus those in their 30 to 40s, or 50s to 60s.

Farewell to the Chinese Dream?

Jonathan Woetzel of McKinsey & Co. sums up the age-based differences by first defining the traditional Chinese values held by the older generations: "China has been a rural society for thousands of years," he points out. From these agricultural roots, he says, a commonly shared "Chinese dream" was formed among previous generations. He explains: "What is this Chinese dream? It still has a solid underlying template of Confucian values and culture—which means that it's very important to be rooted in your peer group and your society. The most important thing is that you are recognized by others for the contributions you make to them. And that they, in turn, reciprocate to you. This is far more important

Part 1: Empowering Millennials (Microsoft)

As an example of the new ways of working that China's millennials can bring to MNCs in China, Microsoft's Alain Crozier tells the story of a fresh college graduate who, soon after joining Microsoft, introduced a client by setting up a meeting in an unconventional way. "This young woman sent a WeChat to the CEO of ByteDance and said: 'I want to meet with you.' And the ByteDance CEO decided, 'I'm gonna answer her, because maybe she has something to offer or to ask.'" The WeChat text soon lead to a 20-minute meeting between that CEO and Crozier, which later led to a new partnership. "In the end, they gained something, and we gained something." That same year, ByteDance acquired a video-sharing app that it renamed TikTok, which went on to become the 16th most downloaded app for iPhones worldwide in 2018.

To show how times have changed, Crozier remembers years back when he, as a junior manager, tried to connect with the CEO of a large retailer by LinkedIn. "The guy didn't answer me. And of course, when I became the CEO in France, then we were LinkedIn friends."

In today's China, the lack of such hierarchical social constraints "tells you a lot about how the relationships develop, the speed of connections." The fact that a busy CEO decides to answer a junior marketer via WeChat also speaks to the general atmosphere of "curiosity" in China, even at the CEO level.

Crozier emphasizes that the change is still new. "Five years ago, I can tell you that the same person sending a WeChat to a CEO would have resulted in a remark from his or her manager as being inappropriate.'" Today, however, a new spirit of "I don't mind if it fails" had taken root. And in this case, it resulted in a happy ending. "It was a win-win for everyone."

than expressing how you, as one individual, feel about something on a given day." He adds: "Where you fit into society is a lot more important than how you feel about it or who you are."

Another part of the traditional Chinese dream, Woetzel says, is the idea that individuals achieve recognition through hard work. He says this commonly held, rigorous work ethic "drives Chinese to be highly competitive within their peer group—to be viewed as the most important person within their workplace, for example." One challenge for employers, Woetzel adds, is that individual contribution has traditionally been measured mainly "within the broader societal sense" rather at the employer level. As a result, individual

Chinese employees may show "less loyalty to a company or an institution" than their counterparts in the West do. He clarifies the traditional Chinese mindset as follows: "You are only loyal to your family and to China." Within that framework, individuals are free to (and indeed are expected to) pursue the best career they can—with the goal of contributing the most to both their family and their country. "Within the private sector, individuals can go anywhere. There's a lot of mobility. It's all about becoming the most productive and most respected person you possibly can be—while supporting your family in the process." This thinking has led China's older generations to place very high importance on salary and benefits to better support one's family.

Self-Expression, Speaking Out

By contrast, China's younger generation of 20- and 30-somethings tend to be motivated by an alternative set of values that differ from those of the Chinese dream. Woetzel explains: "The new motivator of the young Chinese is self-expression. It's the definition of self and an exploration of urban technology, freedom, and global content. So that's a very different mindset for China."

Another characteristic of China's millennials that sets them apart from older colleagues is their willingness to voice their opinions. Alberto Cavaggioni, Maserati's head of China, also clearly notes the generational differences among his China-based team: "In China, fresh university graduates are much more similar—in terms of culture and behavior—to Europeans than to Chinese who are 40 and older." One key generational difference, he says, is that China's younger generations tend to speak out at work, while those over 40 tend to defer to their superiors rather than expressing their thoughts in public. Cavaggioni says he is trying to instill the more expressive, 20-something mindset across the generations at Maserati China in order to improve collaboration and discussion. "We are working extremely hard to instill this habit of sharing ideas, expressing your own opinion, and disagreeing."

"The motivator of the young Chinese is self-expression. It's the definition of self and an exploration of urban technology, freedom, and global content. So that's a very different mindset for China."

—Jonathan Woetzel, Senior Partner, McKinsey & Company

MINI-CASE

Part 2: Recognizing Millennials (Microsoft)

Retaining young talent is one of the key challenges for MNCs in China. Publicly recognizing the good work of the post-90s (or post-2000s) generation is one effective method, but as Microsoft's Alain Crozier shares, it is not without complications.

During the company's largest annual internal sales event, attracting 16,000 Microsoft employees and their guests each year, Crozier was invited to select an outstanding young Chinese employee as a representative of the new generation in a conversation onstage with one of the company's top executives. He chose a young female new hire who had, soon after joining, brought the company the Chinese startup ByteDance as a hot new client (see Mini-Case Part 1).

Crozier describes the scenario at the annual meeting: "We are in a huge arena and we put onstage one of our young up-and-comers, a recent college graduate who was 24 years old. She was interviewed by a direct report to the CEO."

When the Chinese millennial spoke articulately and confidently during the interview, the interview video immediately went viral among Microsoft employees in China. Crozier describes the reaction: "People in China were not just proud but crazy proud! Every generation, every age, every organization, they looked at that video and said: 'Wow. This is just unbelievable!'

"In the US, you have Instagram and Facebook. They are great, but in China we have WeChat—and the speed of distributing information by WeChat is two or three times faster than any other model." Thus, within a matter of minutes, he says, the young woman "became the star not only for the day but for more than the day." Crozier says she not only "won the hearts" of the 16,000 attendees at the event but also became a hero among Microsoft's China employees.

Crozier's plan to "bring the younger generation up front" in order to inspire all Chinese employees had succeeded beautifully for Microsoft China—until the next day.

What happened next? "The next day, she got an offer from one of our competitors who knew that she was onstage the day before."

And then? "Yes, we retained her," says Crozier. But the event clearly portrays the flip side of the "power and speed of social media in China."

Job Instability

According to to employers, the most frustrating quality of millennials is the frequency with which they change jobs. One factor triggering job-hopping is that many workers identified as "post-90s" are financially supported by their families and therefore less motivated by salary either to accept a job offer or to continue in that job. Tata's top executive for China, James Zhan, explains: "When we were young, we appreciated our job very much because we were depending on it. To [members of] the young generation, their life is not depending on this income. Salary, for some of them, is not important. They want to pursue their own interests. So, we have to deal with that." He clarifies: "Usually their family is well-off. Or at least there should be enough money coming from the property they own. So their motivations [for working] are quite different."

Zhang adds that the tendency to job-hop is lessening a bit among post-90s, who are now in their early 30s, as they marry and start families. "The definition of post-1990s covers a wide range. Those in their 30s are becoming more mature, more reliable. But the younger ones, they can quit."

"Stability is a problem," echoes Victoria's Secret's Arun Bhardwaj. His company is deeply familiar with Chinese millennials—both as customers and as employees. Says Bhardwaj: "We have a lot of young people as employees because of the nature of our brands. And our consumers are also young. Therefore, we need to understand what drives and motivates them." He explains that both his China team and his domestic buyers are composed of "people who have never seen flat economic growth or declining growth—people whose incomes have been rising consistently." This creates a degree of instability as many employees feel no risk associated with changing jobs. As a result, one of his key challenges is to address the human aspect of the job, that is, engaging and inspiring employees.

Udacity's head of China also has a front-seat view into domestic 20-somethings. Robert Hsiung says: "The average age of our students is 23—definitely millennials!" He describes this generation as follows: "We see is that Chinese millennials are not as content; they're more willing to take risks and more interested in jumping from job to job to job." He agrees that a significant factor in their lack of stability is relative financial comfort: "A lot of them, especially in China, have the support of two or three generations of parents and grandparents because they are single children. As a result, they don't need to hold down a steady job.

*"Chinese millennials
…[are] more willing
to take risks and more
interested in jumping
from job to job to job."*

—Robert Hsiung,
Managing Director, China,
Udacity

They can take time off to go to school and then find a job." As a result, companies find this group challenging. Says Hsiung: "This makes it more difficult to manage these people. It makes it more difficult to hire them and more difficult to retain them."

Less Motivated by Money

Asked how to retain China's post-90s generation, Udacity's Hsiung clarifies: "In my experience, younger Chinese join our company not just for a salary—not just to make lots of money or to be part of a massively growing startup." Instead, Chinese youth are more motivated by personal fulfillment, he says: "You have to enable your staff to [achieve] self-actualization—really finding a higher calling." He advises MNCs to use the following principles with Chinese millennials: "They find satisfaction from the work by receiving the right amount of freedom, the right vision, and the right guidelines to be successful. The combination of those three things is incredibly important to retaining staff."

"You have to enable your staff to [achieve] self-actualization— really finding a higher calling."

—**Robert Hsiung,**
Managing Director, China,
Udacity

Worldliness is another common quality of China's younger generation that differentiates this population from the previous generations. Explains Tata's James Zhan: "Many of them we hired had education experience overseas—US, UK, Australia. So they have a different mindset, a different understanding of the meaning of life."

Strengths and Weaknesses of China's Talent Pool

When asked to give an overall assessment of China's talent pool today as compared to that of other nations, China CEOs generally described a relatively strong demographic base. Kenneth Jarrett offers a representative viewpoint when he comments that, compared to the workforce elsewhere in Asia, MNCs find that China offers "a hard-working, smart, big workforce and [one] that's pretty well trained." He adds that "even if they are not trained to exactly what you need, they are very trainable."

Next, we recap first the typical strengths, then the typical weaknesses identified by our top executive interviewees in assessing China's domestic talent pool today.

Strong Point 1: Local Knowledge, China Track Record

Of course, one of the key reasons MNCs hire local teams is to gain access to evolving knowledge, insight, and contacts for success in the China market. China CEOs expressed the belief that a strong local team is absolutely essential for success in this complex, fast-changing market. As Jacob Kragh, LEGO's China CEO, states: "Having strong academic marketing knowledge is not enough if you haven't really operated in the China market. Both from a sales and a marketing point of view, things are changing so dramatically that we're looking for functional expertise rooted in very concrete achievements in terms of managing the dynamics of the market. We need people who have experience in and who have already executed in this very dynamic market." In particular, Kragh says his company looks for potential employees with a proven track record in marketing, sales, or operations in China. He says MNCs are generally striving to adapt to changes and to "follow new trends," especially in domestic e-commerce. Says Kragh: "The market is evolving quite fast with the way e-commerce companies are taking over consumers and the retail industry."

Bosch's Chen Yudong delivers this representative comment on the necessity of relying on local talent for domestic market insights: "For 95% of our business, we sell in the local [China] market. . . . If you want to play in the local market, then you want to localize the structure so the team feels like, 'China is my home market. I can fight in this market and grow this market.'"

"If you want to play in the local market, then you want to localize the structure so the team feels like, 'China is my home market. I can fight in this market and grow this market.'"

—Chen Yudong,
President, China, Bosch

Strong Point 2: Can-Do Mindset, Ambition

Another positive quality commonly found within China's domestic talent pool, the leaders of the MNCs said, is a positive, proactive mindset. Microsoft's Alain Crozier explains: "When you are in China, nothing is impossible. You'll get things done. The question is, how is it done?" He adds that while the "can-do" spirit of many employees is a benefit, sometimes top executives must instill more guidelines and standards than they would elsewhere: "As a CEO, you need to provide a bit of boundaries. Because sometimes that aspect is not robust enough in China. You need to bring a bit of execution and robustness to ensure that you build solutions that are going to last." At times, the enthusiasm of domestic teams can lead to a "coup mindset" in terms of focusing on "getting a deal," Crozier says. He warns his China team that "a deal is only great if you can sustain it, if you can provide a service to the customer. You must make sure that you build and develop the capabilities with the customer such that your solution will grow with the customer. Making the deal is not the end, in and of itself. And sometimes, we need to work a bit more on that [in China]."

Frederico Freire of AB InBev also generally finds Chinese employees to be driven and motivated. "We like ambitious people. We like young talents who want to grow. I love to hear from my young talent: 'Fred, my dream is to be you.'" He comments that during the ten years since his arrival in China, Chinese employees at AB InBev have become more outwardly expressive of their career ambitions. "I remember that in the beginning, people were afraid of saying that. They thought it was too much to say that. But I don't see that as too much. I see it as a good ambition. I need ambitious, dynamic people." He continues: "We need people with flexibility, with an open mind, to really navigate and maneuver within the organization, even sometimes making a lateral move. Getting an experience that is not necessarily your core experience but can help you for your next move. People who can transition to different departments and get better prepared for the challenge."

Coca-Cola's Curt Ferguson also notes that, during his two years as the top executive for China at his company, he has seen Chinese employees more actively seeking career advancement and increased responsibility. "In the past, you had to do more team building, more one-on-one coaching. But Chinese employees now want responsibility—they want creativity, they want to see where their careers are going. It's a lot faster pace."

Strong Point 3: Digital Skills

The top executives mentioned that another important asset of China's domestic talent pool is a generally well-developed set of digital skills. In the IT field especially, the China CEOs we interviewed noted that the skillsets and technical level of Chinese personnel is advancing fast. Hiroshi Takahashi, Sony's top China executive, explains: "When China makes a decision to develop something, they put huge money to it. The government is very rich, so they can put huge money into universities and colleges in order to develop so many talents in a very huge volume." The results of this strong government support, Takahashi says, are already visible. "AI is very hot in China. The government is putting a lot of money to develop a lot of AI talents. And they are putting a lot of money into the education of programming engineers. They move very fast. These are the characteristics of China."

"When China makes a decision to develop something, they put huge money to it. The government is very rich, so they can put huge money into universities and colleges in order to develop so many talents in a very huge volume."

—Hiroshi, Takahashi,
Chairman & President, China, Sony

Even in fields outside IT, the generally high level of digital savvy among Chinese citizens today is considered a positive attribute for MNCs. As the CEOs we interviewed explain, many jobs in today's China require some element of digital ability. L'Oréal's China CEO Stéphane Rinderknech comments: "Digital encompasses so many things. There's no more 'my digital team.' It's no more that! Digital is everywhere. People ask me: 'How many digital talents have you got?' Well, we have more than 10,000 employees [in L'Oréal China], so we have more than 10,000 digital talents. Why do I say that? Because . . . in China, digital is the life—this is the life of young people. So, if you want to touch them, you have to be there."

Rainer Burkle of Marriott International agrees that digital skills now extend to nearly all levels of employees in China. Across the company's hotels, some level of digital training is offered to all domestic employees. "This is the answer to tech-savvy Chinese travelers who continue to move away from traditional booking methods, preferring digital booking." He adds that "by constantly developing digital capabilities, we aim to enhance the guest experience through innovation—high touch and high tech." As an example of a digital innovation, he names a new E-Butler initiative launched recently at St. Regis hotels to allow hotel guests to seamlessly request butler services digitally.

Echoing this viewpoint, Coca-Cola's Curt Ferguson simply states that his China team is "so digitally enabled!" while L'Oréal's Stéphane Rinderknech stresses that all employees reporting to him are now categorized as "digital" talent.

Strong Point 4: International Mindset

One change noted by China CEOs who had been in China for more than five years is a newly internationalized mindset among employees, especially those from the younger generations. AB InBev's Frederico Freire explains: "The new generation of Chinese, they are more exposed to the external world." As a concrete example, he cites his company's global management trainee program, which annually identifies around 20 trainees from China. "They are young guys—20, 21, 23 years old—but for those from China, a lot of them have a background of studying in Europe or the US. So they are more exposed to the global world. They are much more open to learning, much more open to flexible problem-solving, much less attached to cultural heritage."

Freire explains the company's goals for this program: "We like to hire people young—after graduation—and forge them within our company, our company culture, our way of managing the company." He adds that developing talent from within is one of AB InBev's central values. "We believe Chinese managers developed internally are going to be much more prepared to take over my role in the future than someone that I hire from the market. This is our company culture—to develop talent from within our company more than from outside."

Advisor Kenneth Yu, former CEO of 3M China, agrees that China's workforce is becoming more global-minded, especially in the country's first-tier cities: "In a place like Shanghai, it's a much bigger workforce, and people move from one international company to another. So they are pretty familiar with everything about how international companies work. They have good English language ability—even down to the support teams." Increasing international travel, Yu notes, has also infused a degree of worldliness into the domestic employee base. "You have so much international travel now. . . . And when you travel internationally, you realize that this is a big world out there, and everything works differently. This can have an impact on the mindset."

Meanwhile, Coca-Cola's Curt Ferguson also describes his China-based team as generally highly educated and internationalized: "Everybody's Western educated. You don't have the old barriers of the past. Everybody has a link to Los Angeles! [laughs] The Chinese now are so well traveled; they know their way around. They know what they want to do."

The China CEOs we interviewed also identified a number of commonly held weak points among Chinese talent as compared with their counterparts worldwide.

Weak Point 1: Leadership Skills

China CEOs and consultants noted a continuing general lack of certain professional skills needed to work effectively in MNCs. Kenneth Jarrett, President of the American Chamber of Commerce in Shanghai, says this problem remains one of the most common issues faced by US-based companies in China: "Talent shortage is the one thing that everyone feels is still a problem." He says the most-named issue from member companies of AmCham Shanghai is "how quickly you can hire fresh graduates and make them useful members of your team. Most companies would say that it takes longer here in China than in other markets."

Which skills are weak or missing in fresh graduates of Chinese universities? Jarrett says leadership-related skills are among those most demanded by MNCs seeking training for their Chinese staff. Among the classes offered by AmCham Shanghai to member companies, he notes that: "A big chunk

"Talent shortage is the one thing that everyone feels is still a problem, [especially] how quickly you can hire fresh graduates and make them useful members of your team. Most companies would say that it takes longer here than in other markets."

—**Kenneth Jarrett,**
President, American Chamber of Commerce, Shanghai

of the training [sessions] offered cover leadership development." Specifically, the courses address a range of topics related to readying employees for the expected job responsibilities in an MNC. Jarrett says: "It can be public speaking, or how you lead teams, or making effective presentations," noting that the weaker skills tend to be those that are not emphasized within the Chinese education system.

One of the most problematic weak spots identified by Western CEOs managing teams in China is the tendency for domestic employees not to freely share their opinions at work. Arun Bhardwaj of Victoria's Secret notes: "In China, people are less open to speaking up. So if you ask for an opinion in a group of people during a meeting, you need to have a very high level of trust and comfort before people will start to speak up. And because it is more of a collectivist mentality, it's much more about fitting in and not sticking out." Kenneth Jarrett agrees, stating: "With the exception of the newer tech-related companies, most Chinese companies are still pretty hierarchical—the boss is the boss and people follow him. Don't be outspoken or challenging. If they challenge, they would do it in a very careful way."

Celina Chew, Bayer's head of China, explains that Chinese employees in her company—especially initially—also tended to be more reserved than their Western peers. Thus, they were less likely to take initiative, work autonomously, or share their own ideas.

"It takes some time for our local colleagues to understand that we are serious about the delegation of powers and responsibilities.... Once our local staff understand that this is the behavior and approach we encourage, I find that they are extremely good."

—**Celina Chew,**
President, Greater China, Bayer

"This is, of course, a generalized statement. But it takes some time for our local colleagues to understand that we are serious about the delegation of powers and responsibilities. We expect these colleagues to act independently—solving problems themselves. Once our local staff understand that this is the behavior and approach we encourage, I find that they are extremely good."

Weak Point 2: Creativity, Innovation

In terms of specific work-related skills, Microsoft's Alain Crozier says that, while China's talent pool is generally strong, several key areas are weaker than in some Western countries. He explains: "If you look at pure creativity, you may have more creativity in some other parts of the world. France, for example, is generally a bit more creative. If you look at the US, maybe a little bit better at the execution."

Other executives have noted that innovative thinking is hard to achieve in China due to traditional business norms. As one manager of a Chinese state-owned enterprise explained to the authors of this book: "If I try a new idea, something innovative, and it fails, I will be blamed by my boss. But if I try something and it succeeds, my boss will take all the credit for it. There is no reason for me to try to be innovative. It's better for me that I do nothing."

Weak Point 3: Cultural Adaptability

While China CEOs name adapting to China as a critical factor for success, interviewees also mentioned that employees within their China team must adapt, in some respects, to the culture of the MNC.

Jacob Kragh, LEGO's top executive for China, explains: "The way we operate in LEGO, we have a distinctive Nordic approach—low focus on hierarchical [structures], not driven by titles, quite informal." The challenge, says Kragh, is that these Nordic values are "sometimes at odds with tradition- al ways of working in China, where hierarchy is felt a lot more." The solution? Finding "people who connect better" with the Nordic mindset. Kragh notes: "When you drive a relatively informal agenda in an organization that's quite flat and quite informal, not all Chinese will thrive in that. Some Chinese will prefer more strict structures, stricter hierarchy to drive decision-making. And I think we're quite different in that respect."

Meanwhile, many China CEOs mentioned the importance among their local team members of being able to adapt to key cultural differences such as sharing their opinions, operating in collaborative and nonhierarchical ways, and demonstrating understanding of and sensitivity toward cultural differences between China and the MNC's home country.

Weak Point 4: Short-Term Mindset

For MNCs, the downside to China's high-energy, fast-paced, and flexible working environment is that these characteristics can lead to short-term thinking, which may damage a company's ability to deliver value to customers. Microsoft's Alain Crozier explains: "Because China is high energy, it is also sometimes short term. Sometimes the mindset of the people is that they are thinking about tomorrow, tomorrow, tomorrow. But you have to take care of the long term as well." Crozier says that a broader, higher-level view is especially critical in IT. "We are in the tech industry. So, very often, the customers are building a system and trusting you for the long term. It's not like providing a pair of shoes; if they break, you buy another pair. No! Our customers run on our technologies—so our responsibilities are much greater."

"Because China is high energy, it is also sometimes short term. Sometimes the mindset of the people is that they are thinking about tomorrow, tomorrow, tomorrow. But you have to take care of the long term as well."

—Alain Crozier,
CEO, Greater China Region, Microsoft

HR Strategies

Given the current challenges for MNCs in today's China, how can they attract top talent? In the following sections, China CEOs share their hard-won advice for successful recruitment and retention.

HR Strategy 1: Rapid Career Advancement

Top executives noted that one successful strategy for retaining top talent in China is rapid career advancement—often more rapid than what takes place in the MNC's home country. The most recent CEIBS China Business Survey found that 55% of WFOEs named "career path" as among the "most efficient" means of retaining employees, while 50% of Chinese domestic firms and 73% of SOEs also did so.[2] Overall, career path was the number-one retention strategy chosen by all three types of companies.

---

[2] 2019 *China Business Survey*. CEIBS

Chunyuan Gu, the head of ABB in China, has also found such results to be true at his company: "Locally, we try to make sure we don't have silo thinking. We are encouraging people who want to work for different functions and different business units. We have created a systematic approach to offer those opportunities, to give employees the chance to develop."

A decade ago, Gu says, it was easier to keep Chinese employees happy via rapid promotions. "In the past, China was about growth, only growth. When the business grows, people have more opportunities for promotion to management jobs, and you can attract good people." This became more difficult after growth-rates across China slowed in 2018 (hitting a 28-year low of 6.6%).[3] "I told [the China team] that, sooner or later, you will go back to normal [company] growth-rates, as our peers in the West [see]. When you don't double the business in three years, you don't create new positions." As an alternative to traditional promotions into the management tier, the company began developing systematic career tracks for different professional positions. Says Gu: "That means we need to think of careers for professionals—engineer, senior engineer, executive engineer, specialist engineer." He says some employees are still not satisfied with the reduction of growth in management promotions. "It's not so easy for some people to accept. In China, even if you have a good pay, if you are not promoted, people don't feel happy. There we have a little bit of a challenge."

Jacob Kragh of LEGO voices a similar concern: "Some people in the organization will perceive that there is a glass ceiling which is keeping them from progressing as quickly as they are hoping to. And that means that we are losing some people." He says LEGO faces a trade-off in balancing the company's global HR systems "in terms of how you quickly you can give key titles" versus expectations in China for faster and more frequent promotions. Being a flat, Scandinavian-style organization, LEGO "doesn't have as many levels in the organization as many Chinese would have hoped, because having many levels

"In China, even if you have a good pay, if you are not promoted, people don't feel happy."

—**Chunyuan Gu,**
Chairman & CEO,
China, ABB

---

[3] Nikkei. https://asia.nikkei.com/Economy/China-s-GDP-growth-slows-to-28-year-low-in-2018.

also presents opportunities for promotions." As a result, Kragh feels pressure to promote faster or lose team members in China. "That's a part of the ongoing challenge we have with the very young and ambitious Chinese who are seeking promotions—since that is, for them, the formal recognition on how their careers are progressing."

At Mango, the company's top executive for China, David Sancho, has found one method of motivating Chinese staff—clarifying job positions within the team. He explains: "Something I found very important in China is to first give clear titles. Job titles in China are very important to make sure that the company 'org chart' is very clear to everyone, and that everyone knows what the other one is doing and what their position is. This gives face to everyone regarding their particular positions." Other China CEOs have also pointed out that job titles can be upgraded, embellished, or changed (especially in English) without a full-fledged promotion, which can also serve as a motivational tool.

Mats Harborn, China CEO of Scania and President of the European Chamber, suggests a different solution for MNCs struggling with high turnover of Chinese staff: hiring the "second tier," the less ambitious employees. He clarifies: "The mistake many companies make is that we believe we should hire the high performers. And high performers are never satisfied. They come, they get [a] high title, a higher salary, and then after a few years they leave." Harborn advises a different tactic when hiring: "The way to work with HR is to look to the next level—people who are solid and whom we can train into becoming genuine members of our global tribes." This strategy, he says, helps to strengthen loyalty because employees can truly grow with the company over time. The problem with top performers, Harborn says, is that "in order not to lose them, we promote them." This, he says, leads to promoting people "too quickly," which in turn leads to people advancing their careers "very easily." He clarifies: "They end up over their competence level—not because they're incompetent but because they simply don't have enough experience. This is not good for [the] individual and not good for the company."

HR Strategy 2: Offer Continuing Education

Given the high value the Chinese society places on education, MNCs mentioned use of continuing education and training as a strongly effective means for retaining top talent. Kamal Dhuper, NIIT's head of China, explains that the high importance placed on education has deep cultural roots in Chinese society. "It's about the culture, the family values—in terms of education being the most important." For Chinese students, he clarifies, "if you have anything less than 95% [as an academic score], you're bad. Because in China, you can't succeed if you're not good in education; you don't get admission into universities. In China, you don't have any other option but to be educated." Most Chinese, he says, grow up with the pressure to succeed academically. "It starts very early for them—their education system instills the idea that 'if you are not good in studies, forget the rest.' That builds a lot of pressure."

Dhuper explains that in China (as in India), families and society see gaining admittance into university as a ticket to success. But only a small percentage of students can enter the university system each year due to China's highly selective exam-based admission system. Although the nation's *gao kao* test has recently opened to admit more students, only around one-third of students sitting for the exam will be admitted into a Chinese university.[4] "That's a problem of a huge, populous country— and India is also similar—with limited resources. There are only so many universities with so many seats." As a result, Chinese tend to grow up under a fiercely competitive education system. "There's a huge model of competition," Dhuper explains. He adds that this highly competitive environment, which begins in primary school, contributes to the relatively high percentage of Chinese and Indian students admitted into top Western universities. "This is probably the reason why Chinese and Indians are admitted in relatively high numbers into Stanford and Berkeley—because they have been competing

---

[4] SCMP. http://www.scmp.com/news/china/society/article/2097512/gaokao-how-one-exam-can-set-course-students-life-china.

since they were young. And if they don't get 100 out of 100, they feel something is wrong." This strong drive to perform academically, Dhuper says, continues to motive Chinese after they begin working, providing employers with an effective retention and promotion tool.

ABB is one foreign company using continued professional training to motivate top talent. The company's China CEO Chunyuan Gu explains ABB's "two level" education-based talent development strategy, offering either local study or international study programs for high-potential Chinese employees. Both levels, he says, offer employees the opportunity to study at respected universities and business schools: "This is a kind of signal to employees that if you are really good, you get a fantastic opportunity to study."

Volvo Cars offers a similar program in China, as well as opportunities to work abroad, as enticements to retain Chinese employees. The company's top China executive, Xiaolin Yuan, explains: "As with any well-established international company, the people development system at Volvo Cars includes training in good schools. And also, we offer job rotation and overseas assignments—all included." Likewise, Andy Ho, Philips' top executive for China, says his company follows a similar strategy for keeping top talent: "One factor helping retention is that we have very good training and talent development." And Bayer's Celina Chew says the wide range of classes offered to employees now includes training in new areas such as digital skills as well as less formal introductions to new tools, such as taking a one-off, Saturday coding workshop or visiting the company's virtual reality room, where employees can experiment with new VR tools.

Stéphane Rinderknech of L'Oréal China also says his company uses professional training as a key retention tool. In fact, he considers professional development as a part of his responsibilities as CEO for China: "The amount of time we spend on learning! That's our job—to make our young talents 'Win-Learn-Grow.' We need to make them feel that they're learning at L'Oréal, that when they have a meeting with me, they're learning something."

To boost digital skills among L'Oréal China employees, the company has introduced a My Learning program for staff. In addition, the company regularly sends high-potential employees abroad. Rinderknech says such training programs quickly pay for themselves in terms of increased motivation and productivity among employees. "They're going to give it back. Once they feel trust, once they feel that they can grow and they can learn, then they give back." One difference between employees in China versus those of other countries worldwide, Rinderknech says, is the sacrifice Chinese employees are willing to make in order to grow and develop professionally. "There's no limit. The class can be Saturday or Sunday night. No problem, no problem! Because they want to win with you. They want this sense of victory."

Marriott International is also among MNCs that actively support China's education system. Rainer Burkle explains the company's three levels of educational support. First is an ambitious training program for trainees. He comments: "Marriott International has always had a reputation of training. Many times, when you talk to people who have been with the company 20, 30 years, when you dig deep, they will probably tell you they started as a trainee." Burkle says the program is expensive, but necessary. "When you look at our hotels, you see a high [number] of trainees. Nowadays, trainees are as expensive as line employees because, in first-tier cities, you have to provide housing as well as food when they work." Second, the company has recently invested several million dollars in conjunction with nonprofit organizations, including the Yao Foundation, to build seven Hope Primary Schools across China. Third, the company organizes a program inviting Chinese teachers to attend information exchanges by Marriott executives. "All of us [executives] join to present seminars about the hotel business," explains Burkle, adding that he himself joins this program. "China has teachers with limited experience in the hospitality industry. They are great teachers, but they have to come closer to the industry and we are committed to helping to close this gap."

At Coca-Cola China, company CEO Curt Ferguson advises MNCs to offer attractive professional training programs even if a certain percentage of Chinese employees will leave after taking the courses. He explains his reasoning: "We have a really cool management trainee program, where we bring in 25, 30 kids a year and we take them through a two-year orientation course. At the end, they are guaranteed a job, and they can choose where they want to go. But we have to realize that—given the pace of China—we might lose half of those kids after the program." Ferguson emphasizes that because of China's bustling job market, his company must factor in a larger percentage of employees changing companies—and then develop creative strategies for fighting back. One strategy, he explains, is to bring the best of those who leave back to the company after they have gained experience elsewhere. "Let's keep the alumni network going. It's like graduation—some will move on, but some will come back. Some will be great ambassadors for our brand." He says understanding and flexibility are key characteristics: "You have to disrupt what you're thinking in order to match the speed of China and what's happening now."

"Before, when I would talk to the kids, they would all say, 'We've got to find jobs in the US.' Now, every single one of them wants to get the hell back to China—and fast—because they see so much opportunity here."

—**Curt Ferguson,**
President, Greater China & Korea, Coca-Cola

Another aspect of Coca-Cola's retention strategy, Ferguson emphasizes, is that the training programs currently offered to high-potential Chinese employees tend to focus on getting jobs in China, not in the US. He explains: "I'm on the board of my business school, Indiana University, the Kelley School. About 20% of Kelley School students are mainland Chinese. Before, when I would talk to the kids, they would all say, 'We've got to find jobs in the US.' Now, every single one of them wants to get the hell back to China—and fast—because they see so much opportunity here."

HR Strategy 3: Sense of Purpose and Strong Company Culture

One strategy mentioned by China CEOs to attract top-tier employees is to ensure that the company mission and vision establish a central sense of purpose clearly supporting social goals, rather than just economic or business goals. In fact, the strategy of "develop a feeling of belonging" was named by WFOEs polled in the 2019 *China Business Survey* as the single "most efficient" measure for retaining employees (56%). Meanwhile, 63% of Chinese private firms and 55% of SOEs also deemed this measure as most efficient.[5]

Andy Ho, the China head at Philips, says his company now emphasizes its social goals when recruiting Chinese talent. Ho says: "People know that we are basically touching our customers and consumers in ways that will make a positive impact on the world as well. Because of this, we are able to attract certain talent to our company."

Celina Chew, the China CEO at Bayer, argues that it is not only China's millennials who seek a clear sense of purpose in their work. "Why do we think only millennials want to work for a purpose? In my experience, most people—including older ones like me—want to work for a purpose, too!" Thus, Bayer strives to provide all employees with opportunities that the Chinese post-90s generation will value. She explains: "Bayer tries to offer many of the things that millennials are known to seek. For example, it is often said that millennials want to have a purpose in their jobs, and not just focus on making money. They want to do something with meaning and impact, they want more autonomy—not to be told what to do. They want to have a voice in meetings and to be taken seriously. They want to use the best tools and most updated technology. We try to offer all of those things—not only to our young colleagues but to all colleagues."

"[Chinese millennials] want to do something with meaning and impact, they want autonomy—not to be told what to do."

—**Celina Chew,**
President, Greater China, Bayer

While the company finds it challenging to compete with the hottest tech companies in terms of attracting talent, Bayer has its own strengths. Says Chew: "We might not be as 'teched-up' as Alibaba and Baidu, but we do try very hard to create a very good work environment for people to come to work every day—to learn and develop their own potential in the context of the company's overarching mission." In addition, the company offers a compelling central purpose. "Our purpose is very strong and well-embedded. Employees have actually told me

---

[5] 2019 *China Business Survey*. CEIBS.

that they joined Bayer because they were inspired by our purpose. 'Science for a Better Life' means that we create innovations which bring a better life to people in society." She adds: "When we really live this mission, and we can show it every day, this really motivates people. So, on the purpose part, we can really attract millennials."

HR Strategy 4: Commitment to Corporate Social Responsibility

Emphasizing active, effective corporate social responsibility (CSR) programs is another strategy that China CEOs use for attracting and retaining Chinese employees. L'Oréal's Stéphane Rinderknech explains the thinking he has observed among post-90s employees: "The young Chinese, they don't care about working for L'Oréal or any name. They want to contribute. That's what makes them wake up in the morning. They can work for a very small company, for a no-name company. What they care about is how they contribute." Rinderknech emphasizes that this drive to make a difference in the company, noted among younger employees, includes a strong ambition to support the growth and success of the company—to play a role in the company's business victories. In addition, China's 20-somethings also tend seek to contribute meaningfully to corporate social responsibility projects. At L'Oréal, one of the most successful and high-profile CSR initiatives has been the company's efforts to adopt green parcels for its huge volume of e-commerce deliveries. (For more information on L'Oréal's green parcel program, see Chapter 5.)

Celina Chew explains the efforts at Bayer to offer meaningful and effective CSR programs. Under the Bayer China Volunteer Association, which comprises over 5,000 domestic employees who are registered as volunteers, the company allows employees to spend two workdays per year (based on their volunteer hours) working on CSR projects of their choice. For example, under the Cinema of the Heart program, which has operated in Beijing for ten years, company volunteers spend one

Saturday per month accompanying a blind person to a movie showing—by serving as narrators during the film. In another example, a Bayer employee located in Zibo used a grant of 5,000 euros from the company's Role Model program to launch a Saturday afternoon Dream Classroom that provides art and calligraphy classes to children with autism and Down syndrome. Chew says: "We give employees outlets to support their own personal causes while also living Bayer's mission of 'Science for a Better Life.' Our volunteer program really allows people to live their own passion in the context of Bayer."

HR Strategy 5: Culture of Innovation

Robert Hsiung of Udacity says one essential strategy for improving retention among Chinese employees—especially among the younger generation—is to establish a corporate culture which nurtures innovation. And part of fostering innovation, he says, is to allow employees to try projects without fear of failing along the way. Hsiung states: "We strongly encourage our staff to go out there, to swing big, to take ownership, and to learn from their mistakes. Then we can continue to evolve and innovate. That shows a lot of trust to the team to push the envelope and continue innovating." In fact, Hsiung says that Udacity has built a corporate culture to nurture risk-taking as a necessary step in the innovation process. He explains: "My team is very focused around innovation. That's key to our success." To foster innovation, he says the company actively rewards employees for experimenting, even when the initial projects fail. "We've had front-line managers who launched projects that just flopped. But we will actually walk the person to the front of a meeting and give him a gift for failing." Such support and recognition, says Hsiung, creates a positive workplace culture and increases retention: "The trust we give to employees is returned. So, as a result, they're much happier. Our retention rates have been very high considering that we are in a sector in which retention is typically not high."

"We strongly encourage our staff to go out there, to swing big, to take ownership, and to learn from their mistakes. Then we can continue to evolve and innovate."

—Robert Hsiung,
Managing Director, China, Udacity

"We've had front-line managers who launched projects that just flopped. But we will actually walk the person to the front of a meeting and give him a gift for failing."

—Robert Hsiung,
Managing Director, China, Udcity

Celina Chew describes a similar pro-innovation goal at Bayer China: "Every company says they are innovative. But if I name the products that Bayer has developed over the years, you will see how much these products touch your lives every day; for example, healthcare products like aspirin and cipro; agrochemicals which transformed the way we feed ourselves; and high-tech materials such as polycarbonate and polyurethane—products which have transformed the way we insulate our buildings, enable mobility and communications. We invented these products. . . So for the 'purpose' part, millennials get the picture."

HR Strategy 6: Create an Inviting Physical Space

Another strategy some MNCs are trying is to attract talent by offering work spaces that support inclusive, flat, and collaborative working styles—in contrast to traditional Chinese work environments that reinforce hierarchy. Bayer's Celina Chew explains: "For the work environment, we do spend some money to make sure that our colleagues have choices in terms of how they would like to work in our office." In fact, some office floors are arranged as collective activity-based workplaces with no private offices. Says Chew: "For example, I do not have a personal separate office, but sit outside in the open space with my management team." The company also offers healthy drinks, a yoga room, a gym, and innovation spaces outfitted with beanbags that allow employees to "choose the spaces in which they would like to work."

Microsoft's new headquarters in the Caohejing district of Shanghai also exemplifies the effort MNCs are making now to create modern, flat, Silicon Valley–style work spaces. The company's China CEO Alain Crozier says, "We tested the design with the younger generation. And they provided a lot of feedback on what they don't want to see." His challenge, then, was to create a space that all generations of employees would appreciate. "How do you make that cohabitation? You need to get those generations to talk to each other. That's important."

And sometimes, he says, MNCs are now deferring a bit to the younger generation in order to send a message of support for newer, flatter ways of working.

HR Strategy 7: Positive Boss-to-Employee Relations

In China, as in other countries, one of the reasons employees often give for leaving a job is poor relations with their direct supervisor. But in China's hot job market, China CEOs noted that even small areas of disagreement or dissatisfaction with an employee's boss can quickly trigger resignation letters. Bosch's top China executive Chen Yudong says this of Chinese talent, especially members of the younger generations: "They jump quickly if they do not feel they have a good boss." One strategy shared by MNCs is to take note of the reporting line when they conduct exit interviews with employees who are leaving. Then the company can analyze which bosses have the highest and lowest rates of employee losses. Coupling this with analysis of leadership styles can provide useful clues about which leadership styles tend to encourage Chinese employees to go or to stay.

Kai Zhang, Manulife's top executive for China, emphasizes that strong relations with one's direct reports is also a key success factor for the China CEO to improve talent retention among the management team. "Here in China, the boss has to make sure to be respected and well-liked [by employees]. I spend more time doing counseling for our employees, which is also related to the fact that they are so much younger than would be the case in the West. They typically are tempted by many job opportunities. After three years, they think they need to get a promotion; otherwise, they feel they are undervalued." Zhang says strong ties between the CEO and members of her or his team can stem the loss of key talent.

Chen Yudong of Bosch China also emphasizes the importance of the behavior of supervisors toward members of his or her team—starting with the CEO. He says: "We can promote the values of the company—we promote openness, we promote

"Here in China, the boss has to make sure to be respected and well-liked [by employees]. I spend more time doing counseling for our employees, which is also related to the fact that they are so much younger than would be the case in the West."

—Kai Zhang,
President & CEO,
China, Manulife-Sinochem

trust. . . . But at the end of the day, how the boss treats subor-dinates is what decides the leadership style." He reminds us that the main reason professionals leave companies, including MNCs in China, is poor working relations with their boss. "The direct boss creates the environment for the team." He recom-mends that China CEOs use a leadership style focused on the "human touch."

HR Strategy 8: Match China's Flexibility, Adaptability

Finally, China CEOs mentioned "flexibility" and "short reaction times" as critical factors in retaining Chinese talent. Carrefour's Thierry Garnier explains the typical Chinese mindset regarding pace of change, especially among younger generations, in this way: "In fact, the Chinese people love change. So, it's rather easy to convince them to change. That's why all these transformations are easier in China." He com-pares the "Chinese impatience" and expectation of immediate results to a person changing from doing no sports to planning to run marathons within a few weeks. He adds: "The most difficult task is to keep a long-term plan when it's not imme-diately successful."

Garnier advises MNCs to understand the value placed on speed among the Chinese team, but also to add a sense of bal-ance. He says: "At the same time, you need to keep your long-term plan." For example, he says: "To adjust your logistics, you need four years. So after six months, [Chinese employees] say, 'Why isn't logistics bringing in more sales? We only have more cost and more problems, so we should stop logistics. It's not successful. Let's move to something else.'" For another ex-ample, he points to supermarket loyalty programs: "You want to build big loyalty programs, but after six months, you have only 10% of the customers using your loyalty card. But you need several years to get up to 70%. Typical Chinese manage-ment will help with the fast change, but they will also chal-lenge your long-term strategy because it's not fast enough.

They can be impatient." Garnier emphasized that being aware of the differing expectations related to speed is an important step toward addressing the potential frustrations of Chinese employees when working at MNCs. IKEA's Freda Zhang, L'Oréal's Stéphane Rinderknech, and Marriott International's Rainer Burkle also emphasized the desire among today's Chinese employees for their employers to adapt quickly and flexibly to market changes.

Summary of Tips

1. **Rapid career advancement**
   Offer a clear, accessible career development path in your organization, with managerial and professional options. Some MNCs use title upgrades or other types of recognition between full promotions to increase motivation.
2. **Continuing education**
   Invest in talent development. For Chinese, education is a deep cultural value. Besides being a motivational tool, training and education improve your employees' performance.
3. **Sense of purpose/strong company culture**
   Emphasizing that your company has a central purpose that contributes positively to society, and an inclusive company culture are two powerful recruitment and retention tools—especially for young Chinese employees. Communicate your central purpose and inclusivity often, and walk the talk in your actions.
4. **Commitment to corporate social responsibility**
   CSR is related to the previous strategy. Today's Chinese employees value companies that care about their social impact beyond business. Create active, effective programs to support social responsibility and involve your staff in the implementation.
5. **Culture of innovation**
   Create a culture of collaboration and innovation by welcoming honest failures and learning from them.

Provide training in innovation, and reward those employees who develop creative ideas and initiatives. Be an innovation role model.

6. **Inviting physical environment**

   The physical environment of the workplace offers another opportunity to instill a corporate culture of collaboration and creativity. Modern office designs emphasize flat hierarchy, as well as boosting the health and comfort of employees.

7. **Positive relations between bosses and employees**

   A bad relationship with the boss remains a key reason for losing talent. Reward those managers who have lower turnover rates among their subordinates. Provide leadership training where needed.

8. **Match China's flexibility**

   Establish and maintain a nimble, adaptable working culture that stresses open communication and fast reactions to market changes.

Chapter 4
China's Digital Revolution

There are some areas in which, truly, Chinese companies are starting to make people raise their eyebrows—areas of true technology advancement.

—**Xiaolin Yuan,** President & CEO, Volvo Cars Asia Pacific (and Senior Vice President, Volvo Cars Group)

China will become an innovation powerhouse in the future. The world needs to realize this and be ready to accept that China's innovation power is growing much faster than the average level.

—**Chen Yudong,** President, Bosch China

INSIDE CHAPTER 4

The Rise of China's Digital Champions

Where Digital China Dominates

Navigating China's Digitized Landscape

Digital Strategies

Summary of Tips

Introduction: A Global Digital Leader Rises

The single challenge most often expressed by China CEOs interviewed in this book regarding leading large-scale operations in today's China concerned the rapid and far-reaching digital transformation that is now underway. Most described the change as a revolution disrupting all business operations, across all industries and functions. In addition, China's digital rise was also seen as deeply influencing consumers, business partners, competitors, and employees in terms of their expectations, demands, lifestyles, and habits.

Consider these facts regarding the growth of China's tech giants Tencent and Alibaba:

Tencent's WeChat app, the most popular social media platform (like Facebook and Twitter combined), boasted these numbers in late 2019:

- Active users: 1.32 billion[1]

- WeChat messages sent per day: 38 billion (26 million per minute)

- Voice messages per day: 6.1 billion

- Calls per day: 100 million

- Corporate accounts: 14 million

- Average number of minutes per day per user: 77

- Percentage of Chinese ages 50 to 80 on WeChat: 98.5%[2]

---

[1] https://www.statista.com/statistics/255778/number-of-active-wechat-messenger-accounts/.
[2] Expanded Ramblings. https://expandedramblings.com/index.php/wechat-statistics/.

Turning to China's e-payment platforms, the nation's two rival platforms—Alibaba's Alipay and Tencent's WeChat Pay—boast these numbers as of mid-2019:

- WeChat Pay: 900 million Chinese users (65% of China's population)[3]
- Alipay: 700 million Chinese users (50.5% of China's population)[4]
- 240 million users outside China (combined, in 40 countries)

In terms of e-spending, China's digital payment market is now worth more than US$18 trillion, of which Alipay controls a 53% share while WeChat Pay takes 40%.[5] In 2017, Alibaba began expanding the Alipay platform overseas, initially to support Chinese travelers. As of mid-2019, both the Alipay and WeChat Pay platforms could be used in 40 countries including much of Asia as well as Europe and North America, albeit primarily by vendors serving Chinese customers (such as duty-free shops). The number of countries and locations was growing fast.

One of the most significant impacts of the rise of Alibaba, Tencent, and other digital champions in China is the superstar status of the founders. For many Chinese, especially younger generations or more entrepreneurially minded people, Alibaba's Jack Ma and Tencent's Ma Huateng are nothing short of national heroes. Other highly regarded domestic companies that have expanded globally—mainly from the tech sector—include Baidu (search engine) and Jingdong (e-commerce). Together, the success of China's Big Four (Baidu, Alibaba, Jingdong, and Tencent, aka BAJT), are a great source of pride for many Chinese.

Xiaolin Yuan, Volvo Cars' top executive for China, sums up the reaction of China CEOs regarding the influence of the digital advancements in this nation when he says: "People are

---

[3] Mobile Payments Today. www.mobilepaymentstoday.com/news/allied-wallet-adds-wechat-pay-with-900-million-active-users/.
[4] China Daily. http://www.chinadaily.com.cn/a/201811/30/WS5c00a-1d3a310eff30328c073.html.
[5] Forbes. https://www.forbes.com/sites/ywang/2018/03/28/is-alipay-losing-to-wechat-in-chinas-trillion-dollar-payment-war/.

really looking with amazement at development of the internet in China, and the rise of local tech companies—Baidu, Alibaba, or Tencent or the smaller ones, the niche players. That's the very reason why in California's Bay Area, the name Shenzhen is being mentioned as a second Silicon Valley. So much is happening." Yuan emphasizes that, in his view, the buzz and hype is warranted: "There are some areas in which, truly, Chinese companies are starting to make people raise their eyebrows—areas of true technology advancement."

At AB InBev, Frederico Freire, the company's China CEO, represents the views of many top executive peers when he describes the mindset of domestic consumers in terms of demanding the constant connectivity and convenience offered by digital platforms. Since domestic consumers are now used to a fully connected life, MNCs supplying B2B must also operate in a digital business model. Freire says, "Digitization in China is not avoidable. We need to go into e-commerce. We need to be where the consumers are. Not doing it is not an option." In the F&B business, digitization means ordering a beer via an app, paying by phone using WeChat or Alipay, and expecting delivery anywhere within 20 minutes. He also says, "This extra-convenient approach, it's unavoidable now." Freire expresses the views of fellow China CEOs in commenting on the extreme connectivity underpinning all aspects of life in today's China—a degree of personal data disclosure which makes some uncomfortable. "It's unbelievable. For digitalization, it's scary, it's scary. At the end of the day, somebody knows everything you do," he says. He comments that even the interviews conducted for this book could be stored and monitored—because they were recorded via mobile phone: "It might be known that you are recording this interview, because you're using an app. And this is somehow scary."

Economist Corporate Network (Shanghai) Director Mary Boyd echoes such thoughts with this comment: "Obviously, the digital platform [in China] is very, very extensive. And it has pushed a lot of the business implications much faster, much further here than elsewhere in the world." She says while this is "definitely" true for retailing—especially in the phenomenon of

"Digitization in China is not avoidable. We need to go into e-commerce. We need to be where the consumers are. Not doing it is not an option."

—**Frederico Freire,**
BU President, China,
AB InBev

"The digital platform [in China] is very, very extensive. And it has pushed a lot of the business implications much faster, much further here than elsewhere in the world."

—**Mary Boyd,**
Director, Shanghai,
Economist Corporate Network

shopping via social media communities—it is also the case for other sectors including fintech.

James Zhan, Tata's top China executive, says there's "no question" that China has advanced technologically in recent years, and is on a trajectory now toward further growth. "There will be ups and downs, but at the end of the day, China will stand out in terms of innovation," he says. Zhan says China is already outstanding globally in key areas including robotics and batteries. In particular, he names BYD and CATL as two Chinese companies excelling in batteries, stating, "They have done a tremendous job in ramping up their operations—in technology and innovation. They will be supplying batteries to us not only in China but around the world." Another sector which is advancing fast in China, Zhan says, is digital maps.

Overall, compared with counterparts in Silicon Valley, Zhan says China's tech players still show a gap in terms of capital efficiency. "For the money you invest versus the technological outcome, probably, Silicon Valley gives a much better outcome." But he believes this gap will disappear over time. "After a certain number of years, some of the money invested in China will hit the jackpot. Because the foundation is there. There are many times more engineers in China, and some of them will break out—maybe not winning a Nobel Prize, but still launching successful applications."

Zhan clarifies: "Even if there are issues with some of the government policies [in China], you will eventually have results." Working in China's favor, he emphasizes, is the try-as-you-go environment in the domestic market. "The best sector, for China, is application technologies. If you don't have a market, you can't grow the technology. Only when you apply the technology to the market, do you have positive feedback." He points out that China's large, open-minded, and accessible consumer base offers fertile ground for young tech companies to test out new apps and products. In another example, he says China's domestic battery companies can launch and sell batteries locally, earn revenue, and then use these funds to cover the cost of improving the product in order to go global. Zhan says, "This positive cycle is important. In this way, the market nourishes the development of technology—and eventually some of them will break through."

Bosch's China President Chen Yudong is also optimistic about China's digital transformation: "China will become an innovation powerhouse in the future. The world needs to realize this and be ready to accept that China's innovation power is growing much faster than the average level." He says this speed of transformation is based on two reasons: "One is that local companies have more money now. So, they can spend more—they hire more people. Second, there are a lot of returnees, globally. You see so many people coming back to China. They bring the know-how and technology back to China." The result, says Chen, is that China is destined to rise technologically. "It's a matter of time." He adds that economic and diplomatic challenges such as trade disputes with the US will actually help China. "Because of that, Chinese people will develop innovation faster."

"China will become an innovation powerhouse in the future. The world needs to realize this and be ready to accept that China's innovation power is growing much faster than the average level."

—Chen Yudong,
President, China, Bosch

From Copying to Improving to Innovating

One important topic in the discussion on China's digital transformation concerns the degree to which the nation's entrepreneurs and inventors have shifted from copying products and services from elsewhere to truly innovating in their own right. China CEOs interviewed agreed that although copying still exists, it has decreased in many industries and sectors, while true innovation has increased. Among our interviewees, opinions varied as to how far along the spectrum Chinese players had advanced. However, all agreed that, as a nation, the country was definitely moving toward greater innovation, originality, and creativity.

Microsoft's head of China, Alain Crozier, explains the unique brand of "made in China" innovations that have shaped the competitive domestic landscape in recent years. In many cases, Crozier explains, Chinese companies are succeeding not by copying international innovations but by substantially improving upon them to create new and better products or services. He points to China's widespread digital bike-sharing system as an example. Crozier says, "Bicycle-sharing was invented in Europe. But originally, you had a bicycle that you had to bring back to a station. And you had a way to connect and disconnect the bicycle through a code. So, China said, 'No more bike station. You can take the bikes from the street corner near your office or home. It's going to be a bit messy, but convenient. And you can access that bike through your mobile phone for two or three RMB per hour.'" The result, Crozier says, is a business model with no heavy infrastructure, and no need to destroy the pavement and build stations. And instead of using codes, users go directly to the cloud to access the bikes. "They took something and transformed it a little bit. This is what China is all about." He adds that the business strategy of Microsoft in China today is to join forces with domestic companies creating such incremental innovations. "For us, it's very important to develop solutions with those companies."

Sony's Hiroshi Takahashi expresses a similar view, recognizing and praising made in China innovation as a bona fide form of invention. He says, "Chinese competitors adapt very fast. That's why, sometimes, they have a conflict with some other countries. They are adapting or learning some technology from outside China, but at the same time adapting it and somehow inventing new technologies." Takahashi, for one, considers adapting and improving to be forms of inventing and creating. "For me, innovation and the adapting is almost the same meaning. It's very difficult to draw a line." He describes the evolution in Chinese-style innovation over the past 30 years. "A lot of innovation in China came from copying in the 1990s. But when you copy something, if you add some new element in, it becomes innovation. This is a very significant nature of Chinese innovation in the past."

Today, he says, Chinese companies are inventing and creating in their own right. "Now, there are some areas—for example, fintech—in which China is already running ahead of the rest of the world." He also sees other developments in hardware launching in China first, then expanding worldwide. "In the hardware field, there are many technologies which are only

"Chinese competitors adapt very fast. That's why, sometimes, they have a conflict with some other countries. They are adapting or learning some technology from outside China, but at the same time adapting it and somehow inventing new technologies. ... Now, there are some areas—for example, fintech—in which China is already running ahead of the rest of the world."

—**Hiroshi Takahashi,** Chairman & President, China, Sony

developed in China. For instance, voice-assisted TV was tried in China first. If they are successful, they will go outside of China and bring the services and systems to the other countries. That's the natural trend."

Other China CEOs also noted rapid advancements underway in their sectors, based on made in China innovations. At Bayer, the company's top China executive Celina Chew told how operations are digitized in China across the company's key sectors of health and nutrition. The company uses robotics as well as automated, driverless vehicles in the warehouse operations of its flagship pharmaceutical plant in Beijing. Meanwhile, in Consumer Health, Chew notes a flourishing of new digital products and services in China. Sharing one example of the spirit of growth and disruption in today's domestic market, Chew recounts how she recently discovered a new medical services company called Ding-Dang which helps patients to find doctors and nurses online, using an app. The app allows patients to purchase medicines as well as to arrange for a professional nurse to come to their home. Chew showed the app to her IT team and, when they tested it, found that patients could buy Bayer products via the app. This is one type of disruptive development taking place in today's China for MNCs. To keep abreast of such developments, Chew says Bayer "proactively scans the landscape for new healthcare-related apps" as well as other developments.

"A lot of work is happening both in a structured way and an unstructured way in China now. Yes, innovation is happening. There is great development—especially in the areas of AI and Big Data, robotics, machine learning—in China. All the key areas the world is talking about today."

—Kamal Dhuper,
President, China, NIIT

In the field of agriculture, Chew also sees impressive advancements being made in China. "Digital farming is going to be massive. It is just starting to take off now." She adds that, looking ahead to predict future digital advancements is a crucial aspect of addressing the China market today. "You go where the customers go. And they are very much going towards a digital trajectory. Both in healthcare and agriculture, we are on the cusp of being seriously disrupted by digital solutions."

Kamal Dhuper, NIIT's top China executive, sums up the overall impression of many China CEOs in assessing the domestic environment for innovation today. He says, "A lot of work is happening both in a structured way and an unstructured way in China now. Yes, innovation is happening. There is great development—especially in the areas of AI and Big Data, robotics, machine learning—in China. All the key areas the world is talking about today."

Innovation Challenges

The transition toward bona fide innovation, for Chinese companies is not, however, without challenges. One difficulty, emphasized by our CEO interviewees, is the fact that the mandatory domestic education system does not emphasize, or even condone, independent thinking among students. Kai Zhang, Manulife's top executive for China, is one CEO who believes that, as a nation, China needs more time before true innovation can take root. "China's biggest technology companies, started by copying the innovations of the West. We need to see more original and disruptive innovations—what China used to be known for." She points out that China is famed for four ancient inventions—printing, paper, gunpowder, and the compass—but creating a fifth one will likely require a shift in the culture and environment. She says, "We need to get to a point where people are rewarded and respected for truly ingenious work—creating value for society which might not lead to commercial success immediately." She says today's "go-go" environment encourages people to make fast money in technology but not to develop true innovation.

The pace of change in today's China, Zhang clarifies, is both strengthening and weakening the nation's tech industry. "In China, the pace of change is very fast. China is like a high-speed freeway; if you're driving your car too slowly, you can get run over. Basically, you have to move very fast." She says those working in China experience the speed of development in terms of tangible changes—the development of logistics, infrastructure, and transportation services—as well as an intangible environment encouraging people to grab opportunities to make fast fortunes. She calls the current environment "immature"

"In China, the pace of change is very fast. China is like a high-speed freeway; if you're driving your car too slowly, you can get run over. Basically, you have to move very fast."

—Kamal Dhuper,
President, China, NIIT

and unable to nurture true innovation: "During the last 20 years, too much money was made in real estate—in flipping the companies or listing shell companies. There are too many zombie companies still operating, too many financial games being played." This backdrop of steep financial gains made from real estate, for example, has skewed the operating environment. She says, "In China, if you compare someone who built a company for ten years against someone who bought a few apartments in Shanghai, the person who bought the few apartments did a lot better. So that's why a lot of businesses, after the initial success, they feel it's so hard to make money. Then, they invest into real estate, or they open restaurants. They get overextended financially and they fail because they're not focused on their core business anymore."

Mats Harborn, Scania's China CEO and President of the European Chamber of Commerce in China, voices a similar concern regarding the mindset and priorities of many Chinese digital entrepreneurs. Harborn says problems exist in both the unregulated and the regulated industries in the Chinese economy. "In the unregulated sectors, there are too many innovators who are not really investing for the sake of providing a good service to the market. They are innovating to create something sexy, to make an easy IPO, or to sell off to make a quick buck."

On the other hand, the areas regulated by the government tend to be over-regulated—thus squelching innovation. Harborn says, "I also see a top-down approach where China is trying to dictate solutions, which makes innovation less efficient. A lot of money is wasted because there's too much top-down approach—too many subsidies in the system." Going forward, he expects a "wake-up call" in the form either of state money drying up or investors losing interest in supporting ill-conceived or ill-managed startups. Ultimately, he hopes to see China developing "a more sensible approach to innovation development."

Other MNCs argue that, ultimately, China's ability to create a nurturing environment to foster innovation will require government support in terms of creating the infrastructure and support systems necessary. Manulife's Kai Zhang explains: "As a nation, China struggles to get to the true innovation without government support." She points out that many Chinese SMEs are ailing due to lack of funding. Zhang believes government funding and support is "necessary" to foster an innovation culture at the beginning stage, even if that support is "government-based instead of market-based." She clarifies, "We need some form of support system—public or private—otherwise we can't create an efficient system for innovation to happen. We need to transform the economy through innovation. Definitely, the government realizes what China needs to do."

Fitting models for China to follow, Zhang advises, can be found in Israel and Germany. Israel offers a model for successfully fostering startups and nurturing new technologies, she says. "In Israel, the government plays a big role in innovation; there's a culture of innovation. And education is very well-regarded in Israel." From the German model, Zhang urges Chinese to learn from the emphasis on quality. "People say Chinese society doesn't have time to pay attention to the fine details. There is a 'fast food' mentality right now; everything is quick." Today's business environment in China, she says, fosters only "small guys with small inventions" focused on short-term commercial success.

While viewpoints varied as to China's progress toward cultivating true innovation, one trend clearly agreed upon by China CEO interviewees was the impact of the country's digital "national heroes," both domestically and globally.

The Rise of China's Digital Champions

One of the most important factors in the rise of Digital China is the emergence, in the past two decades but especially since 2010, of a group of domestic technology giants. These companies have now gained superstar and hero status among many Chinese. In addition to China's top four tech giants (Alibaba, Tencent, Baidu, and Jingdong), other successful tech companies going global include Huawei (telecom), DJI (drones), Didi (share cars), as well as startups including Sensetime (AI) and ByteDance (viral video-sharing apps).

Mini-Profile: Alibaba

- Founded: 1999
- HQ: Hangzhou, China
- Includes: Taobao & TMall, Lazada (Southeast Asia e-commerce), South China Morning Post, AutoNavi (mapping data company), Alipay, Alibaba Pictures Group (Chinese film producer), Aliwangwang, Air Health Information Technology, Hema Supermarket
- Founder: Jack Ma. Ma has been ranked second on *Forbes'* magazine's list of World's Greatest Leaders. Named among *Time* magazine's Most Influential People (2009)
- Employees (2019): 101,958[6]
- Annual revenues (Fiscal 2019): RMB376.8 billion (US$54.74 billion)[7]

Mango's China CEO, David Sancho, expresses the respect which most foreign CEOs have for China's digital leaders: "Look at the giants like Alibaba and Tencent—the way they are producing companies. Look at the Chinese schools that are building a talent pool to drive innovation in China. For sure, China is going to become a powerhouse. It is already."

The rise of China's tech giants has influenced many aspects of the business environment. One far-reaching change has been the blurring of borders between industries and markets caused by the digital revolution. Jerry Zhang, Standard Chartered's top China executive, expresses, "Cross-industry and cross-border collaboration and integration will be a new norm." As an example of fertilization across sectors, she points out, "Five years ago, no one could have predicted that Tencent would invest in a bank. . . . Now Tencent's WeBank is perhaps among the fastest growing lender in China, with NPL rate enviable to most traditional banks."

"Five years ago, no one could have predicted that Tencent would invest in a bank. ... Now Tencent's WeBank is perhaps among the fastest growing lender in China, with NPL rate enviable to most traditional banks."

—Jerry Zhang,
Executive Vice Chairman & CEO, China, Standard Chartered

[6] Statistica. https://www.statista.com/statistics/226794/number-of-employees-at-alibabacom/.
[7] Craft. https://craft.co/alibaba/revenue

Many other MNCs are working directly with China's big digital players to develop customer-centric digital products and services. One such company is Marriott International, which has set up a storefront (via Alibaba's online travel platform, called Fliggy) allowing guests to book hotel reservations digitally. Another aspect of the collaboration—called Post Post Pay—allows qualified users to travel first, then pay after their stay; to book hotels without paying a deposit; and to enjoy a comprehensive wallet-free experience during the stay, as well as express checkout.

In addition, a third joint project with Alibaba now offers guests facial recognition check-in, so far, at two locations in Greater China. Marriott International's top China executive for luxury hotels, Rainer Burkle, explains how it works: "You can check in with just two things: your passport and your face." Most guests make their reservation via mobile phone, receive confirmation digitally, then check in at the hotel using a kiosk in the lobby. They have their face scanned, then receive their room key at the kiosk. Burkle says, "You don't need to queue—so it provides another option for checking in."

L'Oréal is another MNC working with a range of tech companies both in China and abroad as part of the group's Beauty Tech campaign. Stéphane Rinderknech explains: "With digital tech, we are capable to augment the consumer experience." L'Oréal recently bought a Canadian company called Modi-Face which is "leading those technologies which allow users to use augmented reality for makeup simulation on your face and color for your hair." Rinderknech explains that the technology allows users to test out cosmetics and hair dyes realistically using augmented reality. "It's very difficult to know what a hair color is going to look like on you before you dye it. This is beautiful because you move your hair and the augmented reality stays with your image. It's real 3D." Adds Rinderknech: "This is where digital technology is stepping in to really improve the consumer experience. Because when you try lipstick on the back of your hand, there's only so much that you can try that way. When you can try it [virtually] with a mirror, it's

Mini-Profile: Tencent

- Founded: 1998

- HQ: Shenzhen, China

- Includes: WeChat, WeChat Pay, QQ, QQ Wallet, Tencent Games, China Reading, China Comic, Tencent Pictures, Tencent Music Entertainment[8]

- Founder: Ma Huateng. Ma has been ranked one of the most powerful people in the world by *CEOWORLD* magazine. He is the first Chinese citizen to reach *Forbes*' top ten richest men list.

- Employees (2019): 54,309

- Annual revenues (2018): US$47.2 billion in 2018[9]

embedding within the offline. So, again, it's not offline-online. It's O plus O."

Another app will allow consumers with skin problems to receive "skincare diagnosis driven by artificial intelligence." Rinderknech elaborates: "We're launching a project now with Alibaba where we store pictures of tens of thousands of consumers with acne issues. Machine learning analyzes the different type of acne problems on the human face, and crushes that data together. As a consumer, once you say, 'I have an acne problem' and scan your face, the system will tell you the gravity of your acne and recommend a routine customized for your needs." (For serious cases of acne, L'Oréal will recommend seeing a dermatologist.)

Hiroshi Takahashi, Sony's top China executive, explains the impact of China's digital giants on the business operating environment—and on his company's business strategy—in this way: "First, the product itself must be new. China is a very dynamic market, and the key element is speed. Here in China,

"China is a very dynamic market, and the key element is speed. Here in China, new technologies like WeChat or Alipay, Mobike or Didi, those delivery services, they grow so very quickly. That is one of the attributes of China. These are people who like new technology."

—Hiroshi Takahashi,
Chairman & President,
China, Sony

[8] Tencent. https://www.tencent.com/en-us/system.html.
[9] *Forbes*. www.forbes.com/companies/tencent-holdings/#658c5f25158b.

new technologies like WeChat or Alipay, Mobike or Didi, those delivery services, they grow so very quickly. That is one of the attributes of China. These are people who like new technology; they quickly accept new technology and they try new things."

Takahashi describes the breadth and depth of the existing Chinese digital eco-systems, and the impact on Sony's domestic business strategy: "Our products must be capable of accommodating Chinese consumers; we must make them happy. In order to do that, we have to work with Chinese companies. That is my finding after working in China for these years. Our products are no longer independent devices that sell themselves. Here, our products have value only if we can combine our hardware with services and content from other suppliers. And those services and contents are mostly—99%—supplied by Chinese companies within a big ecosystem." He continues: "It is inevitable for us to become a part of a system which is run by Chinese companies."

The strategy for surviving in the China market, Takahashi says, is to join the domestic system: "Our advantage is an excellent hardware technology. With that technology and uniqueness, we can be part of the system run by Chinese companies. They are changing so quickly; that's why we have to work with them. And we must always make sure we are the most accessible to the content and services that China has created." Takahashi says this requires constant upgrading, improving, and inventing. "If you don't have innovation, in China, you die. Innovation must take place every day."

"We must always make sure we are the most accessible to the content and services that China has created."

—**Hiroshi Takahashi**, Chairman & President, China, Sony

SAP is another MNC working closely with China's tech giants. In this case, the company seeks to improve manufacturing efficiencies. Clas Neumann, the company's head of Fast-Growth Markets (including China), comments, "We are in very close contact with Chinese leading e-commerce and cloud providers. What their systems can deliver is amazing—not only in retail but also in improving efficiencies in manufacturing. It is important for China because of rising labor costs." Neumann explains how China is rapidly transforming away from mass manufacturing. "The life-cycle of this model—manufacturer for the world—is coming to an end. It will no longer happen that everything is produced in one place and shipped to the

"We are in very close contact with Chinese leading e-commerce and cloud providers. What their systems can deliver is amazing."

—**Clas Neumann**, Head of Fast-Growth Market Strategy Group, SAP rest of the world." China's new model, fueled by technological improvements, favors higher localization. Neumann says the trend toward improved and localized manufacturing is shaping both the B2C and B2B sectors in China now.

In the food and beverage sector, Frederico Freire, AB InBev's head of China, also describes the unique, fully connected domestic environment created by the predominance of the Alibaba and Tencent digital ecosystems. "The connection which stretches into retailing and wholesaling—the so-called Online to Offline—is unique and unprecedented in any other country. All the way from banking to social groups of friends down to individual communication by voice or video—it is all connected in China." Freire says that because China got a relatively late start in communications, the nation's users—both individuals and businesses—started from scratch and leapfrogged ahead of more mature economies. He says, "China developed without any baggage." As a result, individuals of all ages and demographic backgrounds now use the same digital platforms set up by Alibaba and Tencent. "In China, even 70-year-old citizens use their cell phone to buy things online. I don't see that in any other economies, in any other countries." And this uniformity is both an opportunity and a barrier for MNCs.

One aspect of the dominance of China's domestic digital platforms, coupled with the Chinese government's ban on the use of international platforms (especially Google, YouTube, Facebook, and Twitter) is that China CEOs have had to create alternative and parallel operations in China. Jason Kragh, LEGO's head of China, says, "One of the challenges we're operating with is the fact that LEGO plans to create global platforms. We are sitting here between two chairs, since the Chinese digital ecosystem is not prevalent in other markets. That means: Do we work with a global player to create great initiatives in terms of understanding data, understanding our market, understanding consumers? Or do we work with a partner in China, which is not necessarily operating in other markets? That would mean leveraging technology in a different way than we do with partners in other markets. The way

"...[F]rom banking to social groups of friends down to individual communication by voice or video—it is all connected in China."

—Frederico Freire,
BU President, China, AB InBev

you work with Alibaba in China is different from the way you can work in other countries."

Where Digital China Dominates

In terms of specific areas in which China is leading the digital world, China CEOs mentioned the following developments: fintech, supply chain and delivery, cloud, search, alternative energy and autonomous cars, and IoT.

Sector 1: Fintech

China's advances in financial technologies provide the backbone of the nation's digital revolution, many China CEOs expressed. Recent data from Ernst & Young shows that the percentage of China's digitally active users who are also users of fintech went from 69% in 2017 to 89% in 2019—a much higher percentage than in other key markets including India (87%), UK (71%), US (46%), France (35%), and Japan (34%).[10]

Charles Tseng, Korn Ferry's top executive for China, summarizes the state of China's digitization, especially the development of the two domestic fintech systems, in this way: "There's no question that the digitalization of business, the ecosystem, is far ahead in China than any other country. And the framework is also much more interconnected in China than in the United States, which arguably is the next most developed economy in terms of digitalization." The key difference between the US and China, Tseng adds, is in scope and scale. "In the US, you have relatively small or mid-size tech companies operating in different specialized areas. Whereas in China, you have Alibaba, Tencent, and one or two more huge players. They basically have an interconnected system whereby the entire ecosystem is integrated within their framework. This means that they can move faster, and it means they can move in a more connected way.

---

[10] Ernst & Young. *EY FinTech Adoption Index*, 2019.

I don't know any single Chinese person who doesn't use Weixin (WeChat)."

Not surprisingly, for MNCs in China's B2C sector, e-commerce is becoming increasingly important. AB InBev's Frederico Freire says, "In our industry, e-commerce is now around 2% [in China]. But we see the growth coming. We expect, in five years, to become 10%." As Freire says: "It's where the consumers are. Consumers want the convenience of buying online."

At NIIT, the company's head of China, Kamal Dhuper, points to his own consumer habits as an example of the fintech revolution in China: "I don't even carry a wallet anymore; I use WeChat pay or Alipay. Everything happens online." He adds that transportation and ticketing is all purchased by e-commerce and all tickets are digital in China. "If you go to the railway station or airport, the way they are using technology is amazing. The advancements China has made in terms of technology is very encouraging. Other countries have to catch up."

One of the most important aspects of China's fintech system is the uniformity of virtually all consumers and all businesses using the same two e-commerce platforms (those operated by Alibaba and Tencent), and almost nothing else. The result is unequalled economies of scale. Volvo Cars' top China executive Xiaolin Yuan comments: "Think about how powerful WeChat is, for example. The China market is materializing in certain areas faster than the rest of the world. And these are the areas we need to pay attention to. As a player in this market, we need to be smart enough to leverage these economies of scale." Yuan says that another benefit of the China market is the nation's huge and highly engaged consumer population, which provides an excellent platform for tech companies to test and refine their innovations. "That's the power enjoyed by the companies rooted in China, within this market." He adds, "China's consumer population very much gives the possibilities to scale-up all these technologies, to materialize all these technologies."

Sector 2: Supply Chain and Delivery

Closely related to the rapid development of fintech in China has been the improved efficiencies in the supply chain and in end-user delivery. SAP's Clas Neumann says China is "definitely" becoming an innovation powerhouse in the field of supply chain and distribution. "If you compare the enormous input and the output, China is not as efficient as in Europe or the US. But what you see on the customer side is a huge demand for the latest technology in supply chain."

Neumann continues, "China has excelled in terms of delivery and getting processes into place. You have excellent software and artificial intelligence to order products before they are actually needed. The systems can estimate how many goods are needed in a specific warehouse today, tomorrow, next week. The warehouse is not based on orders but on the AI prediction for orders which will come the following day."

"China has excelled in terms of delivery and getting processes into place. You have excellent software and artificial intelligence to order products before they are actually needed."

—Clas Neumann,
Head of Fast-Growth Market Strategy Group, SAP

In the F&B and retail industry, AB InBev's Frederico Freire tells how end-user deliveries are shaking up business models in China as the methods for reaching consumers have changed dramatically. "It's much easier for you to reach your consumer than before. If you have your phone, you can interact with them directly in this new digital environment. We are spending a lot of time understanding consumers and reaching them using digital touch-points."

As a result, like many MNCs, AB InBev now sells to Chinese customers (both B2B and B2C) via a wide range of channels: website, online store, and digital retail platforms. One issue Freire identifies, however, is that using the full spectrum sometimes leads to "conflicts" with retailers which require creative ways to offer retailers an advantage. "Sometimes you manage with the pricing, or by offering retailers a different SKU, different product, different packaging. But the discussion is not: 'go or no-go' [for digital platforms]. The discussion is: 'How to go?' Of course, you want to protect your market, to protect your base. But it's unavoidable; if you say no to digital, you are out."

"The discussion is not: 'go or no-go' [for digital platforms]. The discussion is: 'How to go?'"

—Frederico Freire,
BU President, China, AB InBev

Sector 3: Internet and Cloud-Based

One MNC with a clear view into China's transition from traditional IT toward digital—and the growth of digital in China—is Tata Consultancy Services (TCS). James Zhan explains the shift: "At TCS, we have more than 700,000 employees. Most of them are software engineers. They are all working on the computer, IT, digital areas. And some of their businesses are moving. There's a strategic shift from traditional IT services to digital." He explains the difference in this way: "Digital is going to internet-based, cloud-based. Traditional IT is: you have your mainframe; you have your database in-house. Now, traditional IT is moving to the cloud." And while this transition is taking place in technology centers worldwide, Zhan says China is one of the key locations worldwide where the shift is under way.

Another key area of cloud-based technological advancement underway in China is improvements to search engines. According to Microsoft's China head Alain Crozier: "Search is also something that we are doing very, very intensely here in China." Crozier explains that the search technology is evolving fast, from its original starting point (as a method of locating links to information on specific topics) toward more robust, intuitive, and intelligent compiling and summarizing. He explains: "Intelligent search will mean interactions between [users] and the search engine allowing you to refine your search very quickly—not by the user typing again and again, but by the machine talking to you, asking you one or two questions, then sorting better what you're looking for."

In the future, Crozier continues, search will also be able to summarize articles or even books. "You'll be able to say, 'Hey, can you give me, in 200 words, a summary of this book?' With a search engine, AI, and another set of technologies, we can do that." The implications, for researchers in fields including education and law, are very important. "Today, the way search works is that users are the one doing the sorting by clicking. The search is not summarizing, it's just send links which you have to click, and you have to read. That's basic search."

Intelligent search, he clarifies, will be intuitive and responsive to users. For example, if a user wants to research a potential client before meeting him or her, intelligent search can help. "In intelligent search, we say: 'Can you give me a summary of who she is?' The response will be: 'Boom, I'll get that sorted out.' You'll get a résumé because the intelligent search compiles the information chronologically." Going even further, he says, intelligent search will also separate the information found in terms of personal and professional data.

Sector 4: AI and IoT

One of the hottest tech fields worldwide today, artificial intelligence, is rapidly becoming a strong suit for R&D in China, say China CEOs. One top MNC executive in China describes the high-profile role the nation is playing globally in advancing this important technology: "What people are working on in China is fundamentally going to change drastically how we will be impacted by technology—and AI is one of them."

Regarding IoT, other China CEOs including Microsoft's Alain Crozier also recognize China's potential. Crozier points to the agricultural sector to illustrate the high potential of this technology in China: "To make sure we can feed the planet—which is going to be a challenge—we really need to increase productivity in agriculture." Instead of accomplishing this goal by enhancing productivity via chemicals, which may not be optimal for human health, he says, IoT provides another avenue for increasing yield. He explains: "IoT can help by allowing you to know exactly your soil. You can treat your soil differently from one parcel to another parcel—at a very sophisticated level." The way IoT assists, he says, is by allowing agriculturalists to access data on soil composition even in remote areas where 5G communications may not now reach. "I am talking about remote areas in Central China, in Africa, and parts of Europe and the US," explains Crozier.

How will sensors boost productivity? "What you need are sensors that are almost autonomous in capturing information and computing that information. Sensors with some intelligence, which can send some summarized information to the cloud." To overcome the challenge of limited connectivity in remote rural areas, Microsoft is conducting research to make use of unused excess bandwidth from televisions to expand IoT via sensors in agricultural fields. He says: "We are using very, very, very low bandwidth that doesn't require a pipe. We are going to use this space that's available to transmit information." The beauty of this innovative approach, Crozier says, is that: "You don't need an infrastructure; you don't need 5G." Once the sensors transmit data, agriculturalists will access many key data points. "We're going to make sure that, if you are in remote areas, you will know how to water your soil differently, to seed differently, to protect your fields differently against extreme temperatures or wind."

The implications for IoT research in China reach far beyond agriculture, he adds. "IoT will play a strategic role in providing technology in areas where we didn't have any." And as sensors become more intelligent, smaller, and more prevalent, they will allow objects and devices to transmit and share information without accessing the cloud. In the future, Crozier envisions a world in which objects such as pens, coffee cups, and cell phones share information. "We are definitively going to have more connection between different devices." Another important future development, he says, is that intelligent objects, outfitted with sensors, will be able to conduct some computer activities within the device, without accessing the cloud.

Sector 5: Electric Vehicles, Autonomous Cars

One of the most discussed, highest potential areas of technology development in China, China CEOs said, is in the arena of cars. Both the fields of electric vehicles and of autonomous cars are expanding rapidly in China now. Since 2017, China has been the world's largest consumer of e-vehicles, purchasing more than 579,000 units per year.[11] The next closest market, the US, purchases less than 200,000 units yearly.

---

[11] Forbes. https://www.forbes.com/sites/niallmccarthy/2018/06/01/electric-car-sales-are-surging-in-china-infographic/#624c17c3d1f7.

One MNC supporting the development of alternative energy cars in China is Tata. The group's James Zhan explains that Tata Technologies, which focuses on designing cars, is currently geared mainly toward new energy vehicles: electric cars and hybrids. He adds, "Especially in China, there's a big push toward electric cars."

A second, related project is Tata's work to develop lighter-weight, aluminum-based vehicle bodies to run on a battery. Zhan says, "For a battery engine, you need a lighter vehicle." For this reason, Tata Technology is now helping to supply auto makers with aluminum auto bodies.

Third, Tata is also working in the sub-sector of e-vehicle charging systems. Zhan explains that Tata Technology is designing drive-in battery-charging stations in China operated by robots, and is already providing these stations to Chinese customers including Nio.

Regarding autonomous cars, another Tata subsidiary provides the software for e-vehicles to OEMs. This business has been growing fast in India and is now "also moving to China," according to Zhan. The company creates accessories for e-vehicles—including sensors and cameras—which are designed to "help relieve the driver from the burden of driving."

One benefit China can offer to attract cutting-edge R&D in emerging technologies is the nation's long history as a back-end OEM manufacturer for the world's top car brands. Zhan says, "We are in a good position because we've had the in-house capability for so many years."

Another MNC focusing on both electronic vehicles and autonomous cars in China is Volvo Cars. Commenting on the complexity of this emerging sector in China—as it includes both auto makers and digital companies—Xiaolin Yuan says: "This only shows that technology proliferates into all areas and many people see possibilities just as we do. And of course, those from different industries will have different strengths."

The secret to success in emerging technology–focused sectors, in Yuan's view, is not to over-extend the business strategy. He explains, "The beauty of being open-minded company without big concerns regarding heavy investment in the traditional areas is that we are free to invest into areas that are very future-oriented." One piece of advice for MNCs in China is not to try to develop across all areas at once. "Whether you call it a humble or wise, we believe we cannot do it all. We need to do what we do best." Thus, Volvo Cars remains focused on ensuring safety, health, and functionality in its cars. "We know it is not about the fluffy extras, but the truly functional."

Finally, Yuan emphasizes that those in the auto sector must not work in silos, but must collaborate with the tech sector. He clarifies: "We cannot create systems that are not congruous with other popular systems. We need to cooperate with the best-in-class in those areas." For that reason, Yuan says, Volvo Cars has partnered with Google to accelerate innovation in connectivity and to foster the development of applications and connected services. Yuan adds, "We ourselves are very much looking to the future—to think carefully about what role we should play and what kind of relationship we need with all these tech giants involved in this future mobility world."

Bosch is also investing into autonomous cars and e-vehicles in China. Chen Yudong, the company's top executive for China, explains that out of the company's 60,000 employees in China, 7,000 are engineers. Although Chen says domestic R&D focuses mostly on the D and less on the R, the company still does some China-based research. Key areas for Bosch China include autonomous driving, electrification, and connective services.

Navigating China's Digitized Landscape

Given China's extremely fast and extremely broad technological development, coupled with market dominance of its domestic digital giants and the proliferation of disruptive young tech startups, the China CEOs interviewed in this book identified two key challenges they face while leading large operations amid China's tech revolution.

Challenge 1: HQ Gap in Understanding Digital China

Against the backdrop of China's dynamic and vast digital transformation, one challenge for China CEOs is to ensure that their global headquarters understand and support the necessary efforts to keep pace. Economist Corporate Network's Mary Boyd comments: "The problem for many MNCs is that what they see happening here [in China] is so far ahead of what they see happening in their home market or the corporate headquarters. They are constantly having to explain stuff and having to redesign or reinterpret things that may come up from headquarters because initiatives need to be at a faster pace or using different channels in the China market." Many MNCs, she says, end up operating at "two speeds"—the speed in China and the speed at headquarters.

Kenneth Jarret of AmCham Shanghai says one of the challenges noted by member companies is not being fully up to speed with China's digitization. Jarrett says MNCs typically face two disadvantages. First, culturally, they approach both the Chinese digital platforms and the Chinese social media as outsiders. "For foreign companies, it's hard to keep up with Chinese companies in leveraging social media. Chinese companies just have a better feel for it than the multinationals." Second, some MNCs still face a lack of understanding of the digital revolution in China. "From corporate headquarters, there are still a lot of people who don't know WeChat. . . . So there might still be an under-estimation about how integral it is in the lives of people in China."

ABB's top executive for China, Chunyuan Gu, voices a similar concern regarding a "digital divide" between China operations and headquarters for some MNCs: "The interest of our customers in using new technology is enormous. And this is not fully understood by our Western colleagues. The China market is more advanced than many multinational company headquarters." Gu gives one example, in robotics: "When I came to Shanghai 15 years ago, my job was to set up a factory manufacturing robots. Everybody said, 'Why do you need to do that?' Because China was then

> "The problem for many MNCs is that what they see happening here [in China] is so far ahead of what they see happening in their home market or the corporate headquarters."
>
> —**Mary Boyd,** Director, Shanghai, Economist Corporate Network

> "For foreign companies, it's hard to keep up with Chinese companies in leveraging social media."
>
> —**Kenneth Jarrett,** President, American Chamber of Commerce, Shanghai

> "The interest of our customers in using new technology is enormous. And this is not fully understood by our Western colleagues. ... For the past three or four years, China has been world's largest market for industrial robots. The interest—the pressure—to adopt this new technology is enormous."
>
> —**Chunyuan Gu,** Chairman & CEO, China, ABB

a low-cost manufacturing country. But today you can see that for the past three or four years, China has been world's largest market for industrial robots. The interest—the pressure—to adopt this new technology is enormous. We have a major responsibility to drive this and develop it here. We need to invest more in the future technology in China. It is our task to really push for that."

He adds that new technology tends to bring about a faster ROI in China than the home markets of many MNCs. "We have been driving digitalization for two years [in China]. After two years, when you see the dollar value coming from China, it is outstanding. I gave this as a little piece of advice for my international colleagues: Compare China to any country in Europe. The ROI is very good." He concludes: "We believe China is the long-term future for R&D—but I'm not so sure every company sees this."

Manulife's Kai Zhang says part of the trouble in securing understanding from headquarters is that the pace of change in many home markets is so different from that of China. "If you live in China, you know the pace of life here. I have a house in New Jersey and I go back to New York every other year. And very little changes there. The roads are the same, the buildings are the same; so are the tunnels and bridges." Not so, in China, she says. "Here [in China], you always have something new. It's not only the change itself; it's the pace of change. Because China is just in a different stage of development. The US went through that in the early years, but now is quite stable."

Many China CEOs describe the strong reaction of executives from their corporate HQ when they are exposed to China's digital transformation. NIIT's Kamal Dhuper tells of a recent visit of his global CEO to China: "After a few days in China, he told me, 'Kamal, I'm surprised! The kind of progress—not only the infrastructure created—but China is probably the most technologically advanced country I have been to in the past five to six years." Even the US, the CEO said, is far behind. "He says, 'In the US, I don't see the adaptation of technology happening at this pace." Especially impressive, for incoming executives, is China's "complete switch" to e-commerce by mobile phone via

WeChat and Alipay, Dhuper says, and the use of e-tickets for the metro and high-speed train.

Dhuper compares tech advancement in China against the other hubs of tech advancement worldwide: "In the US and Europe, there is a structured way of innovating and bringing about advancement. In China, it's also happening, but we don't know how and where. But if the [Chinese] government is putting their support behind it, something will come." Given the size and clout of domestic technology players, and the fact that Alibaba and Huawei have already gone global, Dhuper believes that "a lot of innovation is going to come from China."

Challenge 2: Automation versus Job Security

Another issue identified by China CEOs as adding challenges to their work in leading large operations in China is the issue of automation disrupting or replacing human labor. As the nation rapidly digitizes, this is an issue to grapple with for MNCs as well as domestic players, and the Chinese government.

One MNC facing the human trade-off companies face when automating their operations is Scania, the Swedish automotive parts manufacturer. Scania's China top executive Mats Harborn, who is also President of the European Chamber of Commerce Shanghai, says use of robotics in manufacturing is now "an obsession" in China. "If you don't have robots, you give up on quality and you're not cost efficient. But when you put in too many robots, the process becomes too inflexible. You need the right balance depending on what sort of production you have. At this moment, the approach towards production is too simplistic."

However, a parallel issue facing companies using robotics in China is social stability. Chinese blue-collar workers understand well the risks for them, in terms of job security, as the field of robotics advances. Harborn says, "The increase in robotics is now happening in same places where the working population is shrinking. The challenge for the state is to create a transfer system so that the benefits of automation actually come to the state. Then the state can distribute these benefits to those in society who do not see the benefits. Otherwise, we would have social upheaval."

SAP's Clas Neumann voices a similar concern: "With every industrial revolution of the past—and people now speak about this fourth industrial revolution—you had the same issue, basically. There are people whose skills are not as relevant as they used to be." Neumann is optimistic overall, stating: "You might need half of the number of people in a factory now, but you might need double the number of factories to serve your demand. You still need sufficient workers." However, he does recognize that finding a new role for every worker will present challenges. "The new technologies, of course, don't mean that everybody will become a data scientist. You can't make today's unskilled laborer into tomorrow's IT specialist."

Even in highly skilled positions, jobs may well be lost across industries. Neumann says, "A lot of software engineering will be done by machines." However, he argues that technological advances, including in robotics, will also lead to the creation of new jobs. "Technology also allowed us to include people into the workforce who could not be included before." He gives the example of a housewife from India who can now work from home using new technology—a job which previously did not exist. Emerging developments in blockchain and other technologies, he asserts, are also creating new jobs that will "democratize" the workforce. He asserts: "I believe there will be a lot of additional jobs also for people who have no university education or vocational training but can participate in the global workforce because they can participate from wherever they are. It is true that some factory jobs will not be required. But that doesn't mean that we don't require workforce in other areas."

While upheaval in the job market based on disruptive technology is taking place worldwide, China CEOs believe it is happening more deeply here. Robert Hsiung, Udacity's head of China, says, "The major revolution that's happening—not

> *"The new technologies, of course, don't mean that everybody will become a data scientist. You can't make today's unskilled laborer into tomorrow's IT specialist."*
>
> **—Clas Neumann,**
> Head of Fast-Growth Market Strategy Group, SAP

> *"The major revolution that's happening—not only in China, but it's going to affect China the most—is the revolution in AI and robotics."*
>
> **—Robert Hsiung,**
> Managing Director, China, Udacity

only in China, but it's going to affect China the most—is the revolution in AI and robotics." He says the disruption caused by these two technologies "is going to impact a lot of people's jobs," citing expectations that robots will replace up to 50% of jobs in the future. And the jobs to be lost, he stresses, are not only blue-collar. "The 50% of jobs are mostly low-skilled labor, repetitive jobs. But those repetitive jobs are not limited only to manufacturing and blue-collar jobs. They include white-collar jobs as well: accounting work, legal work, even in healthcare. This is coming soon. It's coming faster than we think."

What does this change mean for MNCs in China? Hsiung says, "For China, it's going to bring incredible challenges. Firstly, social. You're going to have a lot of people out of work, especially the lower end of the socioeconomic stream." He says the first category to lose their jobs, most likely, will be those in hard labor positions such as at meat packing plants. He says, "I have lots of friends in South China who own factories. They say, 'People born in the 1990s don't want to work in factories, so I'm buying robots to replace our workers. Robots are reliable and don't complain.' That's transforming the workforce."

Hsiung adds, "This change is forcing these [Chinese] young people to find other jobs. They need to move to a higher level of work skill. We talk about digital transformation, but I think it's really about stepping up to a more intellectual level of creativity and problem solving, innovation, system thinking, critical thinking—all the things that robots cannot do." At the end of the day, Hsiung remains hopeful that the digital transformation will create more jobs than joblessness. "The tenet behind AI is that AI is largely based on historical data and historical information. So basically, by analyzing all this historical information, they can guess what's going to happen in the future and make the decisions based on that. But creating new things and innovating in ways that have no patterns is a key area in which humans still need to play."

Digital Strategies

Strategy 1: Invest in R&D in China

One oft-repeated piece of advice given by China CEOs regarding how best to compete in today's fast-digitizing China is to invest in domestic R&D. One such MNC making a clear commitment to investing in R&D in China is ABB. Chunyuan Gu, the company's top executive for China, explains that his company's R&D operations in China employ 2,000 researchers. In addition, ABB operates one of the largest research centers in Shanghai and is developing digital solutions for other areas, including HR (for recruitment) and marketing. Gu explains, "We are in transition from an electrical and automation company to a digital company."

The biggest challenge for ABB now, Gu says, is to shift into digital while maintaining efficiency for customers. "There are many new things we need to learn. . . . We need to change our production processes but we also need to manage the business model." Despite the challenges, the company feels pressure to make these transitions—and to do so from China. Gu says, "We need to develop our digital solutions. It is even more important in China that we have the ambition and the plan to be the leader on certain things—to make sure ABB is still one of the technology leaders in the world and in China."

ABB's strategy in China has been a high-profile approach, Gu says. For example, to solidify the company's reputation as a digital leader, they hold large-scale customer events in China— attracting up to 6,000 Chinese customers per event "to show them ABB's portfolio of digital solutions."

Another MNC committed to participating actively in digital R&D is Microsoft. Alain Crozier explains that innovation is part of the company's domestic business strategy: "Our organizational footprints are very similar in China and the US. What does that mean? It means we are not only a 'sales and marketing' organization in China." He clarifies that sales is actually the company's smallest employee group in China. "Very early, we decided to come to China with a long-term mindset. That means making sure our engineers are also based in China.

And not only developers doing code. We also decided—and this was one of the core decisions of Bill Gates—that we are going to make sure our research can be done in China. So, for 21 years, we have had true research, fundamental research, here in China." Today, key areas of made-in-China research for the company include AI, IoT, cloud computer, and machine learning. Crozier says, "A lot of research for Microsoft is done in China. When Microsoft decided to come to China, it was with the idea that we will do everything the same as we are doing in the US."

"For 21 years, we have had true research, fundamental research, here in China."

—**Alain Crozier,**
CEO, Greater China Region, Microsoft

Philips is another MNC operating a "top" R&D center in China. Andy Ho, the company's head of China, emphasizes that the R&D undertaken there serves not just China, but global markets—especially in the field of medical devices. In some cases, Ho says, China-based R&D is exported abroad, within the group. "I have a team here doing material research for global needs. We do have local teams creating global research—it depends on the product."

"I have a team [in China] doing material research for global needs. We do have local teams creating global research—it depends on the product."

—**Andy Ho,**
Leader, Greater China, Philips

At SAP, the company employs 3,000 engineers in China—most focused on product development. The company's Clas Neumann emphasizes that this reflects about 10% of the company's global R&D. He says there is a "good match" between SAP and "Made in China 2025"—referring to the Chinese central government's initiative to solidify the nation as a global powerhouse in technology. From that point of view, and because there are so many private and public sector initiatives in China for AI, digital supply chain, digital warehouse—these kinds of products are very important for companies.

Strategy 2: Innovate in China for the World

Even MNCs that have not invested into formal R&D centers in China emphasize the importance of conducting product development or introducing creative new business strategies or digitally focused initiatives in China. AmCham Shanghai's Kenneth Jarrett says more MNCs are developing innovations—especially digital improvements to their operations—in China first, then applying them globally. He shares a typical example regarding an American IT company. "They were quite proud . . . they're doing a lot of local innovations to make their production line more efficient. And the innovations developed in China were being applied by that company globally." Jarrett says such a scenario "makes sense" in today's business environment "because whatever they were producing here was being produced in the factories elsewhere. So that definitely there is, in that particular company, very high receptivity to anything that works."

For MNCs operating in China, the discussion regarding digital upgrading is now an interactive dialogue between headquarters and China, Jarrett says. "Whether it's new forms of marketing, or the use of new digital products, it's definitely now a two-way flow. I wouldn't say that its equal because I still suspect that, for the big multinationals, even if they respect the need to know their clients in China, it's still a psychological hurdle to say 'This is a China innovation—and this is actually great anywhere.'"

One MNC focused on innovating in China for global operations is Bayer. The company's Celina Chew mentioned an innovative new technology developed in Italy based on the idea of a plant having a digital twin. Bayer engineers can first manufacture virtually at the digital twin site; then, after tweaking the process to maximize efficiency, they can undertake actual manufacturing in the real plant. Chew explains, "If you want to test something, you do it first at the twin plant. Then control what happens in the real factory."

In the field of healthcare, Bayer is also developing innovations in China. For example, one app recently introduced domestically helps diabetes patients to better manage their postprandial blood sugar through real-time interactions with doctors. "Using the app, patients and doctors work more closely together to build an 'information bridge.' Most patients don't measure their glucose regularly or accurately after meals, so they don't actually know when it goes up and down. This app measures the glucose levels of the patient, then delivers this information directly to the patient's doctors." The result is a significant benefit for patients: "Doctors can really tailor your medication and your treatment exactly to your own post-meal glucose spikes. The interaction is individualized, which is excellent."

In the beauty industry, L'Oréal's Stéphane Rinderknech also says more innovative ideas for the group are initiating in China, then spreading internationally. He explains that L'Oréal's Research and Innovation Center, launched in Shanghai in 2005, is now the Group's largest R&D facility in the Asia Pacific and is one of the Group's six regional hubs for research and innovation networks worldwide. The center was set up to provide "better insight into Chinese consumers" and to adapt products to meet their "specific demands." But in recent years, the findings and results produced in the center have spread beyond China. Rinderknech says "The center has produced lots of outcomes which are innovated in China, then promoted to other markets to benefit consumers worldwide."

Another example shared by Rinderknech is "end-to-end forecasting"—a system in which L'Oréal uses data to track consumer purchasing, then deliver predictive analytics. "The machine does the forecasting for you. Artificial intelligence will power your forecast by accumulating all the relevant data." In creating sales forecasts, Rinderknech says AI can efficiently factor in such information as the likely impact of future weather forecasts on sales. "The machine will adjust much better than marketers can. Marketers can create concepts but they don't necessarily know how to factor in all related aspects."

At LEGO, Jacob Kragh, the company's top executive for China, expresses a similar commitment to innovation in China. He says, "We're making sure that China is influencing the global innovation as one of the key markets."

In the education field, Kamal Dhuper of NIIT explains why it is important to innovate in China: "Today, we have brought to China many newer models—models in which some part of the learning happens online." For example, he points to one online platform in which students can access content, including course-work as well as MOOCs and videos as many times as they want. Dhuper says, "It's a flipped classroom model where the learner comes to the physical classroom after having learned some of the concepts online. Which means that, in the classroom, you have more of a stepped-up discussion rather than just learning the basics."

Another way NIIT is digitizing its operations in China is through its "synchronous learning technology platform," in which teachers reach broader groups of students via video conference. Dhuper explains: "Today, our classrooms may not be only one teacher standing in front of 30 students. Today, our faculty sit in our studios—we have four such studios across China—and their lectures are beamed to remote classrooms connected to that studio." The benefit, Dhuper says, is that the number of students to be reached expands greatly. "We reach multiple classrooms across China. Each of those classrooms will have 30 students on average."

Strategy 3: Prepare for a Cash-Free China

One of the key messages voiced by China CEOs is that the nation's domestic consumer market is now virtually cash free—a factor which MNCs must fully accept and embrace. As one CEO comments, since Chinese consumers make nearly all transactions via Alipay or WeChat, employees at most retail shops no longer handle cash. Several CEOs agreed with media predictions of the coming eventual elimination of money in China. Warns one China CEO: "MNCs need to react to this. If you don't, you're going to be out of business."

Strategy 4: Tap the Digital Natives

One strategy used by MNCs to stay abreast of China's digitization is to leverage their own in-house digital natives. Bayer's Celina Chew encourages her team-members to bring the "very digital mindset" they use after hours to the workplace. "A lot of our colleagues are really very digital in their personal lives. But when they come into the company, they sometimes leave this ability at the door and work within our ecosystem." Chew's challenge is to convince employees to "bring their digital selves into the company—to find solutions that leverage and embrace the digital part of their lives." She adds, "We expect a high level of customer service in our personal lives—for example, fast delivery of products we have ordered online. But at work, we are often still thinking in the context of how we were set up in the past, old ranges of solutions." In contrast, she says: "I'd like to see alternative, tech-driven options proposed more often. I'm not that digital, but I believe that there must be some other solutions that we're not probably exploring. It cannot be that we have a similar range of solutions now—with so many new tools available—as compared with 10 years ago." How to foster more digital thinking? One method preferred by Chew is to engage actively with the start-up community. "To encourage outside-in thinking and external innovation, we hold Lunch-and-Learn sessions and invite speakers on a broad range of topics including digital. We run a Reverse Digital Mentoring program in which young digital natives in our company act as mentors for senior managers." Such efforts allow Bayer to "leverage the natural digital skills and outlook of our younger, more digitally savvy colleagues."

MINI CASE

Reverse Mentoring on Digital (L'Oréal)

Given the breakneck pace of digital revolution underway in China, with new apps grabbing attention and shifting consumer loyalty almost daily, how can MNCs (and their teams) catch up? L'Oréal China uses an innovative reverse mentoring solution. Stéphane Rinderknech explains, "Usually you have a mentor who is older, who has experience. Here is it the reverse." The company appoints Generation Y employees to introduce new apps or new micro-bloggers. "We ask them: 'Tell our leaders what is coming in the digital world—this is what's coming: this brand, this product—and why.'" The goal is a clear view into ongoing and emerging consumer trends, says Rinderknech. "The point is to know what's happening and why. Why are people shifting?"

The program is part of an overall strategy of recognizing and valuing younger staffers, Rinderknech adds. "We empower young employees. We love the bottom up. Bottom up means you plant the seeds of what you want to do, you let them cultivate and grow." With the right employees, showing trust and allowing a bit of freedom typically leads to more innovative and more impactful results, he says. "Even when what they present to you is what you wanted to do all along, you can smile and say: 'Good idea. It's great. Let's do that.' If they understood well your strategic direction, what you expect, the image that you have for the company, then they will come back with something that you want."

Summary of Tips

1. **Invest in R&D in China**
   Innovate in China to take advantage of the thriving domestic digital ecosystem and to keep up with the world's digital leaders. Embrace the digital transformation taking place in China.

2. **Innovate in China for the world**
   Invest in R&D in China. Use China as a testing ground for innovations which you can then roll out in other markets around the world.

3. **Prepare for a cash-free China**
   Adapt your payment systems for a cash-free China. Use this learning in other markets in which you operate. What is happening now in China will likely happen soon in other markets in which you operate.

4. **Tap the digital natives**
   Take full advantage of your Chinese talent's digital savvy. Allow them to lead the digital transformation and use them as reverse mentors to your senior executives.

Chapter 5
The Transformation of Chinese Consumers

China's future generations will grow up used to the living environment of today—used to mobile shopping, used to home delivery speeds within 30 minutes. . . . When they grow up, they will integrate worldwide, making the world change even quicker.

—**Freda Zhang,** Country Commercial VP, China, IKEA

The growth here is exponential. The difference in China is the speed and the scale. That's what really strikes me. There is no other place in the world—not one—where you have both. . . . I'm talking about billion-euro companies that can grow in double digits—even 30% per year—in China. Real scale and real speed.

—**Stéphane Rinderknech,** CEO, China, L'Oréal

The whole central part [of China] is not well developed, and the western part is completely undeveloped. And I'm not even talking about the northwest and southwest—completely new areas of development. The size and scale of the country is enormous.

—**Charles Tseng,** Chairman, Asia Pacific, Korn Ferry

INSIDE CHAPTER 5

Profile of Today's Chinese Consumer

Strategies for Winning Chinese Consumers

Summary of Tips

Introduction: China's High-Potential Domestic Shoppers

To understand the importance of Chinese consumers for multinational companies worldwide, consider these trends:

> In 2020, China is expected to have the world's largest middle-class population, anticipated to make 16% of global purchases among this shopping category and overtaking their counterparts in the US (accounting for 11% of global middle-class spending).[1]
>
> Chinese compose the world's largest population of outbound travelers. Regarding overseas travelers, the population grew from 34.5 million outbound Chinese in 2006[2] to 150 million outbound Chinese in 2018.[3] And among these, around 21% stay in luxury hotels.[4]
>
> Car ownership in China went from 37 million cars in 2006[5] to 235 million cars in 2018,[6] including 2.82 million luxury cars.[7] In a show of the speed with which Chinese adopt new technologies, China is also the world's leading purchaser of electric vehicles, buying more than 1 million EV cars in 2018 (56% of global purchases).[8]

---

[1] Brookings Institute. *Global Economy & Development Working Paper 100.* February 2017.
[2] World Tourism Alliance. http://www.wta-web.org/eng/sjzx_4026/lytjgb_4027/201710/t20171013_842568.shtml.
[3] Travel China Guide. https://www.travelchinaguide.com/tourism/2018statistics/.
[4] McKinsey & Co. https://www.mckinsey.com/industries/travel-transport-and-logistics/our-insights/huanying-to-the-new-chinese-traveler.
[5] Michigan Technological University. https://digitalcommons.mtu.edu/cgi/viewcontent.cgi?article=1443&context=etds.
[6] Ministry of Public Security, China. http://autonews.gasgoo.com/china_news/70015270.html.
[7] Mordor Intelligence. https://www.mordorintelligence.com/industry-reports/china-luxury-car-market.
[8] Automotive News Europe. https://europe.autonews.com/automakers/china-set-dominate-electric-vehicle-battleground.

In the area of luxury, China has reigned as the world's number-one market since 2015.[9]

In 2018, Chinese consumers purchased 32% of the world's luxury goods, spending RMB500 billion.[10]

In terms of lifestyle, a growing percentage of Chinese live an always on life in which they are constantly connected digitally and engaged in social media (including at work or school, at home, and when with family or friends). The average Chinese now spends 3:02 hours online[11] per day (compared with 3:27 hours in the US)[12] including via computer, phone, or other devices.

Looking ahead, China's consumer base is poised to grow even stronger. At one end of the spectrum are the sustained efforts of the Chinese central government to eradicate poverty nationwide. While 66% of Chinese were categorized as "poor" by the central government in 1990,[13] by 2014 the percentage had improved to 1.4%.[14] In addition, in 2014 the central government announced that a key objective of the 13th Five-Year Plan (2016–2020) was to lift all Chinese citizens above the poverty line by 2020. Achieving that goal would mean raising the family income level of all citizens above RMB2,300 (US$362.50) per year. By 2017, the nation's officially recorded poor population had shrunk to 3.1%[15] and the government announced that it was on track to meet its 2020 goal.

---

[9] Bain & Co. https://www.bain.com/insights/whats-powering-chinas-market-for-luxury-goods/.

[10] McKinsey & Co. https://www.mckinsey.com/business-functions/marketing-and-sales/our-insights/chinese-luxury-consumers-more-global-more-demanding-still-spending.

[11] E-marketer. https://www.emarketer.com/content/in-china-adults-spend-half-their-media-time-online.

[12] MIT. https://www.technologyreview.com/f/610045/the-average-american-spends-24-hours-a-week-online/.

[13] China Daily. http://www.chinadaily.com.cn/a/201903/14/WS5c89b8dea3106c65c34ee93a.html.

[14] World Bank. https://data.worldbank.org/topic/poverty?locations=CN.

[15] World Bank. http://povertydata.worldbank.org/poverty/country/CHN.

Consumer Trend 1: Super Well-Informed

For a glimpse of the highly engaged way in which today's Chinese go about shopping, consider that the average domestic consumer takes part in a complex combination of online and offline information gathering, typically consulting an average of 16 different social media and online sites before making a purchase.[16] These sources include domestic and international sites, paid and unpaid sources, key opinion leaders (KOLs), and social media influencers, as well as onsite salesclerks. Shoppers also regularly consult their own personal social network, mainly via WeChat groups, for advice before purchasing.

For China's middle-class population—the target market for many MNCs—another promising message issued by the central government in conjuncture with the 13th Five-Year Plan was the goal of creating a "moderately prosperous society." Many MNCs have been encouraged by the government's official blessing of prosperity, expecting this to help fuel the ongoing expansion of the nation's middle class.

One factor boosting the growth of middle-income families is an easing of the one-child policy—a change which is expected to increase the birthrate. Under the one-child policy, China's birthrate fell from 6.4 births per woman in 1960 to around 1.5 from 2000 to 2014.[17] After new regulations eased the policy in 2015, the birthrate rose to 1.68 by 2017[18] and is expected to rise moderately going forward.

Looking further ahead, by 2040, analysts expect half the world's middle-class population to come from China and India.[19] In terms of spending power, the value of purchases made by China's middle-class shoppers is expected to jump from US$6.8 trillion in 2020 to US$14.3 trillion by 2030.[20]

---

[16] McKinsey & Co. https://www.mckinsey.com/featured-insights/china/how-young-chinese-consumers-are-reshaping-global-luxury.

[17] World Bank. https://data.worldbank.org/indicator/SP.DYN.TFRT.IN?locations=CN.

[18] World Bank. https://data.worldbank.org/indicator/SP.DYN.TFRT.IN?locations=CN.

[19] Brookings Institute. *The Emerging Middle Class in Developing Countries.* June, 2011.

[20] Brookings Institute. *Global Economy and Development Working Paper 100.* February 2017. In 2005 PPP dollars.

For the China CEOs interviewed in this book, targeting today's Chinese consumers means facing a highly promising but highly complex market characterized by a number of challenges. They describe a market which offers an unprecedented scope and scale as well as continued growth potential as China's economy continues to develop. As well, MNCs are generally encouraged by the openness and curiosity of Chinese domestic shoppers but also warn of three key challenges: high demands (for convenience, quality, customization and low price), fickle behavior (easily distracted and influenced by competing brands, social media), and complexity (displaying vast generational differences).

The views that Freda Zhang, IKEA's top executive for China, expresses about the potential of China's consumer market for her multinational company are representative of those of many China CEOs. Zhang recommends that her global executive board should consider China as a global innovation center because the domestic consumer population in this country is evolving so fast and is, in many ways, pioneering key consumer trends that will likely emerge in other markets later. She argues that the fast-growing middle-class populations of both China and India make these two countries universally important for MNCs. Forward-looking international companies can thus begin preparing now for the coming of age of Chinese young shoppers by understanding them. Zhang says: "China's future generations will grow up used to the living environment of today—used to mobile shopping, used to home delivery speeds within 30 minutes." And when today's Chinese children come of age, she stresses, they will influence consumption patterns not just in China but beyond. "When they grow up, they will integrate worldwide, making the world change even quicker." Smart MNCs, Zhang says, will prepare now for the altered consumer profiles of tomorrow.

The primary drive behind the call of China CEOs for MNCs to focus on Chinese consumers is the sheer number of citizens who are expected to have strong spending power in the coming years. IKEA's Freda Zhang reminds that "in China, in one province, the GDP equals that of an entire country in Europe. For

"[I]n China, in one province, the GDP equals that of an entire country in Europe."

—Freda Zhang,
Country Commercial VP,
China, IKEA

Consumer Trend 2: A Bright Future for Luxury

As evidence of China's voracious appetite for luxury, consider that average Chinese consumers now spend three to five hours online per week educating themselves about luxury products.[21] Most luxury purchases in China are now made either by the post-80s or post-90s generation. An encouraging sign for luxury brands is that 50% of millennial shoppers who bought luxury products during 2018 were making purchases in this category for the first time, and a full 92% had begun spending in this category within the past three years.[22] This trend means that as newcomers, China's younger generations are likely to expand their appetite for luxury shopping in the years ahead.

"One Chinese entrepreneur told me: 'We don't even have to expand overseas. We can grow double digits for the next 10, 15, 20 years in China.'"

—Charles Tseng,
Chairman, Asia Pacific, Korn Ferry

"At that time (2007), in the first-tier cities, most of our customers were foreigners. Today, 77% of our customers are Chinese, throughout China."

—Rainer Burkle,
Area Vice President, Luxury, Greater China, Marriott International

example, the GDP of Shandong Province is almost twice that of Switzerland." Meanwhile, in his role placing top-level executives into positions across China for both MNCs and domestic companies, Charles Tseng, Korn Ferry's top executive for China, stresses that many of his China-based clients have made the domestic market a prime focus of their business strategy. He shares the thinking of one such client: "One Chinese entrepreneur told me: 'We don't even have to expand overseas. We can grow double digits for the next 10, 15, 20 years in China.'"

One China CEO who has witnessed first-hand the growing spending power of Chinese consumers in recent years is Rainer Burkle, Marriott International's top executive for luxury hotels in China. He describes the transformation that has occurred since his arrival to China in 2007. "At that time, in the first-tier cities, most of our customers were foreigners. Today, 77% of our customers are Chinese, throughout China. So this is a major change." He adds that the luxury hotels sub-segment is particularly booming across China now, fueled mainly by domestic guests.

A clear glimpse into the potential offered to MNCs which successfully cater to Chinese consumers can be seen in the

[21] McKinsey & Co. https://www.mckinsey.com/business-functions/marketing-and-sales/our-insights/chinese-luxury-consumers-more-global-more-demanding-still-spending.
[22] McKinsey & Co. https://www.mckinsey.com/featured-insights/china/how-young-chinese-consumers-are-reshaping-global-luxury.

rapid growth of L'Oréal China since the group's initial arrival in the late 1990s. In 1997, the first China CEO of L'Oréal, Paolo Gasparini (who was interviewed in the first edition of this book), arrived in China with one assistant from Hong Kong, a suitcase full of make-up samples, and a "vision to put a lipstick in the hand of every Chinese woman" (in the words of current China CEO Stéphane Rinderknech). At the time, L'Oréal's current global CEO, Jean-Paul Agon, also established the group's Asia Zone and boldly forecast that China would become number one both in terms of the world economy and for L'Oréal.

Twenty-two years later, Asia Pacific sales for the L'Oréal Group exceeded 7 billion euros (due mainly to China), overtaking North America. And in Q1 2019, Asia Pacific overtook Western Europe to become the company's biggest zone worldwide. As of 2018, China was L'Oréal's second-largest beauty market worldwide after the US and was the number-one market for four brands: L'Oréal Men Expert, Lancôme, HR, and YSL Beauty. Today, Rinderknech adds that 35% of sales in China now come from e-commerce.

As L'Oréal's third China CEO, Rinderknech tells of the phenomenal expansion the group has achieved in this market: "I guess no one at the time could imagine that we would be where we are now." To explain the pace of growth during his eight years at the helm of L'Oréal China (from 2011 to 2019), he states that achievements made in the early years of his term seemed "like peanuts" just one or two years later: "Like, when we celebrated our first billion euro turnover for China. By 2019, we more than tripled that figure. Or we made a celebration for the sales on 11-11 Day. But by the next year, you look back and say, 'That was actually nothing compared to what we are doing now.'"

Although other markets have also experienced fast growth, Rinderknech says China is unique: "The growth here is exponential. The difference in China is the speed *and* the scale. That's what really strikes me. There is no other place in the world—not one—where you have both." He clarifies: "I'm not talking about American speed. There is some speed in the US, but I am talking about much faster speed. I'm talking about a billion euro companies that can grow in double digits—even 30% per year—in China. Real scale and real speed."

"The difference in China is the speed and the scale. That's what really strikes me. There is no other place in the world— not one—where you have both. … I am only the third CEO in China for L'Oréal. By the time we have the fifth or sixth China CEO, China will be the number-one market in the world for the group, by far."

—**Stéphane Rinderknech,** CEO, China, L'Oreal

And despite such growth, Rinderknech says the company is still "just scratching the surface" in China. Looking ahead, he expects this growth rate to continue. "I am only the third CEO in China for L'Oréal. By the time we have the fifth or sixth China CEO, China will be the number-one market in the world for the group, by far."

The main reason for his confidence is the current strength and expected continued growth of China's consumer base. Rinderknech emphasizes the increased spending power of Chinese consumers since he arrived. "I have seen the improvement in the past eight years—in the people," he says. "Do people live better? Yes. Do they have more purchasing power? Yes. Are they happier? Yes. I have no hesitation to give three yeses for the years since I arrived in China. If you look at other places in the world and ask yourself the same three questions, I'm not sure you will answer yes to each of them." Such growth, he says, offers vast potential for companies targeting Chinese consumers. "The thing is, there are so many Chinese consumers. There is so much elevation in the middle class, so many new consumers coming up."

From Tier 1 to Tiers 2, 3, and 4

Jonathan Woetzel, Senior Partner at McKinsey & Company, says one important aspect of the evolution of Chinese consumers has been the rapid geographical expansion of the country's middle class: "Consumers are far richer, of course. But the main point is that the Chinese middle class has expanded geometrically as income has grown." This has left China with a more geographically diverse, more culturally "heterogeneous" middle-class population. He explains: "Before, a certain consumer could be precisely identified within three or four Tier 1 cities. They were all between the ages of X and Y, and they all had certain types of occupations, and lived in certain kinds of buildings. . . . Today, it's far more dispersed. There are tens if not hundreds of cities [across China] where you'll find this new consumer driving trends."

"The Chinese middle class has expanded geometrically as income has grown. ... There are tens if not hundreds of cities [across China] where you'll find this new consumer driving trends."

—Jonathan Woetzel,
Senior Partner, McKinsey & Company

Consumer Trend 3: The Power of Key Opinion Leaders

In China, perhaps more than anywhere else, the opinions of social media influencers matter greatly among consumers. Among the nations' most impactful KOLs is Beijing Central Academy of Drama graduate-cum–social commentator Papi Jiang. Jiang's microblog has attracted an astounding 31 million followers[23] who tune in for her frequent posts on social issues, including the generation gap (she was born in 1987) and social pressures on singles, as well as her thoughts on entertainment and lifestyle. As this book went to press, one post by Jiang in which she raps about her mother's tendency to say "no" (to the food she likes, to the pastimes she enjoys) was viewed by 100,000 Chinese during the first day of posting.[24] Other microbloggers have built followings for their thoughts on specific consumer topics. Automobile commentator Chen Zhen, for example, had 4.43 million followers as this book went to press,[25] while the Tongdao Dashu site (delivering horoscope readings) had 17 million followers.[26]

Korn Ferry's Charles Tseng adds that many China-based companies are planning to continue growing in the coming decade and beyond simply by following the increased spending power of citizens in the nation's Tier 2 and Tier 3 cities. As Tseng explains: "The whole central part [of China] is not well developed, and the western part is completely undeveloped. And I'm not even talking about the northwest and southwest— completely new areas of development. The size and scale of the country is enormous."

Marriott International is one MNC that is banking on the economic development of China's less urbanized areas in the short term and midterm. In fact, the group expects to jump from operating more than 350 hotels (across 22 hotel brands) in China to doubling that number in the coming years. Rainer Burkle says: "We cannot only look at the first-tier cities. We have to

---

[23] Culture Tip. https://theculturetrip.com/asia/china/articles/why-is-the-chinese-internet-going-crazy-over-papi-jiang/.
[24] *China CEO II* authors' research.
[25] *China CEO II* authors' research.
[26] *China CEO II* authors' research.

look at second-tier cities. For second-tier cities, it's a relatively simple decision—they are really thriving." Burkle adds that his company is seeing high growth in China's Tier 2 cities. "There has been a lot of effort in building infrastructure in these second-tier cities. So, one side is the government but on the other side, we also see the middle class growing very strong. People have come from the countryside to move into those cities." Burkle has seen demand for luxury hospitality rise with the expansion of China's middle and upper-middle classes and their increased domestic travel. With this in mind, Marriott International opened a new W hotel and a Ritz-Carlton in Xian in 2018, and a Ritz-Carlton in Nanjing in 2019.

Tier 3 cities in China are growing as well, says Marriott International's Rainer Burkle: "For the third tier, it's city by city. But there are also opportunities there." As one example, he names the company's new Ritz-Carlton in Sichuan Province's remote Jiuzhaigou National Park. "This is really not a metropolis. It's the countryside, but it's a beautiful, unique place."

For B2C providers, including L'Oréal, China's rural areas are offering a rich ground for increasing market-share because of the country's rapidly expanding use of e-commerce. Stéphane Rinderknech, comments: "Today, 60% of China's 15- to 34-year-olds are in China's Tier 3 and Tier 4 cities and below. That's the next population we're talking to: this 60%. And that's where digital and e-commerce is so important for us—because it allows us to penetrate faster, deeper—and to go and get these people." Rinderknech gives one example of the power of e-commerce across both rural China: "About 50% of YSL sales in China are in places where we don't have sales counters, no physical presence. It's all by e-commerce. If we were limited to the offline world, it would take four times longer to get to those consumers."

Rinderknech sums up the promise of China's consumer market in this way: "This is why beauty growth is accelerating—it's a mix of rising middle-class purchasing power, millennials coming into the picture, and the capability to reach consumers faster, deeper. All of these combined, when you multiply,

"About 50% of YSL sales in China are in places where we don't have sales counters, no physical presence. It's all by e-commerce."

—**Stéphane Rinderknech,**
CEO, China, L'Oreal

Consumer Trend 4: 11/11 Day

As a show of both the marketing prowess of Alibaba and the vibrant enthusiasm for shopping among Chinese consumers, consider the rapid rise of 11/11 Day. Started as a celebration of China's not-yet-married population (because of the repeated number 1 in the date), Alibaba launched a special sales day for unmarried singles on November 11 back in 2009. The one-day e-commerce discount shopping event, aka Singles Day, soon caught on virally, with shoppers prepurchasing via the digital giant's B2C platform, Tmall. By 2017, 11/11 Day attracted sales of US$25.3 billion in 24 hours;[27] by 2019, that figure had soared to US$38 billion during the day,[28] thus becoming a major shopping phenomenon for all B2C retailers in China, including MNCs.

multiply, multiply, that makes an enormous market which is growing at the speed of light." He adds that the growth L'Oréal has so far experienced in China is just the tip of the iceberg. "We are just scratching the surface because the income per capita, the penetration of makeup—these are still at a very, very early stage in China."

Mary Boyd, Economist Corporate Network's Director for Shanghai, has also witnessed a closing of the gap between rural and urban China in recent years. "In the past, we might have seen a divide between first-tier and second-tier populations, but now it's probably fair to say that if it's a big hit in the first-tier cities, it is probably going to be a big hit in the second-tier cities and towns." These new shared purchasing behaviors, she says, are due mainly to the growth of e-commerce.

Besides growth in sheer purchasing power, China's domestic shopping population has also changed dramatically in its mindset. The evolution of Chinese consumers in recent years has, on one hand strengthened the position of MNCs in China but, on the other hand, brought new challenges to their business models. A recap of the key characteristics that

"[I]t's probably fair to say that if it's a big hit in the first-tier cities, it is probably going to be a big hit in the second-tier cities and towns."

—Mary Boyd,
Director, Shanghai,
Economist Corporate
Network

---

[27] CNBC. https://www.cnbc.com/2018/11/11/alibaba-singles-day-2018-record-sales-on-largest-shopping-event-day.html.
[28] CNBC. https://www.cnbc.com/2019/11/11/alibaba-singles-day-2019-record-sales-on-biggest-shopping-day.html.

China CEOs identified as shaping the domestic B2C market for MNCs follows.

Profile of Today's Chinese Consumer

Characteristic 1: Informed and Sophisticated but Fickle

McKinsey's Jonathan Woetzel sums up today's Chinese urban consumer with these three words: "increasingly globally aware." He says ubiquitous and constant access to the internet, social media, and other technologies, as well as increased outbound international travel, have "allowed Chinese consumers to start to gain a point of view." He elaborates: "There are some new, modern trends—such as a much greater awareness of the importance of taking care of the environment, of food safety, of exercise. The [Chinese] consumer has started to become more self-aware."

The trouble for MNCs, says Woetzel, is that "fickleness" is another aspect of today's Chinese consumer mindset: "It's still easy for [consumers] to change brands, to trade off and on. . . . This month, they'll try this new product. Next month, they'll try a different one. Brand loyalty is very challenging to maintain."

Another challenging characteristic, Woetzel notes, is that China's dynamic consumer population also makes traditional marketing segmentation less relevant. Simply put, China's domestic shoppers tend to follow purchasing patterns less rigorously—sometimes behaving like price-conscious decision-makers, other times behaving like luxury shoppers. He says: "Customer segment identification is difficult in China because Chinese consumers tend to move up and down within a brand hierarchy on a monthly, if not weekly basis. So identifying who is the 'premium customer' is not easy." In addition, he says, the "online-offline transition" also adds complexity. "At this point, every consumer uses both online and offline to learn of, try, and ultimately purchase items." The challenge for MNCs is that domestic consumers often learn of their products via their one online platform, then purchase through another, lower cost platform.

Many China CEOs expressed the view that, while China's consumers are becoming savvier, better informed, more demanding in terms of gathering information from multiple sources, ultimately, they are also growing more willing to make purchases. Tata's top China executive James Zhan expresses the dramatic change he has seen in domestic consumers during his time in the role: "Since 2010, the Chinese economy has grown to a very different level. Disposable incomes are much higher: You can feel it; you can see it. Consumers are not trying to negotiate for a little discount. Now they want to have a certain lifestyle. Or they want to have long-term value. They pay more attention to real quality of life instead of artificial value. They are more mature—they are willing to pay more for good products."

LEGO's Jacob Kragh is another top China executive with high hopes for the nation's domestic shopping population: "China has gone from being a small emerging market for LEGO to a large emerging market—and it is still not finished." While the US remains the company's largest market, followed by Germany, expected economic growth rates place the country on a path toward becoming number one for LEGO by 2030. Kragh says: "We're starting to deal with the China market in terms of its potential more than its current size. We set resources based not on the market today but on what the market can be in the future." This is one reason why, in 2015, LEGO altered its global structure to place China on par with other regional geographies, including Asia Pacific, Europe, and the US, in terms of using a direct reporting line to corporate headquarters.

Another China CEO with a front-row view into the changing mindset of domestic shoppers is Frederico Freire of AB InBev. He notes a shift in viewpoints after leaving China for Korea between 2016 and 2018. "When I came back [to China] in the beginning of 2018, I could see a lot of differences in the country overall. Consumers were getting more exposure to the external

"Since 2010, the Chinese economy has grown to a very different level. Disposable incomes are much higher: You can feel it; you can see it."

—**James Zhan,** President, China, Tata Sons

world, they were travelling much more than before, they were becoming more conscious of quality."

Today, Freire describes a new spirit of experimentation and curiosity among domestic beverage drinkers. "They are looking for diversification. They are trying more new things." In the F&B industry, especially in the beer sector, this open mindset means trying new products such as lager beers, wheat beers, dark beers, and ales. Freire says Chinese consumers are now "much more curious to learn, to try than before." And price? "They are willing to pay more if they believe that there is a benefit in that product—either the quality, or a new beautiful package, or another reason."

In the investment and insurance industry, MNCs still find a gap between the mindset of Chinese consumers versus their Western counterparts. Kai Zhang, Manulife's top executive for China, explains: "One thing which is still true regarding Chinese investors is that they are less sophisticated. They are still looking for an absolute return, even for insurance. They often treat insurance as a 'savings replacement' product." Today, she says, "they are starting to understand the health protection component of insurance, and about the wealth transfer, legacy planning, and estate planning aspects." Meanwhile for investment products like mutual funds, Zhang still finds that some domestic consumers complain about returns of 3%—a rate which Western clients would find acceptable. "Some clients still expect a yield at least matching the deposit; otherwise, they feel that they have been cheated and will complain," she says. "This sort of situation has started to get better as the market matures. Today, you may not hear those rudimentary complaints anymore. But still [Chinese] people think less about long-term asset allocation. They think more about short-term, absolute returns."

Characteristic 2: Digital and Demanding (Convenience Is King)

One of the most challenging aspects for companies dealing with China's domestic shoppers is their high level of expectations

MINI-CASE 1

Coca-Cola Delivery Challenges in China

Curt Ferguson, Coca-Cola's China CEO, tells how distribution demands in China have evolved in recent years. "At Coca-Cola, we pat ourselves on the back and say: 'We have 12 million outlets which we deliver to on a weekly basis in China—and that's a lot.' But distribution is turned totally upside-down now. Today, I have to have 450 million outlets to reach every Chinese household. Or now maybe 1.4 billion outlets to reach everyone with a cell phone." In other words, today's Chinese consumers demand at-home, on-site, or even individual delivery—anywhere, anytime, within 30 minutes, and for a nominal, added fee.

Ferguson explains the new mindset: "Here's a story that really hit home for me. I was standing in line for a movie in Shanghai. And all of a sudden, a guy delivers a Coke to the man standing in line in front of me. And I'm paying a marketing fee for product availability per movie outlet to have a Coke cooler installed there. And the guy in front of me just got delivered everything he wants while waiting in line. Of course, nobody's going to stop the delivery guy from taking that Coke into the theater, right? So hold it: my business model is really upset."

fueled by the country's ongoing digital revolution. Mats Harborn, President of the European Chamber of Commerce in China, explains the trouble this mindset can cause for unprepared MNCs: "Thirty years ago, [Europeans] did not understand that Japanese customers were the most demanding in the world. We learnt some lessons in Japan—realizing what we thought was good quality was seen as shoddy at best by Japanese. Today, in China we see the same thing. But here, consumers demand convenience, fast delivery times, flexibility. China has a very developed consumer culture in that regard."

For Philips, digitization has changed the company's outreach to Chinese consumers in two ways. Andy Ho, the company's head of China, first notes that the best and only way to reach consumers with a marketing message today is via WeChat. "If we want to register a consumer for Philips and you send them an email, it doesn't work. You need WeChat to approach the consumer." Second, Ho says that after attracting the interest of Chinese consumers, most actual sales will be completed online: "In Hong Kong, 20 to 30% of sales are made online. In China,

"[Chinese] consumers demand convenience, fast delivery times, flexibility. China has a very developed consumer culture in that regard."

—**Mats Harborn,**
President, European Chamber of Commerce in China

"In China, almost 70% of Philips' consumer products are being sold online—and more than 80% of these purchases are made via mobile."

—**Andy Ho,**
Leader, Greater China, Philips

Mango's Delivery Challenges in China

David Sancho, China CEO of Mango, calls distribution and delivery "the key to success" in China. "In China, the logistics capabilities of distribution companies are amazing. Today, in China, you deliver clothing to shoppers in less than 48 hours, no matter where. This is really the power behind the growth of e-commerce in this market."

This power of distribution is forcing Mango and other MNCs to change their business models to match the expectations of Chinese consumer. "Globally, e-commerce accounts for 20% of our sales; in China, it accounts for 30% and it's growing tremendously, tremendously."

With online sales doubling and tripling yearly now in China, will brick-and-mortar stores continue to serve a purpose? Sancho notes: "We are now in the middle of a transformation [regarding] what role the physical store will play in this new strategy." Shops will play a role, he says, in terms of allowing customers to "play with the product, interact with it, test it, understand the brand." Going forward, stores will also serve as "digital warehouses" used as pick-up points for final on-site delivery.

almost 70% of Philips' consumer products are being sold online—and more than 80% of these purchases are made via mobile."

One characteristic of Chinese consumers, exacerbated by the highly digitized environment, is "short-term" mindset. James Zhan, Tata's top executive for China, used this descriptive to explain the mindset among domestic automobile shoppers (relevant for Tata as the parent company of Jaguar Land Rover): "Chinese people are probably more 'short-term thinking' than 'longer-term thinking.'" He gives the example of Shanghai residents buying electric cars because the city government offers them a free license plate. The problem, Zhan says, is that they may actually "not be getting a good car." He says: "People just react to the short-term gain; they want to try the new alternative energy vehicle. But that vehicle is not mature." More mature consumers, he adds, would research the car further before buying, finding out how many miles the car runs without recharge, confirming its reliability, and understanding where and how to repair the car. Zhan says: "Many [Chinese consumers] just jump into the new technology."

Another MNC adapting to China's new consumer demands is Coca-Cola. Worldwide, the company has long been known for extremely widespread distribution via its sales outlets—even reaching the base camp at Mount Everest and locations in the Amazon forest. But today's Chinese consumers present a new level of distribution challenges, says the company's top China executive, Curt Ferguson: "Our past chairman, many years ago, said: 'Coke should always be within an arm's reach of desire. If it's not there, we're doing something wrong.' So, Coke should be where you want it. But now, in China, 'arm's reach' means in somebody's pocket—they want it brought to them." In China, the demand for at-home or on-site delivery is now huge and highly competitive. "If one guy can get it there in 30 minutes, another will get it there in 20 minutes. Right?" (See "Mini-Case 1: Coke's Delivery Challenges in China" earlier in this chapter.) Ferguson muses, half-jokingly, that the next step in China's mobile shopping evolution will be predictive sales targeting individuals based on their behavior. He explains: "A smart-phone could detect, for example, when someone goes out for a bike ride. After 30 minutes of cycling, a message could be sent to his or her phone, asking 'Are you thirsty?' and offering drink delivery en route." He adds: "We are getting to those kinds of levels, which is kind of spooky even."

In the insurance sector, Manulife's Kai Zhang also describes a rapid evolution in Chinese consumer tastes based on digital tools: "The biggest change is the way the technology is changing everybody's life in China. In terms of behavior, they are using everything digital. In the future, I don't think the younger generation will go to branches. You have tele-presence, so people can face each other [virtually] from different locations. With that technology, in my view, you don't need physical branches anymore." She describes how China has surpassed other markets in terms of digitization. "China has leapfrogged ahead of other countries," she notes, basically going from a cash-based system directly to digital. Zhang says: "We never used checks in China. We skipped checks and we are even skipping credit cards. Now, it's the digital wallet."

"After 30 minutes of cycling, a message could be sent to [the consumer's] phone asking, 'Are you thirsty?' and offering drink delivery en route."

—Curt Ferguson,
President, Greater China & Korea, Coca-Cola

"China has leapfrogged ahead of other countries. ... We skipped checks and we are even skipping credit cards. Now, it's the digital wallet."

—Kai Zhang,
President & CEO, China, Manulife-Sinochem

A key factor in the fast rise of digital wallets in China is the high value that consumers place on convenience vis-à-vis privacy. Sony's China CEO Hiroshi Takahashi comments: "Relatively speaking, Chinese consumers don't pay too much attention to protecting sensitive personal information, if I compare [them] with the rest of the world. Because if you use We-Chat, you expose almost everything."

Manulife's Kai Zhang agrees: "Chinese people are willing to give up a lot for convenience." She explains the different mindset of Chinese versus Western consumers: "In China, people already assume that they don't have privacy. So they are less concerned about people sweeping your QR code, exposing where you are." By contrast, digital wallets have not taken off in the US and Europe, she says, mainly for cultural reasons. "One, because people's behaviors or habits die hard. They are very used to their plastic cards already. Second, [Western] people are a lot more conscientious and conscious about their privacy. They may not want to use mobile phones for payment everywhere."

Interestingly, it is mainly cultural reasons that prevented credit card usage from catching on in China. Kai Zhang says: "In China, people don't like the concept of borrowing. When they borrow, they feel anxious. That's why the credit card was not really accepted, and people did not have to give up anything to switch to digital. They don't have a credit card because it's already built into the phone. So it's convenient."

Jerry Zhang, Standard Chartered's top China executive, says one reason Chinese consumers have higher and higher expectations for convenience is because Chinese e-commerce companies have developed so rapidly. "In some areas, turnaround time for delivery and logistics management for example, they are leading the world." Zhang mentions JD.com's "impressive" 24-hour delivery pledge, and Alibaba's "magnificent" storage and distribution centers in key logistic hubs. She expects consumer demands for speedy, convenient delivery to quickly expand in neighboring Asian countries—a process that has already begun. One example: in 2018, Alibaba increased its investment in Lazada, the biggest online shopping website in ASEAN. Zhang says: "By expanding into overseas markets,

"In China, people already assume that they don't have privacy. So they are less concerned about people sweeping your QR code."

—**Kai Zhang,**
President & CEO, China, Manulife-Sinochem

these Chinese e-commerce companies have a chance to upgrade the retailing model in these markets, to bring about a better consumer experience, and to contribute to commercial prosperity."

The downside of rapid acceptance of digital payment systems has been a level of misuse by providers. Tata's James Zhan comments: "[Chinese consumers] just accepted the digital payment; they are very easy to trust." But he points out that some Chinese families have lost their fortunes in this way, by trusting their savings to fraudulent digital P2P organizations. "In a less mature market, people trust the players too easily."

Another impact Coca-Cola is feeling from the e-commerce and delivery revolution is a loss of their traditional salesforce to new employment models. Curt Ferguson says: "We see a huge mass transformation in the loss of salespeople who would rather drive a motorbike [making e-commerce deliveries] because they feel they are in business for themselves. That's better than sales pressure."

Another challenge exacerbated by mobile shopping has been the ease and frequency with which consumers jump from one product to another. Sony's Hiroshi Takahashi comments: "Chinese are very, very agile consumers. They quickly abandon you to try a new thing tomorrow. So we have to deal with that."

"Chinese are very, very agile consumers. They quickly abandon you to try a new thing tomorrow."

—**Hiroshi Takahashi,** Chairman & President, China, Sony

If shopping is done online these days in China, does that pertain to all purchases? Even luxury sports cars? Maserati's top executive for China, Alberto Cavaggioni, says yes, telling of Maserati's dramatic entry into Alibaba's Tmall platform in 2016. When the company introduced its Levante model car into the e-commerce system that year, there was a dramatic reception: "We sold 100 Maserati Levantes in 18 seconds. We were the first [luxury auto brand] to use Tmall on Alibaba's online platform."

While Cavaggioni admits that his company does not sell a large number of cars via Tmall, it is an important part of the company's overall China marketing strategy. "It's something you need to do because people surf, people look for the brand. . . . People may surf online, and then the final part of the purchasing process is done at the dealership." Cavaggioni says the internet is where Chinese "do their homework" by "making comparisons with the competitors." In China, he adds, internet research has become a necessary part of consumers' buying processes "to a higher degree and more advanced level than the rest of the world." Today, China represents around 30% of Maserati's total worldwide sales. Cavaggioni calls China "the most important market in terms of volume in the world." He explains that the actual volume of sales is close to that of the US, "but in terms of overall results, China is so important that it's considered not only as a single market, but as a region—like the Europe region. So China has become the most important market for Maserati."

Another new initiative for Maserati is the new collaboration with Alibaba to create the i-store, a system allowing access to customer profiles. Cavaggioni explains: "When you walk into one of our showrooms, with i-store, we know who you are, your consumer behavior. We may know that you are a 40-year-old gentleman, a professor with this level of income, who buys this and that. . . . We understand your consumer habits and we can guide you to the type of product you could be interested in. Are you more of a sporty guy? Are you more an elegant guy? . . . The i-store is an extra support. If the sales team really leverages this tool, they will understand who the customer in front of them is."

"When you walk into one of our showrooms, with i-store, we know who you are, your consumer behavior."

—**Alberto Cavaggioni,**
Managing Director, China,
Maserati

Once in the showroom, potential buyers can interact with the cars by activating augmented reality to access the information they are interested in. Cavaggioni notes: "You scan parts of the car, and you get the information from the website. You scan the seats, and you see which seat models are available, which colors are available. . . . It explains the history of Maserati." In this way, technology offers another interactive touch point with consumers—methods that are increasingly expected by Chinese shoppers.

Characteristic 3: Price-Conscious vs. Quality-Conscious

One of the most complex characteristics of today's Chinese consumers, as described by the China CEOs, is the combination of their being very demanding on price (and very well informed via social media) and their growing understanding of and appreciation for high quality. In other words, our interviewees describe savvy and tough domestic consumers who make full use of online information to compare prices and other features before purchasing. At the same time, a rising number of Chinese consumers are able and willing to make very expensive high-end luxury purchases.

A growing appetite for luxury shopping also adds to the complex mindset of Chinese shoppers. Mats Harborn, President of the European Chamber of Commerce in China, explains that although Chinese consumers can be very well informed and demanding on price, they can also, in some circumstances, prefer to pay a high price for luxury goods. He explains: "The basic behavior of a Chinese customer is always price conscious. But when you connect a buying decision to giving face to yourself, or giving face to somebody else, then all of a sudden it becomes very important to pay a high price. This is the concept of 'ostentatious consumption,' a term I really did not understand until I saw this new Chinese consumer class." Harborn refers to the emerging group of Chinese who are wealthy enough to purchase the world's flashiest sports cars, highest-end designer bags, and most expensive prestige watches.

"[W]hen you connect a buying decision to giving face to yourself ... all of a sudden, it becomes very important to pay a high price."

—Mats Harborn,
President, European Chamber of Commerce in China

One trend that clearly benefits MNCs in related fields is the growing appetite among Chinese for luxury travel and high-end accommodation. Rainer Burkle of Marriott International comments on this new demand: "In the hotel business, generally, every sector has grown in China since around 2010, but luxury hotels have grown extremely well. That is the good part of the business."

Xiaolin Yuan, Volvo Cars' top China executive, explains the challenge of China's dual-minded, price-conscious/quality-conscious shoppers in this way: "There's a lot of talk stating that: 'Nowadays, Chinese are not brand sensitive. It's so convenient for them to go to the internet to buy cheap things, for quick satisfaction.'" He adds that these concerns are particularly targeted toward Chinese millennials. But Yuan advises MNCs to stay "clear headed" regarding Chinese consumers' willingness to pay. He describes two trends shaping consumer behavior in today's China: "The China market is getting more mature each day. Of course, there is one dynamic part focused on buying cheap stuff, but the trend is also becoming more 'premium' and more 'individualized.' These two keywords are very relevant for our market."

As a result, Volvo Cars is promoting both premium-ness and individualization in the China market. Yuan explains: "As people's income becomes more stable and more people can afford a quality lifestyle, the market for 'premium' is growing. This is the reason China has surprised the world with its consuming power compared to countries like India." He gives this example: "India's total premium market size is around 40,000 luxury cars. That's one-ninth the market size of Zhejiang Province (in China). So, you can imagine the potential that the China market has now. I'm not talking about unrealized potential. No, this is the size of the China market now. And it's growing." He adds that the pace of growth is also remarkable in China. "Maybe the pace of growth in the premium auto market is not that surprising for the Chinese, but people look with amazement from Europe and the US."

Yuan is particularly optimistic about the changing tastes of Chinese consumers. "When I say premium, it is premium with quality—beyond bling, bling. [Chinese] people are starting to think, 'I need to have things with taste instead of labeling which shows that it is expensive.' Now, it's about taste." He adds: "This is supporting the strong growth of brands like Volvo, because we offer good products with taste and individualization." On the other side, he says, Volvo Cars is competing against, for example, German premium cars via increased individualization. "Chinese people would like to seek their identity instead of using brands to give themselves an identity. They want individualization, they want taste. They want people to recognize them differently. I think these are all striking characters of the nature of the China market now."

Safety is another quality-related selling point promoted by Volvo Cars. Yuan explains that Chinese consumers have been shaken by a number of scandals regarding product safety— a factor which can pull them toward trusted foreign brands.

"Particularly in China, the brand means you can trust their product and services in terms of safety and health. That's extremely important in nowadays China because people are not feeling assured about product safety. You can trust no one in terms of safety: for the food we eat, the cars we sit in. With the Volvo label on it, that gives people a lot of assurance that 'Now, we're covered.'" Asked whether Chinese consumers consider Volvo, which is Chinese owned, as a foreign or domestic brand, Yuan comments: "Very much a Swedish brand."

Philips is another MNC that has witnessed first-hand the complex mindset of Chinese consumers today regarding price. The company's top China executive, Andy Ho, explains: "A certain portion of the population likes price/performance, even likes cheap products." But he emphasizes that a spectrum of buying habits exist. For example, in the household appliances sector, he says, one sees Chinese consumers purchasing in the RMB100–200 range (US$14.55–US$29.10) as well as the RMB3,000–4,000 range (US$437–US$582). "You get certain people who actually like to buy at the RMB3,000 range," he says, naming both quality and prestige as motivations for purchasing high-end household goods. And among certain consumers, Ho says, quality standards and expectations have risen dramatically with digitization and increased access to comparative information: "Today, Chinese customers, especially retail customers, are more aware of their rights. In the past, they were not that picky. But now, some of customers are very picky. You have to really manage your product quality carefully."

The key to engaging and satisfying Chinese consumers, Ho says, is to allow them to first gather information easily and fully online. He explains: "People use their mobile phones to compare prices. . . . People enjoy the experience of surfing via mobile phone to learn about a product: How trendy is it? How good looking? How easy to use?" After comparing carefully, consumers then purchase online.

Stéphane Rinderknech, L'Oréal's China CEO, agrees that increased demand for high quality has been one of the biggest changes among Chinese consumers since 2010. Rinderknech says: "Quality, quality, quality. That's probably the biggest revolution in China. I think Chinese consumers will be even more demanding on quality than Japanese consumers. China is really following that trend. It's amazing, the difference I see in my eight years . . . in China."

Maserati's Alberto Cavaggioni explains the complex nature of the Chinese consumer purchasing process. "Customers are much more careful in buying—it doesn't matter what. What they do is: they search, they compare, they try to make a deal. And before making a deal with you, they have already tried to make a deal with somebody else. They try to make the best deal." He says although some auto buyers are "very passionate," most are quite calculating when it comes to purchasing.

> *"What [Chinese consumers] do is: they search, they compare, they try to make a deal. And before making a deal with you, they have already tried to make a deal with somebody else."*
>
> —**Alberto Cavaggioni,**
> Managing Director, China, Maserati

Another challenge is that brand loyalty tends to run low among Chinese shoppers, making it easy to lose a buyer to another brand. Cavaggioni says: "At the moment, the level of loyalty is not yet there. We need to work on the loyalty." He continues by explaining that Chinese consumers tend to seek constant variety and novelty—posing a challenge for his company. He says: "We have a limited product lineup, and Chinese look for novelty. The customers, if they really want product novelty and another brand that fits their social position, then they go and buy that brand." Maserati is now using a strategy to leverage the fact that China's super-luxury car shoppers often change automobiles every two or three years. "This is good but at the same time, challenging. You need to also find a way to create new interest and have them repurchase the latest version of the same model or to walk across to another model."

In the fashion industry, Mango's top executive for China, David Sancho, sums up the "amazing change" he has witnessed in Chinese consumer tastes: "When we got here in 2010, one of our visions was to educate the Chinese customer with Western taste. It was very important for us to give Chinese customers a sense of fashion: how to dress, what is fashionable." Not so today. "After ten years, those customers have evolved so much. They have embraced a lot of information, a lot of taste. They have become very ambitious and very strong demanders of fashion. They understand what they're looking for. We came from a point where they needed to be educated to a point where they know so much that they are asking for a lot. They very important to the market because they know what they want."

In the healthcare sector, Chinese consumers have also grown more difficult to keep up with. Celina Chew, Bayer's top executive for China. explains that domestic consumers "adopt new things very, very quickly" based on several factors: "First, in general, Chinese consumers now have more money to spend, given their rising incomes. They also have an increasing desire for quality: quality in healthcare, in food, in quality of life. And they also expect variety, choice, and access. They are very demanding." She says Chinese consumers can sometimes be seemingly paradoxical in terms of simultaneously "wanting and valuing tradition and reliability" while also "wanting to try new things and novel experiences."

Because of the fast-changing, highly competitive environment, Chew says members of her salesforce sometimes struggle to follow conflicting consumer trends. "It's really not easy for my guys to read what consumers need. We have brands that are more than 100 years old. How to refresh these constantly so that people are constantly interested in them, yet preserving the heart of the tradition? The adoption of new trends and new ideas is very, very fast in China."

Adding complexity for MNCs is a growing demand among Chinese consumers for a continuous stream of fresh and engaging online content. Chew says: "The content part of communication these days is difficult. It's not just a matter of having a phone and connecting. If I don't have something new to say all the time, it's very difficult. . . . You can have WeChat channels, but if there's nothing new to say. . . . The attention span of customers these days is very, very quick. You're competing for eyeballs all the time, and you're not the only one in the market. Everyone else is also talking to them. So how to capture them?" In the field of healthcare, Chew hopes to see a shift from digital-style messaging back toward more substantial, traditional information-sharing. "If I look around the world, there's a swing towards more traditional communication. Because there's so much digital that it is nice to have something more concrete, more real. Maybe that will also come to China: the convenience of digital plus something more lasting."

"The attention span of customers these days is very, very quick. You're competing for eyeballs all the time, and you're not the only one in the market."

—**Celina Chew,**
President, Greater China, Bayer

Udacity's Consumer Engagement Challenges

The story of Udacity's launch in China holds several lessons for MNCs. The company's China CEO, Robert Hsiung, recounts: "It's actually a funny story. When we launched Udacity, we had huge hopes for China. As soon as we opened our doors, we got thousands of students signed up for trial accounts. The number of trial accounts in China eclipsed the total number of students globally at the time. The leadership was extremely excited. We thought we would be making billions of dollars."

But one month later, a different scene emerged. "After those trials expired, no one put the money down," says Hsiung. "We expected tens of thousands of students by the end of August 2016, and we ended in September with a couple of hundred."

What was the learning point? "We realized that the US model—in terms of how the product was packaged, how the product was sold, how the student was served—did not match the needs of the China market." The company's mistake, Hsiung says, was in "taking the US model and just launching that in China. That's one of the challenges that a lot of US companies face in China. . . . A lot of US businesses feel they have an amazing product that's going to sell itself. They think: 'If I sell this for $1 to 1 billion Chinese people, I'll make it big.' But it's not that easy."

Udacity's next move in China was to "start over from zero" to create a true "product-market fit." The three years that followed, Hsiung says, led to "a continued evolution of the way we work, the way we sell, the way we serve our students. And it's still evolving today."

One of the innovations launched in China after the revamp was later launched globally by the company. Hsiung explains that, in order to increase the completion rate of students taking their online courses, Udacity China began dividing participating students into groups of 15, then assigning a coach and mentor to each small group. Hsiung notes: "We created these roles to work with the student to resolve two key areas: First, to keep the students really, really motivated and engaged in their studying. Second, to identify the learning blockers that prevent students from mastering concepts and skills." Hsiung says the combination of online courses plus offline group work helps the overall program succeed. "By working together in close groups, they build friendships. And that keeps them engaged." The new system creates "a much more effective teaching environment for our students." The results have been impressive: "Those two key roles have made a huge difference in increasing our graduation rates from 30–40% to 80–90% of students." Today, this "launched in China" strategy is used by Udacity elsewhere worldwide.

In the field of education, NIIT's head of China Kamal Dhuper finds his domestic customers increasingly concerned with brand name and quality—two trends that are promising for his company's offerings in the sectors of IT training and degree courses. "The Chinese consumers now, by and large, have become more aware and more brand conscious. They want the best. In our industry, much like other industries, if you have a good brand, if your brand gives value, and they can trust your brand to give good quality, they will come to you." Dhuper observes that consumer preferences in education are similar to those in other sectors today: "If you look at cosmetics, at cars, at Prada and Gucci, . . . Chinese don't want to buy the fakes. They want to buy the genuine stuff." In today's world, he says, many Chinese consumers have no appetite for counterfeits: "It's a disgrace for Chinese to buy fake stuff. They have become very brand conscious. They would rather go for a good quality brand [or] not buy at all."

This discerning attitude among consumers, Dhuper notes, has resulted in a shrinking pool of education providers in China. "In our industry, we have seen competition consolidate. Fifteen years back, there used to be a lot of local players. But there were quality issues." Those remaining, he says, have "invested in building brands" and have become more serious competitors.

For NIIT, the company leverages two tools that help to attract and retain Chinese students in its IT training courses and programs. First is the international scope of the company. Dhuper notes: "Being global brings a lot of strength to our products." Second is the company's proven track record in helping their students to secure either improved employment or placement in continuing education. NIIT's placement and employment rate is "four times higher than that of a normal university graduate," Dhuper says. "In education, your consumer is going to value you based on the outcome he gets at the program's end. And our differentiation is our unique pedagogy—the way we teach, our methods, it almost guarantees better outcomes."

Characteristic 4: Generational Diversity

One emerging challenge that China CEOs described as intensifying is the "generation gap" in Chinese society. Economist Corporate Network's Mary Boyd says despite the "unifying" effect of digitization, one countertrend in Chinese society has been the emergence of more clear socio-cultural differences between China's older and younger sets. "There are some pretty clear generational markers," she says, adding that today's Chinese society displays more generational groupings than geographic groupings. "What might be attractive to one particular age group is going to be probably true for all urban people [Chinese] at that age group."

Victoria's Secret is one MNC that is directly taking note of the generational differences within Chinese shoppers. The company's top executive for China, Arun Bhardwaj, identifies three different consumer groups existing in parallel in Chinese society today. "First, there are those born in the 1950s and 1960s, who went through the hard times and have seen China evolve. Their consumption habits and how they see the world are a little bit different. They tend to save money, they tend to plan for the future, and invest in their kids."

Second, the generations born in the 1970s and 1980s were the first group to again enjoy a stable education (not interrupted by the Cultural Revolution) as well as increased exposure to the outside world. Today, Bhardwaj says these consumers tend to exhibit both the values of their parents and more international thinking: "They're the ones traveling the world today. They have enough income, and they've achieved a degree of security in their life. They bought their apartment, they have cars, and they have young kids who they're trying to send to good schools, so they have a much more balanced consumption pattern." Compared with younger consumers, he says, "they tend to be a bit more loyal, a bit more stable." However, compared with older generations, they tend to "explore and try new things, but still have some traditional values."

Finally, China's "post-1990" consumers display very different values. Says Bhardwaj: "This group doesn't tend to save a lot of money. Their main focus is: 'What can I get today? What can I enjoy today? What can I experience that is totally new and different?' They are very experimental; they don't fit a particular mold." Creating challenge for MNCs, he says, is the fact that China's post-1990s generation "is not the generation who would automatically gravitate towards a Western brand." Instead, all brands must earn their interest. "They are very curious, but they also expect very high-quality product and service, as well as newness and innovation. And they very easily switch brands and try different things. There's a lower degree of loyalty." (For more on China's generation gaps, see Chapter 3.)

At IKEA, top China executive Freda Zhang shares her personal and professional observations regarding the generation gaps among shoppers. "Regarding consumers, we focus on the young generation in China. In the European market, it's not like that. There, we think that we need to provide more for the aging, for the seniors." Zhang says the focus is different in China for generational reasons: "My parents' generation, they don't spend money. And my generation is still very conservative. The biggest consumption is coming from those born after 1980, 1985. They grew up in a society full of resources. When I grew up, food was still limited. So, of course, I still have the mindset of wanting to save money instead of spending."

China's younger generations have grown up with vastly different priorities, Zhang explains: "Those born after 1985, they want to consume more. This group of people created new rules for the retail game. That's why, even for me at the age of 40, I need the fresh eyes of those born after 1990s—to understand the consumer behavior better."

She adds that, in other parts of Greater China, the mindset is also different. Zhang compares the behavior of her mother (who lives in mainland China) with that of her mother-in-law (who lives in Taiwan) in this way: "In Taiwan, my mother-in-law spends a lot of money. But my mom will never do that. The history they grew up with is different."

Marriott International is another MNC studying new generational groups in Chinese society in order to best match the different demographics. The company's top China executive for

> *"[Millennial consumers'] main focus is: 'What can I get today? What can I enjoy today?'"*
>
> —**Arun Bhardwaj,**
> President, Greater China,
> LBrands International
> (Victoria's Secret)

> *"The biggest consumption is coming from those born after 1980, 1985. They grew up in a society full of resources."*
>
> —**Freda Zhang,**
> Country Commercial VP,
> China, IKEA

luxury Burkle describes the new mindset of consumers born after 1990 in this way: "Young people feel that, 'I think of it now and I get it now.' With a snap of the finger, I can connect with someone who can provide what I need, fast." What kind of requirements? Burkle says: "They want everything—many individual requirements, spontaneously." For example, he says: "They might ask the staff at the W, 'What's happening in Shanghai tonight? I want to go clubbing.' And the one recommending really has to know what's going on—ideally, the person is an insider who knows the coolest places, places others wouldn't know." Burkle says: "That's the idea—you have it all at your fingertips."

"They [young Chinese consumers] want everything—many individual requirements, spontaneously."

—**Rainer Burkle,**
Area Vice President, Luxury, Greater China, Marriott International

On the positive side, he notes that the younger generation has embraced his group's luxury facilities not only for travel accommodations but also for dining or night-clubbing. "In China, it is clear that younger guests frequent our luxury hotels more than in other places in the world. The youngsters have really embraced our brands." He points out that weekend parties at the W in Shanghai, with a deejay, can attract more than 1,000 young customers. He says: "The brand is a big draw."

L'Oréal's head of China, Stéphane Rinderknech, echoes the words of fellow China CEOs in his description of the post-90s generation: "They are very different from the Confucian norms of before. Before, you had to be like everyone else: Your haircut, your hairstyle, no makeup, no color, no differentiation. You fit within the mold." By contrast, the post-90s generation has a different set of priorities: "They love beauty. They want to express their difference. Before, it was us, us, us. Now, it is me, me, me."

"Before, it was us, us, us. Now, it is me, me, me."

—**Stéphane Rinderknech,**
CEO, China, L'Oréal

For L'Oréal, the new consumer mindset translates into a new interest in cultivating an individual style. Rinderknech explains the mindset: "So it's: 'I'm different, I'm unconventional. And I want to find everything—my dress code, fashion, makeup—to express that difference. My lipstick color will not be the same as yours because I'm different. I will color my hair. I will have many facets. That's the revolution."

In addition to spending money differentiating their appearance, China's post-90s generations also tend to support a new social agenda. For example, L'Oréal faces a new pressure to support environmental protection and sustainable business operations. Rinderknech explains the priorities of Chinese youth: "They have financial power. They have four grandparents who save money and two parents who save money all for them, the one child. So, they have big money to spend. And they want brands that socially contribute to make the world a better place. . . . They travel abroad. They are knowledgeable—about brands, about products, about the world, about ingredients and about safety. All of these have become extremely important topics impacting purchasing for consumers. Is this company contributing to the world? What's my connection to the brands, the heritage, the authenticity, the history, the uniqueness?"

"[Young Chinese] have big money to spend. And they want brands that socially contribute to make the world a better place."

—Stéphane Rinderknech, CEO, China, L'Oréal

Special Advice for Winning China's B2B Customers

MNCs targeting B2B clients in today's China have also noted a transformation in terms of expectations. Tata's James Zhan describes the challenges created for MNCs by the changing mindset of this category of customers. "For corporate customers, it's challenging because the structure of the market has changed so much in recent years. In the past, multinationals were playing a very important role in the economy. They [were] very influential. But during the past two years, many multinationals are not growing." He says this lack of growth has triggered a loss of clout for some MNCs among local customers.

Regarding Tata, Zhan comments: "We're fortunate that we are growing, but we still feel the pressure." By contrast, many of the client companies that MNCs serve in China are growing—especially state-owned enterprises. Zhan explains the flip-flop in roles: "Ten years ago, many SOEs were just poorly managed. They have become more professional; they have gained a lot more capabilities. They've become international." Meanwhile, he adds that the past decade also saw rapid development and maturation of China's private companies, including Alibaba, Tencent, Baidu, Xiaomi, Meituan, and 360.com. "Before 2010, the internet was just starting, and these companies were not in our radar," Zhan says. "But now, our customers have changed so much." He says Tata has had to adapt to new ways of selling to both evolving SOEs and ambitious, "very entrepreneurial" tech companies. Zhan says the solution is a work in progress: "We have not solved it yet. . . . We are still struggling. We are still trying to figure out the best way to win major contracts from these two changing centers."

Jerry Zhang, Standard Chartered's top China executive, says one strategy for MNCs serving B2B customers in China is to grow with their domestic clients, especially as they seek to expand overseas. She says: "Standard Chartered has been able to enjoy the fruits of China's success" as more domestic companies "go global," especially in the wake of the government's promotion of the Belt and Road Initiative (B&RI). Zhang says her bank has focused on serving as a partner for domestic companies supporting the B&RI and seeking the right banking partner to serve this region.

Microsoft is another MNC that has based its business strategy in China on selling to Chinese companies via partnerships and co-development. Alain Crozier, the company's top executive for China, says: "Partnership is another aspect of why we are successful in China. We provide our partners with the tools, platform, and capabilities to develop solutions, as well as a large ecosystem. We are very much a partner-led company." In China, Microsoft works with 17,000 partners, ranging from very large infrastructure companies to small startups.

What is the outlook for MNCs focusing on B2B sales to Chinese clients? For those in tech-related industries, the outlook is bright, says Crozier: "This richness in the diversity of Chinese partners has accelerated a lot in the past three years. Why is that? One big reason is the strength of China's tech industry. When you look at the tech industry, you have a very, very strong position in the US—where you have the main players—but if you look just beside the US, the next country is really China."

Another challenge faced by MNCs in the B2B market is the Chinese client's demand for high quality at a low price. One China CEO, who witnessed an evolution in thinking from his Chinese customers since around 2000, explains the change in this way: "Fifteen or 20 years ago, price was not an issue;

Chinese customers just bought what they needed. Then gradually they became much more price demanding. Also, the government's procurement program for state-owned companies became more rigid. So basically, they didn't know how to do procurement; the only thing they knew was price."

Today, this China CEO says the mindset among domestic B2B clients is again shifting: "Now, they are becoming more focused on quality, but they still complain about price." The challenge for MNCs, he says, is that costs in China—labor costs, costs of repairs—are rising. "We have to balance costs, quality, and performance." The China head says that the nation is now in "an interesting period economically," in that MNCs need to persuade their clients to accept a reasonable balance between quality and price. "We need to educate the market, and we cannot do it alone. We are working with other companies to push customers toward a more mature procurement process."

Strategies for Winning Chinese Consumers

Strategy 1: Customize for Chinese Tastes

Alongside digital expectations, China's consumers are also demanding customization to suit their cultural preferences. Marriott International's Rainer Burkle, for example, explains how his company's new Li Yu program caters specifically to individual Chinese travelers: "It's a program for Chinese travelling abroad—to ensure that they feel comfortable by providing them a special concierge service in their language and following customized standards." So far, the program is offered at over 1000 group hotels worldwide and is growing. "Today, more and more Chinese travel individually. So we really want to make their travels smooth."

The service, accessed by WeChat, offers Chinese travelers a virtual service assistant to provide Mandarin-language destination information. The program also guarantees Chinese travelers certain food and beverage (F&B) norms in the 1,000 member hotels (such as Chinese tea and teaware in the rooms) and recommendations for finding Chinese cuisine locally.

Victoria's Secret is also becoming more active in adapting to domestic tastes, changing not only in terms of sizing, colors, and styles but also running seasonal promotions based on Chinese holidays and altering their business model to match cultural norms. Bhardwaj notes: "Obviously there are differences between East and West in terms of the social context—how boldly people are dressing." As a lingerie company, he says, "we need to be mindful of the culture."

Coca-Cola is also taking customer engagement and customization to another degree, including in China. Curt Ferguson explains: "It's amazing now the level of 'mass customization' that people are doing in China. And now, they're taking it to the next level by customizing it online, for individuals." He notes that in China, consumers can order individual gift cans of Coca-Cola printed with a friend's name on it, for example, for a birthday party or wedding.

Ferguson describes how the concept of custom printing has turned mass manufacturing on its head worldwide in recent years. He describes his own experience in Nigeria (several years ago) when the central government approached Coca-Cola with a special request. Ferguson says: "It was National Day and the President of Nigeria said to me: 'Can you create a green Coca-Cola can?' I said: 'What a great idea!' because Nigeria's national flag is green." At that time, it was impossible for Coke to make such a change, but today, times have changed. He says: "Nowadays, we could do it, and we'd have his name on the cans. It's just one of the things we are working on."

In fact, Coke takes customization so seriously that one of the company's newest plants, a massive new facility in Kunming (built with 12 assembly lines), is located adjacent to one of Coke's smallest plants—a facility where the company is producing small batches of customized beverages. Thus, Ferguson says Coke is developing two value-streams at once in China—mass production characterized by greater efficiencies, and high-end, value-added customization.

"Can you order Coke just the way you want it on Alibaba? With a little bit of cinnamon and a little bit of vanilla, for example? We're doing that today," he says. Ferguson explains that Coke has customized a special Coca-Cola flavor for Alibaba to sell on November 11, China's famous Singles Day for online shopping.

> "Can you order Coke just the way you want it on Alibaba? With a little bit of cinnamon and a little bit of vanilla, for example? We're doing that today."
>
> —Curt Ferguson,
> President, Greater China & Korea, Coca-Cola

Strategy 2: Engage and Interact

In today's digitized society, interacting with customers is another key component to successful business strategies in China. AB InBev gives another example of meeting Chinese consumers' new demands for customization and innovation. The company's head of China, Frederico Freire, tells of the new "digital interaction with consumers" that allows them to create their own beer: "We have initiatives where consumers produce our beers. They say: 'I want a beer with this color, this taste, this aroma, these ingredients.' And then we have a kind of contest with consumers—which is the best beer that consumers can create? We then choose one of them and produce that beer as a small batch, sold as a seasonal item." He says the campaign increases interaction with consumers. "If you don't engage consumers, you lose." In the future, he expects consumers to ask for an even higher degree of customization. "It's unbelievable. I'm not talking about craft beers. They want something totally unique. They want a product made just for them."

> "If you don't engage [Chinese] consumers, you lose."
>
> —Frederico Freire,
> BU President, China, AB InBev

For Coca-Cola, another made in China digital campaign involves highlighting a group of key Chinese cities via specially printed cans featuring scannable QR codes. Curt Ferguson explains: "When you scan that can, you can take a little virtual tour online through the cloud, seeing the cool aspects of Chengdu, or Shanghai, or Xiamen." Ferguson says the campaign caught on by interacting with consumers and also tapping into Chinese pride for its cities. "It's a cool little tour. And people are proud of where they're from."

In the field of fashion, Mango's David Sancho shares his vision of a future in which customers will use 3D printing on-site, in retail shops: "The horizon is going that way. 3D printing is evolving, amazingly. Some gurus are describing a future in which retailers just have a showroom, and customers will personalize their shoes and have them printed there in less than an hour." He says this is "something that we're working on," as one example of "how innovation is changing the way we shop." And he adds that, considering China's fast-paced, experimental environment, such changes may well take place in China first.

Strategy 3: Understand China's Generational Differences

One success factor in engaging Chinese consumers mentioned by the China CEOs is to carefully track and understand the country's emerging generational groups. As L'Oréal's Stéphane Rinderknech explains: "In this job, the pressure to understand the different generations is tremendous." He explains that his group studies the new demographics in terms of five-year groupings. "In China, it's such a big revolution that we split to every five years. Before, we talked about post-70s, post-80s, post-90s. Now, we have the 'post-95' and the 'post-2000' because it's changing so fast."

Digital technology plays into this increased understanding of generational preferences by allowing MNCs such as L'Oréal to customize their offerings per generational groups and subgroups. Says Rinderknech: "Digital brought the capability to customize, to do precision advertising that really fits specific needs." As a result, Chinese consumers begin to demand new levels of individualization. "We came into the world of personalization, of customization. . . . [The belief that] I'm me and I'm worth it. So bring it for me."

Strategy 4: Leverage Big Data

Increased data tracking of Chinese consumers is another aspect of the China market that is creating new opportunities for MNCs. Jonathan Woetzel, Senior Partner at McKinsey & Company, says: "The market is so much more transparent today than it was before; there's so much more data." He emphasizes that data can be collected on the purchasing patterns and demographics of individual consumers in China, thus allowing MNCs to "develop better approaches" to meet customer needs. But for most companies, placing data analytics at the center of the business strategy is still new. Woetzel says: "It's flipping the organization on its head—to become a much more analytics-driven organization—a data-based organization as opposed to any other organizing principle. That is the opportunity and the challenge."

Meanwhile, L'Oréal's Stéphane Rinderknech comments on the power of WeChat to encourage consumers to form their own spontaneous social groups. "WeChat did not exist before 2011. Today, it has more than 800 million active users sending 38 billion messages per day." Most importantly for his company, the platform "allows people to create their own communities, to customize your phone for your own needs and desires." Rinderknech explains that many consumers now use their mobile phone through the whole shopping journey, from searching for advice from friends, to actually making purchases. "As a company, we have to enter this world."

When describing the proliferation of big data made possible by mobile usage, Rinderknech also emphasizes that data analytics are only useful if companies know how to analyze it. "A lot of companies accumulate data for the sake of saying 'We have data.' But how you make sense of it is another thing. If you are organized in the analysis, then it's amazing what you can do." He gives a recent example of analyzing a certain eye cream for L'Oréal Paris. "We totally customized the mix based on a population in which our market-share was low. We then used big data to better understand consumers' changing demands and behaviors." The goal, Rinderknech explains, is that L'Oréal is "always the first to provide customers with what they need most" while at the same time protecting consumers' data privacy.

> *"A lot of companies accumulate data for the sake of saying 'We have data.' But how you make sense of it is another thing."*
>
> —**Stéphane Rinderknech,** CEO, China, L'Oreal

Strategy 5: Appeal to China's New Social-Mindedness

One strategy, especially for appealing to China's younger, more socially minded population, is to place social goals clearly into the business strategy. For example, Coca-Cola's Curt Ferguson says corporate social responsibility, especially environmental protection efforts, has become an increasingly important part of the company's domestic marketing strategy, because China's younger generations have increased concerns about sustainability. Thus, in China, the company has made concerted efforts to improve waste-water treatment to replenish water resources. Today, he says Coke's track record in China—where the company replenishes 25% more water than it uses—boosts its image with young consumers.

Another area of focus for Coca-Cola is recycling. Ferguson notes: "Our goal now is a 'world without waste.' We seek to recycle all of our packaging and get it out of the waste stream." One advantage of launching sustainability efforts in China, Ferguson says, is that it is possible to leverage economies of scale. "It's more challenging, believe it or not, in a lot of other countries that don't have the big ecosystems that China has." He also says that the receptivity of local governments has helped as Coke has worked with local governments to develop a collaborative system. "We actually help the government to brainstorm on the best system for individual locations: 'Do we set up a deposit system? How we can get the empty bottles in the right place?'" In many locations across China, Coca-Cola is now creating products such as carpets from its recycled PET.

At L'Oréal China, the company recently launched an initiative to use green parcels, referring to using recyclable or reusable containers when delivering product orders to individual shoppers. Rinderknech chose to support this project because "it is a mega-problem of sustainability" since traditional packaging relies on one-time-use of paper, plastic, tape, and other materials, all of which contribute greatly to physical rubbish in China. Rinderknech says his company is quickly ramping up the green parcels initiative in China, delivering 20 million green parcels in 2019, then 40 million in 2020, until eventually L'Oréal China shifts to 100% green parcels in China.

Strategy 6: Develop Soft Skills to Counteract Digitization

Along with the digitization of Chinese consumers, MNCs also noted a rising counter demand for "human" skills. As Marriott International's Rainer Burkle explains, his luxury hotel staff is focusing on carefully gauging the increasingly complex needs of hotel guests given today's blurred lines between business and leisure. He explains: "Ten years ago, business and leisure were really separate, but now [they have] grown together. Everything is done at the same time."

For hotel management, this presents a challenge in training staff. Good hotel staff need a higher level of sophistication to sense the needs of guests today. "I just make one example: you might find a gentleman or lady sitting in one of our club lounges in a Ritz-Carlton, for example, drinking a glass of red wine. . . . She might get a call from her husband and the kids while she is doing this, so you could consider this as leisure time. But actually, all this time, she is writing the speech which she is going to give the next day to 2,000 delegates. . . . Your first impression is that this is lady is taking a break, but actually she is working. So the staff has to sense this." He adds: "My time as a waiter was much easier because I was able to identify a guest—to know when I do not disturb this guest, or when this guest wants me to interact. Nowadays, the nuances are much smaller, and you really have to understand those differences because they might change within a few minutes."

Such sophisticated awareness and polished reactions from hotel staff, Burkle explains, cannot be outsourced to artificial intelligence (AI) but instead require excellent soft skills training for his team.

Summary of Tips

1. **Customize for Chinese tastes**
    Chinese customers expect MNCs to cater to their preferences, even when they travel abroad. Meanwhile, the new digital culture is creating new demand for customization, or mass customization. This has encouraged Chinese shoppers to demand innovative ways to cater to their individual tastes.

2. **Engage and interact**
    Engage customers in your product design. Provide channels for them to give feedback to your company and for your company to react.

3. **Understand China's generational differences**
    Each generation of Chinese requires a different approach as consumers due to significant differences in backgrounds, priorities, and lifestyle. Some MNCs even segment Chinese consumers by five-year groupings (post-1995, post-2000) to better track and match evolving tastes.

4. **Leverage Big Data**
    Fully utilizing the enormous amount of data on consumer behavior requires teams to not only assess trends but share them internally to maximize benefits. Transform the data into knowledge and apply it to your market strategy.

5. **Appeal to China's new social-mindedness**
    Younger Chinese are more social-minded than members of previous generations. Emphasize your company's central purpose and/or corporate social responsibility initiatives in China to appeal to consumers.

6. **Develop soft skills to counteract digitization**
    Technology is not a substitute for human interaction. Customers are calling for a human touch alongside digitally enhanced convenience. The moment of truth is the personal interaction with your customer, which cannot be outsourced to AI.

Chapter 6
Competing in China

In literally every sector now, you find Chinese companies ranked among the top worldwide. It's a very significant change for us. We have to learn how to engage them.

—**James Zhan,** President, China, Tata Sons

The signals to change were very strong—especially in digital. What nobody expected at that time is that your competitors would be the guys working with computers.

Thierry Garnier, President/CEO, China; CEO Asia; Group Vice President, Carrefour

INSIDE CHAPTER 6

Why Multinational Corporations in China Have Lost Ground

Why Chinese Players Have Gained Ground

Strategies for Facing Chinese Competitors

Summary of Tips

Introduction: Evolution of Chinese Competitors

When asked to summarize the competitive strategy in China among the MNCs they represent, most China CEOs interviewed for this book described a dramatic transition from following a business model based primarily on fast growth (during the 1990s and 2000s) to one of innovation and digitization since the 2010s. The shift is triggered by several factors: the maturation of China's economy, the overall shift away from an export-based model and toward targeting Chinese consumers, and the dramatic rise in competitiveness among Chinese players—across nearly all industries.

One China CEO who witnessed first-hand the transformation away from a pure growth strategy is IKEA's top executive in China, Freda Zhang. A PRC citizen who came of age in the 1990s, she explains: "The 1990s was an interesting decade in China's history because it was the change from the old economic system to the new economic system. So, all the foreign companies in China grew superfast. The growth was mainly from foreign companies. Companies from Hong Kong, Taiwan, South Korea, Japan all opened manufacturing here."

In terms of economic impact, the influx of foreign manufacturers led to a ripple effect across the Chinese economy, fueling the upgrading of state-owned enterprises (SOEs) seeking to serve the new demand for manufacturing as well as the launch of domestic private companies jumping into manufacturing. By the late 1990s, China had secured its position as the factory of the world; this eventually fueled the development of Chinese manufacturers such as Haier, which started by producing for international brands.

Zhang, who then worked in the purchasing department of another international company, describes the charged work environment back then: "As a buyer in that market, the only thing we saw was growth. Basically, you didn't need to care about anything else. We only looked at growth." This growth-mindedness impacted all aspects of operations, she recalls. "So, when I was working in the factory, I did not care about waste on the production floor or lean manufacturing. I didn't have time to think about that; there were orders waiting outside the factory. I really needed to finish the order. Productivity and volume were the only things I focused on. Price was not an issue, because whatever we quoted, we were competitive," she says with a laugh.

For MNCs selling into the China market, the strong position held by foreign manufacturers during the 1990s and early 2000s also triggered increased demand for foreign products from the nation's burgeoning consumer class. Kenneth Jarrett, President of the American Chamber of Commerce of Shanghai (which represents some 1,500 American companies with operations in China), explains that MNCs have lost two types of benefits over the past 20 years: superior processes and superior brand image. The next section covers these losses in detail.

Why Multinational Corporations in China Have Lost Ground

Factor 1: Loss of Superior Processes

For most MNCs, Jarrett says that the most significant difference they now feel in China compared to 20 years ago is "speed of change in the marketplace." He explains: "Two decades ago, American companies felt pretty confident that they knew how to operate in markets outside the United States. They typically came here after opening up other non-US markets. And that's what they brought to China." For many MNCs, this strategy initially "did work," Jarrett says. "Because, back then, they [MNCs] had bulk. They were big, very complete organizations. Very efficient. And they understood marketing and product development—all of that. They were well financed and they had good products. So there weren't many competitors among local companies."

Today, however, "All of that has changed," Jarrett says. He explains that, in many cases, processes that work well for an MNC in other markets prove flawed in China—especially in terms of not matching the domestic pace of reactivity and speed-to-market. He adds: "The foreign process is still a positive, but it does bring with it some definite downsides as well—in terms of slowness, in terms of responsiveness." In the worst cases, he says, MNCs fail to adapt their processes to match China. "For some big multinationals, they might still suffer from the hubris of feeling that they need to do it their way as opposed to the China way. Every company has to come to grips with that. But companies are much more aware of that as a danger. Many companies have failed because of that. They've seen the pretty dramatic rise of Chinese companies and they operate their own way. And they're quite successful at doing it. And some Chinese companies are starting to go overseas as well."

"The foreign process is still a positive, but it does bring with it some definite downsides as well—in terms of slowness, in terms of responsiveness.... Every company has to come to grips with that. But companies are much more aware of that as a danger. Many companies have failed because of that."

—**Kenneth Jarrett,**
President, American
Chamber of Commerce,
Shanghai

Factor 2: Loss of Superior Brand Image

Regarding the formerly strong brand image of many MNCs in China, Kenneth Jarrett of the American Chamber of Commerce in Shanghai recalls the situation: "In the early 1980s, when foreign products were just being reintroduced to China, the belief in high-quality foreign products probably was not questioned. People would always favor them over a local brand." He says this generally continued into the 2000s for many companies in many sectors.

During the 1990s and 2000s, another benefit for foreign companies was the favorable impression they held within the employment pool. Freda Zhang, IKEA's top executive for China, describes the mindset of young Chinese employees (such as herself) back then: "At that time, working in a foreign company was a kind of fashion. For university students, after graduation, if you could work in an international company—an American or European company—it was considered even better than working in a Taiwanese or Korean company." Thus, a benefit enjoyed by MNCs companies was their ability to attract top talent.

But 2008 was the year many analysts describe as the end of the pure high-growth period for Chinese manufacturing. In this year, MNCs were hit both by the global financial crisis and the Chinese government's decision to trim key tax advantages for foreign manufacturers. In addition, profit margins in many sectors fell due to a combination of rising production costs across China and the growing capabilities of local competitors who began offering improved quality at still-low prices. The result was fewer advantages for MNCS and slimmer profit margins for their China operations.

If we fast-forward to today, says Kenneth Jarrett, we find that MNCs have lost much of their brand capital among Chinese consumers. He describes "evolving consumer attitudes" in this way: "Chinese consumers feel that there are good Chinese brands now. That's a change. MNCs didn't face many branded Chinese companies in the past."

Jonathan Woetzel, Senior Partner at McKinsey & Company, agrees that domestic consumers now have a new mindset: "From a consumer point of view, I don't think that the origin of the product or the foreign-versus-local branding is the most important factor now in most sectors," he says. "In fact, many Chinese consumers have no idea whether the product is owned by a foreign or a Chinese company now. Many Chinese think MNC-made products are Chinese—even everyday items such as toothpaste." And while some high-tech sectors may still give foreign brands an advantage, Woetzel says this advantage is shrinking. "There are some segments where nationality might make a difference, such as technology. But even technology is changing. Before, there was a big premium on foreign smartphone technology, for example. But now, that is actually going away. So, at this point, I don't rule anything out."

Overall, Woetzel advises MNCs that the "most important change" impacting the China market during the past 15 years has been the "growth of China's private sector." He explains: "We've seen a transformation of the economy from state to private—and continuing in that direction. That stems from the ability of the private sector to better meet the rising needs and expectations of the Chinese consumer." Another

"Before, there was a big premium on foreign smartphone technology, for example. But now, that is actually going away. So, at this point, I don't rule anything out."

—Jonathan Woetzel,
Senior Partner, McKinsey & Company

related change—also raising the level of competition faced by MNCs—is the strengthening of domestic SOEs. Woetzel notes: "State enterprises are in a bit better shape now than they were [in 2006] largely because the less profitable and the less efficient ones have been restructured and, in some cases, shut down. There's still plenty out there but there's less. And the larger ones are by and large quite profitable. So the state sector looks slightly different than it did then." The result, Woetzel says, is that "China is probably one of the world's most competitive environments."

Such changes are reflected in annual business confidence surveys conducted by associations and chambers of commerce. The results of the 2019 *China Business Survey* by CEIBS (one of the largest such surveys, based on more than 1,000 responses from both Chinese and foreign enterprises), portrays the weakened positions that many MNCs now face. When asked "How intense is the competition you are facing in China?" only 2% of foreign firms answered "not intense," while 88% said "very intense" or "intense." (Among Chinese firms, 87% also said "very intense" or "intense."[1])

"China is probably one of the world's most competitive environments."

—Jonathan Woetzel, Senior Partner, McKinsey & Company

Factor 3: Loss of Superior Innovation

Even in the area of innovation—a realm that used to be considered a stronghold for MNCs—Chinese competitors have recently not only gained ground but surpassed Western companies in their own view. The European Chamber of Commerce China's annual business confidence survey for 2019 produced surprising results regarding the image of Chinese competitors among foreign member companies. Firms were asked, "Within your industry, how innovative do you feel Chinese firms are compared to European firms?" Of those polled, 34% said "significantly" or "slightly" more innovative, while another 28% said "equally innovative." Thus the overall positive response was 62% in 2019, an increase from 47% in 2017.[2] Mats Harborn,

---

[1] CEIBS. *China Business Survey*, 2019.
[2] *European Business in China Business Confidence Survey*, 2019.

the chamber's President, calls these results "very surprising," adding: "It means member companies are trying to tell their headquarters: 'Don't believe that just because China is a one-party state with a controlled internet, Chinese companies are not innovative.' On the contrary, these people are hungry, they are clever, they are innovative, and the landscape here is extremely competitive. So, if we are not on our toes in our own organizations, we may be exposed to disruptive innovations here." Harborn also warns MNCs that "when it comes to ideas, we cannot be nationalistic. We should pick up as many new ideas and innovations in China as possible or form partnerships or cooperation with good Chinese companies."

As a measure of the arrival of Chinese companies, Tata Group's China CEO James Zhan points out that more domestic Chinese firms are joining the global lists ranking the world's largest companies. In terms of revenue, Zhan emphasizes that more Chinese companies now populate the Fortune 500 list. Meanwhile, among companies in the engineering and construction industry, roughly half of those in the global top-ten list are now based in China, while a growing number of domestic enterprises in the tech sector now also boast the highest market capitalization for companies worldwide. Zhan adds that, while Alibaba and Tencent may see their market cap fluctuate, the overall shift is a "very significant positive change from ten years ago." He concludes that "in literally every sector now, you find Chinese companies ranked among the top worldwide. It's a very significant change for us. We have to learn how to engage them."

McKinsey's Jonathan Woetzel further elaborates on the evolution of Chinese companies, explaining that most domestic firms on the *Fortune* 500 list are there mainly because "China is a very big market." He explains: "These companies may technically be multinationals, but let's call them 'multilocal,' because most of their revenue comes from China. They have a little bit of an international footprint, and their management structure reflects that." However, he adds that this is changing as Chinese companies rapidly internationalize. "One of the characteristics of many of the newer Chinese companies is that they have

"In literally every sector now, you find Chinese companies ranked among the top worldwide. It's a very significant change for us. We have to learn how to engage them."

—**James Zhan,**
President, China, Tata Sons

Chinese on their management teams, but with global experience. They have work experience outside the country or they have international language capability." In addition, there are also some Chinese companies "that are genuinely global in their outlook, their management team, their revenue footprint, their technology sources. Over time, we'll see more of that. The more highly digitized the sector, the more likely it is to generate truly global Chinese companies." Sectors that are likely to foster truly multinational Chinese companies, Woetzel predicts, include financial services, media, and value-added manufacturing. Less likely sectors include construction and agriculture, but he adds that "even in these sectors, we may see individual stand-outs."

> *"The more highly digitized the sector, the more likely it is to generate truly global Chinese companies."*
>
> **—Jonathan Woetzel,**
> Senior Partner, McKinsey & Company

The results of respected business confidence surveys also bear this out. In CEIBS' 2019 *China Business Report*, companies were asked: "Who are your main competitors in China?" Foreign firms first named Chinese private firms (67%), followed by foreign companies (57%), SOEs (29%), and imports (25%). Meanwhile, Chinese companies rated their key competitors as domestic private firms (80%), SOEs (44%), and foreign firms (16%).

In his role as an expert on executive recruitment, Charles Tseng, Korn Ferry's China CEO, tells incoming foreign middle-and upper-level managers to China to prepare for "a very competitive market, because you're dealing with very, very competitive-minded local players." He says this applies across nearly all sectors today. As a consequence, Tseng warns: "You really need to move fast—with speed, with agility, with flexibility—in order to adjust to the Chinese environment."

Factor 4: Sleepless Nights Across Sectors

> *"For sure, Chinese competitors are getting better. Some are getting so good, that you wake up in the night."*
>
> **—Chunyuan Gu,**
> Chairman & CEO, China, ABB

In the manufacturing and industrial sectors, the comments of Chunyuan Gu, ABB's top executive for China, are typical: "For sure, Chinese competitors are getting better. Some are getting so good, that you wake up in the night. Absolutely." Gu says that across ABB's key sectors— power grid, transition, distribution, heavy equipment—Chinese players are improving. Although one reason for the advancement of Chinese players has been the support they enjoy from the Chinese government, Gu says a bigger concern for ABB now is the measurable advances domestic companies have made through improving and developing operations, coupled with their rapid expansion. "In the automation field, I have seen companies develop from nothing to as big as some of ABB's businesses within just a few years. And some are now even better than us."

In the technology sector, Chinese competitors are now widely recognized as operating at an international class. Clas Neumann, SAP's head of fast-growth markets strategy (including China), explains the evolution of the sector in this way: "It started with technology companies, which learned by producing for others. By now, they have a big competitive advantage. And now it is also happening in other industries as internet companies follow their globalization strategy. It is only a matter of time before China's smaller internet companies learn how to approach the international markets."

In the food and beverage field, AB InBev's head of China Frederico Freire says his biggest competitors in China are now Chinese companies. "And I do see that they are catching up quite fast." In years past, when local players "used to be more [producers of] low-end products," he says, AB InBev followed a strategy of differentiating in China via premium brands. "We see the Chinese companies waking up to 'trade-up' or 'premiumization' opportunities," Freire says, adding that foreign brands offer fewer clear advantages today. "Being honest, Chinese competitors are increasing the quality of their products, and they are investing in innovation more than before. I see an evolution among Chinese companies."

The other trend AB InBev is exploiting is to develop the Chinese market for craft beers—a high-end niche that is small but "growing fast." Freire says: "They help us to create a beer culture, to boost the curiosity to learn about the brewing process, different colors, aromas, and tastes. . . . And Chinese customers are open to pay more, open to try more."

Even MNCs in sectors related to hard sciences—such as healthcare and agricultural development—find competition to be fierce in China. According to Celina Chew, Bayer's top

"In the automation field, I have seen companies develop from nothing to as big as some of ABB's businesses within just a few years. And some are now even better than us."

—Chunyuan Gu,
Chairman & CEO, China, ABB

"It started with [Chinese] technology companies, which learned by producing for others. By now, they have a big competitive advantage. And now it is also happening in other industries as internet companies follow their globalization strategy."

—Clas Neumann,
Head of Fast-Growth Market Strategy Group, SAP

"We see the Chinese companies waking up to 'trade-up' or 'premiumization' opportunities."

—Frederico Freire,
BU President, China, AB InBev

executive in China, local players "have learned very fast, and they have even moved beyond us in some ways." In the healthcare market, Chew says Bayer still maintains an advantage with consumers, but that lead is narrowing: "If patients or consumers have an illness or a medical condition, and they want an innovative product to address it, they will still seek out solutions from a Bayer or another MNC healthcare company because we have the expertise and experience in the molecules that deal with such illnesses or conditions," she says. "These molecules still count, and our brand still counts for a great deal. In this way, we are still leading." In the agricultural sector, which is "much more fragmented," Chew says Bayer also maintains certain advantages over domestic players regarding customer preferences for innovative and effective modern products. But she adds that "it may be that Chinese competitors will catch up sooner rather than later." She also notes that for MNCs in some other sectors or industries, local competition may be "much more challenging."

In the services sector, such as banking and insurance, China CEOs also now find highly competitive local players. Manulife's China CEO Kai Zhang says local banks "learned from the Citibanks of the world very quickly. They have upgraded their branches very, very quickly." She says that the only area where local banks cannot compete with foreign ones today is "the fact that their branches are uneven because they are in so many different cities." But this advantage is ebbing away, she adds: "If you go to a nice China Merchant's branch, it's as good as a Citi or Standard Chartered branch." Even more important, she says, is that Chinese banks now offer for the domestic market products that are "better, more diversified" than those of international banks, and that domestic banks are more flexible and adaptable. "What's most important is that they don't have a legacy system," which allows them to leapfrog into using the best new technologies. Zhang notes: "When Chinese banks upgrade, they use whatever is best at the time. They can use the best hardware and software—with more computing power, more flexibility and agility—to introduce new products and adapt to market changes. Meanwhile, global companies struggle with systems they built many years ago—because it takes

"If you go to a nice China Merchant's branch, it's as good as a Citi or Standard Chartered branch."

—**Kai Zhang,**
President & CEO, China,
Manulife-Sinochem

such high cost and disruption of business to migrate from an old system to a new system."

IKEA's Freda Zhang offers a clear summary of the evolution of domestic competition, which she sees as running parallel to her own professional development: "During my first ten years at IKEA [from 2000 to 2010], I learned the most. It was a knowledge injection from an international company." After 2010, however, she began to learn from domestic competition as well. "Over the past ten years, I started to realize that I need to step out, to learn from the new fast-growing Chinese brands. They have their typical qualities which we need to learn from. That is my reflection."

Looking ahead, Freda Zhang expects the years leading up to 2025 to be a crucial period for China-based retailers of consumer products—especially in home furnishings. During this time, she expects traditional home furnishings companies in China to move aggressively into online sales, in order to keep up with China's digital companies. Meanwhile, she expects that young Chinese companies will strengthen their capabilities in two domains previously dominated by MNCs: the offline shopping experience and the quality of their supply chains. For the moment, Zhang says that IKEA still enjoys an advantage over local competitors because of its well-established supply chain and its offline shops. Over time, however, she expects domestic competitors to catch up on both fronts. "Let's not deny that they can manage. Chinese entrepreneurs have the spirit; they will manage everything. Among these new Chinese brands, maybe not all of them, but some of them will become super-giant in the future."

Finally, interviewees confirmed that there is still a role for MNCs in China. McKinsey's Jonathan Woetzel comments that foreign companies "can still be an important part of the corporate landscape." He explains: "There are many sectors where multinationals lead—especially in sectors where technology is important." He adds that most global brands "are now firmly established in China" and that this market remains very important for many. "For multinationals, China represents, typically, somewhere between 10% and 30% of revenues. And so it is an important contributor." Thus, learning to compete against

"Among these new Chinese brands, maybe not all of them, but some of them will become super-giant in the future."

—**Freda Zhang,**
Country Commercial VP, China, IKEA

"There are many sectors where multinationals lead— especially in sectors where technology is important."

—**Jonathan Woetzel,**
Senior Partner, McKinsey & Company

Chinese competitors is a part of the global MNC agenda now. (For more on the future of MNCs in China, see Chapter 9.)

In summing up the competitive environment for MNCs in today's China, the China CEOs described four key advantages enjoyed by local competitors—advantages that are weakening the position of MNCs, not only in the China market but worldwide. The key advantages of Chinese domestic firms (as outlined below) are: speed to market, Chinese-style innovation, digital adoption, and international expansion.

Why Chinese Players Have Gained Ground

Factor 1: Speed to Market

Speed of adaptation to changing market conditions and consumer tastes is one area where many interviewees see MNCs now struggling to compete in China. IKEA's Freda Zhang explains that to those in headquarters, the China market can look "crazy" in terms of the speed at which market conditions shift, spurred by aggressive local companies. She tells of a recent meeting among IKEA's top management during which the global head of purchasing announced to those gathered that, so far, no furniture manufacturer had found a way to deliver a sofa to an end-user within 12 hours of placing the order. "But after he spoke, we told him that Jing Dong is already doing that. The speed is so quick in China."

Increasing speed—in terms of delivery times, product development, reaction to consumer demand, and other aspects—is causing concern for IKEA and other MNCs. Zhang says: "I am very much observing all the new Chinese brands right now. Their growth index is amazing." One key advantage for domestic brands, she says, is their "startup" mentality. "They have speed, plus resources, plus an open mind. They don't have limits; they can try different business models." As a specific example of speed, Zhang points to how Chinese companies have rapidly adopted "so many different online payment models." By contrast, she says IKEA cannot as easily test different payment models: "Our speed will never be the same."

Speed of product development is another area where MNCs struggle to compete. Zhang explains that IKEA and other large-scale MNCs tend to follow a linear organization in which "one department does one thing and then passes [it on] to another department." In developing a new product, for example, the sales team typically serves as the only channel interacting with customers and passing customer feedback to the product development team. The product development team then designs the products based on the customer needs that the sales team described. Then the product is passed to the supply chain, and then finally reaches the customer. "That's why we need two years to develop one product, because we need internal alignment between organizations, between departments."

By contrast, China's young tech companies can achieve much faster product-development cycles by operating more collaboratively. Freda Zhang notes: "When you are in a small company, everybody is multifunctional. All the product developers, sales team, everybody is talking with the customer at the same time. They are working as a circle with the customer in the center. This is disrupting the linear organization." Even as China's tech companies have grown in size, Zhang says many have maintained an entrepreneurial mindset. She explains: "The good part is that all of them are still in the growing mode. Although they are big already, like Alibaba and Tencent, they are still run by the first-generation founder. This is very different, to be honest, from the situation of most MNCs in China." Even as Alibaba, Tencent, and Huawei have grown and are now run by management teams, not just by their founding fathers, their success is tied to maintaining the spirit and mindset of a startup. "They . . . all have the founder's mentality; they are all founders." She points out that they do not need to adapt an entrepreneurial spirit because "they were born that way." All they need to do is maintain their core spirit as they grow.

One key success factor, IKEA's Freda Zhang notes, is the focus of Tencent, Alibaba, and Huawei on using a "project-based"

"[China's young tech companies] are working as a circle with the customer in the center. This is disrupting the linear organization."

—**Freda Zhang,**
Country Commercial VP,
China, IKEA

organization. She says: "They operate more like they are floating. Their people are working in one organization today, and tomorrow they change. If one project doesn't sell, they quickly change." In this way, the structure remains lean and flexible. "Within their company, they have so many small, small companies. And the leaders of these small companies operate like inventors—they need to prove their business case in order to get funding from the big company."

The speed and nimbleness of China's digital giants give them another competitive advantage, Zhang says: a more attractive corporate culture for employees. "We also lose people from IKEA to Chinese companies such as Tencent and Alibaba. . . . The trend in the past years is that the competence flow is very, very heavy, mainly from the international companies to Chinese digital giants. Very few move from them to us."

Bayer's Celina Chew agrees that MNCs are often slowed down by three issues: first, their need to align with global and/or regional headquarters; second, the very high-quality standards that MNCs apply; and third, a fear of failing. In contrast, she says, local competitors are more likely to try as they go. Chew notes: "We try to get a product perfect before it gets to the market because it is in our DNA to deliver excellent, high-quality products from the start. And because of the potential risk to our reputation for reliability." By contrast, many domestic companies release their product as a test. They gauge the reaction from customers, then refine the product. "For example, consider the iterations that Xiaomi does with its products," says Chew. "They get the product out there and receive opinions from their customers. Based on this feedback, they adjust and develop the product until it is something the customers want." China's digitized consumer market offers a range of channels for collecting a wealth of feedback instantly, she emphasizes. "If a product does not generate the level of acceptance the developer was expecting, it is good to consider the feedback and see if the issues can be addressed, rather than continuing to push it to consumers."

Chen Yudong, Bosch's head of China, echoes the same frustration regarding speed. "I do see the local companies become stronger. You can see this in the market-share of our own components and products. And local [companies] have an advantage in that they are quicker and more flexible in terms of sensing the product, in terms of decision-making."

The speed advantage seems to be a reality across sectors, according to China CEOs. In the insurance industry, Manulife's Kai Zhang says she has "tremendous respect" for Chinese competitors in terms of developing at a far faster speed than have insurance companies in the West. "I find it amazing, the execution capability of Ping An—the culture it has built, the talent it can attract, and the transformation it has gone through with just a 30-year-history. It has become one of the most valuable insurance companies in the world, in terms of rankings, during that time." The transformation, she says, is hard for many people outside China to fathom: "Manulife, for example, has over 130 years' history. It's very hard for global companies with a long heritage to accept that, suddenly, a young Chinese competitor has a bigger market cap. They may not even think they are in the same league. But I'm sorry, that's the case." In addition to rushing to catch up, she notes that Ping An is also seated in a market offering "huge opportunities" compared with those available to Western insurers.

Another aspect of the competitive environment in China, Kai Zhang says, is the ambitious mindset of competitors. "Here, you are basically leapfrogging. The mindset is: We want to be number one, we want to be the biggest. The stress level in China is way higher [than in the West]. . . . What people in the West don't understand about the difficulty of operating in China is that you're competing with companies like Ping An, like Alibaba, and Tencent. People are in such a hurry! People don't sleep here!"

In the fashion sector, Mango's China CEO, David Sancho, explains the rise of domestic competition as "brutal." Describing the changes since he arrived in China in 2011, Sancho says: "When I first got here, there were six or seven local players. Now, not only are they real competitors, but they are becoming international competitors. The change has been amazing: the way they have grown, the way they have evolved—even to be

> "Local [companies] have an advantage in that they are quicker and more flexible in terms of sensing the product, in terms of decision-making."
>
> —Chen Yudong,
> President, China, Bosch

> "It's very hard for global companies with a long heritage to accept that, suddenly, a young Chinese competitor has a bigger market cap."
>
> —Kai Zhang,
> President & CEO, China, Manulife-Sinochem

> "When I first got here, there were six or seven local players. Now, not only are they real competitors, but they are becoming international competitors."
>
> —David Sancho,
> CEO, East Asia & India, Mango

"*Chinese competitors have a speed-to-market which is amazingly faster than Western companies.*"

—**David Sancho,**
CEO, East Asia & India,
China Mango

much better than us in a lot of ways. And they know the local market much better." Even though Mango has the advantage of deeper resources, Sancho says it has "really become complicated" for his company to compete. "Chinese competitors have a speed-to-market which is amazingly faster than Western companies." He gives two examples of speed. The first is customer relations management. "Loyalty programs in China are digital. Nobody has a physical loyalty card anymore." The second is methods of payment. "Nobody's using credit cards in the stores in China. It's all WeChat or Alipay or Tmall. Local players have embraced that at a much faster pace than Western companies."

Another factor slowing the speed of MNCs is the time required to educate headquarters on China and convince them of the need for change. Sancho notes: "Global headquarters implement global strategies, but China requires a local strategy. What you are doing globally doesn't really help or cannot really be implemented in China. You have to convince the board: 'Look, guys, this has to be done now because it's already being done by local competitors. And it's the only way to adapt in China.'"

One fashion-oriented change Sancho has noted is that, spurred by e-commerce, Mango is adapting more to Chinese tastes. "We've been using international patterns, but the trend is toward adapting more and more to local tastes. Not only with shape, but also with styles, colors, and trends. . . . It is necessary to really adapt part of the collection to the China market. It's still a very small portion [of the global market], but because of e-commerce, local production for local adaptation is going to be really key."

Retailers are well aware of the transformation within their industry, especially those serving the supermarket sector. (See "Mini-Case 1: Learning from Mistakes [Carrefour].") Arun Bhardwaj of Victoria's Secret says he and others witnessed Western consumer products suppliers for this segment being suddenly short-circuited by China's shift to online shopping. "These guys were not ready. They still had only bigger pack sizes and giant boxes for delivery to supermarkets. That's not how the customer shops anymore. So it was easy to get caught short." He explains the new mindset necessary in retail in this way: "With the evolution that's taking place, retailers must think proactively in terms of store size, store design."

Throughout China's retail business today, from supermarkets to fashion, Bhardwaj says that the role of brick-and-mortar locations will now be linked to online shopping experiences. He explains that for retailers, the secret to surviving in China is "constant innovation to stay ahead of local competitors," adding that "the speed of evolution in China is faster than most other places."

Factor 2: Chinese-Style Innovation (from Copying to Incremental Change to True Innovation)

Given China's long history of intellectual property rights infringements, innovation has long been considered an area in which MNCs prevailed and domestic companies competed more by copying than by creating bona fide innovation. But China CEOs across industries say that times have changed, spurred largely by China's own home-grown digital transformation.

In one example, Alain Crozier, Microsoft's top executive in China, describes the case of China's massive increase in online food delivery shaking up the restaurant business. He says China's offline-to-online (O2O) channels for home food delivery are now far more advanced than those in the West. "Let's say you want to buy dinner using O2O. If you are in the US or Europe, you can buy a pizza. But basically that's it. In China, you can say, 'I want a bit of sushi, I want noodles, I want dessert, and I want two drinks.' . . . You use a platform connected to different restaurants. You design your menu based on thousands of items coming from thousands of restaurants. At the end of the day, you're going to get exactly the menu you really want, with one click, delivered to your place." This kind of innovation in digital technology is shaking up traditional industries—in this case offering an alternative to shopping in supermarkets or

"If you are in the US or Europe, you can buy a pizza. But basically that's it. In China, you can say, 'I want a bit of sushi, I want noodles, I want dessert, and I want two drinks.'"

—**Alain Crozier,**
CEO, Greater China Region, Microsoft

dining in restaurants—and must be noted by MNCs. As Crozier warns, the mobile purchasing models now launching in China will soon be adopted worldwide. "This emerging business model is very strong in China. And I can see this one going global."

Kenneth Jarrett, President of the American Chamber of Commerce in Shanghai, agrees, explaining that MNC members of the chamber have noted that in many sectors, Chinese competitors now not only match MNCs in terms of quality but have added a digital aspect to their business strategy. As one example, he points out that Starbucks has been experiencing increased competition in China from local players, including Luckin Coffee. This online-focused player is "giving Starbucks a run for their money," says Jarrett. He explains: "It began as a pure digital play—you just order coffee drinks on-line. They're actually having an impact on Starbucks because they deliver. So they're fully capitalizing on e-commerce and social media and the fact that China's delivery speeds are incredible."

McKinsey & Company is one organization actively tracking China's rise in innovation capability. Senior Partner Jonathan Woetzel, who frequently writes on the changing business environment in China, explains the meaning of the McKinsey Global Institute's phrase "the China effect." "What we mean by that phrase is, first of all, China is innovative. But China is not only creating a broad spectrum of innovative new products and services but is also actually changing the process of innovation itself. If we define innovation as 'the development of changes to products and services that create commercial value,' then the way China does that is essentially cheaper, faster, and more global than was the case before."

Asked how exactly China innovates faster and more cheaply than other nations, Woetzel names the combination of China's well-established manufacturing base with a large and highly accessible consumer base easily reached via digital channels. He points to the emerging "innovation clusters" developing in Shenzhen and Shanghai, which allow for extra-fast product development cycles. "You can test something, then immediately pilot it, then develop the prototypes, get feedback, and repeat

"[In China] you can test something, then immediately pilot it, then develop the prototypes, get feedback, and repeat the cycle."

—Jonathan Woetzel, Senior Partner, McKinsey & Company

the cycle," Woetzel says. "This speed, plus the digital economy, means you can shorten the process—prototyping something in half the time as it might take you outside of China."

Woetzel adds that one of the reasons behind China's rapid adoption of technology and constant improvement is its long tradition of a "global attitude toward technology." He points out that China went from containing essentially no technology in 1949 to teaming up with the Soviets, then with other sectors of the outside world in the decades that followed. He comments: "China's technology has long been developed in a global context." Woetzel believes that this historical background has currently created another beneficial legacy, in that China's high-tech parks tend to feature very international staff, making them "at least as global as one would typically see in London or Silicon Valley." He adds: "In addition, China has long been the greatest source of foreign students globally, many of whom are now returning." For all these reasons, China is becoming an innovation powerhouse.

Factor 3: Digital Transformation

Closely related to China's rising innovation capabilities, in terms of adding competitiveness to domestic companies, is the nation's ongoing digital transformation. Our CEO interviewees noted that this adds another layer of competitive pressure on MNCs.

Bayer's Celina Chew explains the new environment for her company in China. She describes increased competition via digital channels because China's tech giants are now entering both the healthcare and agriculture sectors. Thus, the pool of competitors for Bayer in China has expanded to include Baidu, Alibaba, and Google, as well as tech startups. "Now, we need to look at competitors not in our normal market, but also across a much broader market." Today, she says, "disruption often comes from somewhere you don't expect because digital companies are focused on addressing unmet needs." The point that her team should learn, she says, is to follow trends in all sectors

"Disruption often comes from somewhere you don't expect because digital companies are focused on addressing unmet needs."

—**Celina Chew,**
President, Greater China, Bayer

of the China market, not just her industries. "In China, it's really important to be well aware of what's going on outside your industry—because competition is broader than that. Somebody from the outside just thinks: 'I want to solve this problem.' That's where we may not be doing so well."

Microsoft's Alain Crozier uses the French word *creuset* (a mixing pot for cooking) to describe the creative, messy, but fruitful environment in today's China, where ambitious, consumer-focused startups make use of the nation's growing technological capabilities. "You see Chinese startups coming to market, succeeding, growing, and becoming really big. Or disappearing because it's maybe not the right time or maybe not the right model." When the model works, Crozier has seen Chinese companies grow extremely fast. He points to Byte-Dance as an example—a Chinese viral app viewing company that acquired Musical.ly in 2017 from an Indian company. Byte-Dance then replaced Musical.ly with its own TikTok platform the following year. By mid-2019, TikTok had attracted 1 billion users, becoming one of the top 20 downloads of the year on iPhones according to Apple. This kind of growth is possible in today's China market when fueled by technology. And Crozier reminds us that across a spectrum of tech subsectors—including advancements in search, cloud, machine-learning, IoT, and computer vision—some of the world's most advanced research and development is now taking place in China, in collaboration with Chinese companies.

Factor 4: International Expansion

One message from the China CEOs is that MNCs should now prepare to find an increasing number of Chinese competitors going global. In fact, several commented that the process of domestic companies gaining ground internationally, often by offering lower pricing, is well under way.

In manufacturing, Bosch is one MNC that has seen its Chinese domestic competitors entering international markets in recent years. The company's China CEO, Chen Yudong, says:

"They are starting. For automotive components, for sure they are willing to buy international companies. They are now quite aggressive." He points to several recent "big acquisitions," which include Chinese companies purchasing the Japanese airbag maker Takata in 2017 as well as Nissan's battery division in early 2019. Chen notes: "So I do see them getting stronger. We also feel the competition from local players."

Even in the toy industry, a sector in which Chinese competitors have not yet achieved a global presence, MNCs are preparing for Chinese expansion. Jacob Kragh, LEGO's top China executive, says: "We are seeing the early signs of [going global]. . . . We haven't seen the 'Xiaomi of the toy industry' just yet. Most Chinese competitors are still building on the local base—doing a lot to create a strong home market to give them the platform for growth. Most are not creating any real impact internationally yet, although their vision is clearly there."

In the electronics and entertainment fields, Sony's China CEO Hiroshi Takahashi says that Chinese competitors are already operating in Japan: "It is a natural trend. The China market is saturated. So to take more market-share, inevitably they have to go out. That also means they have to adapt to different cultures."

In banking, Jerry Zhang, Standard Chartered's top China executive, says domestic competitors are both gaining ground locally and also preparing to head overseas. "Chinese companies have grown rapidly in recent years and are playing an increasingly important role, not only in China but also worldwide." She also points to the efforts of domestic banks to partner with Chinese digital giants—especially BATJ (Baidu, Alibaba, Tencent, and Jingdong)—to "build scale for the future."

In fashion, Mango's David Sancho is also seeing more Chinese brands going global. He names Lily and Bosideng as examples. "They are now becoming global. I can see the willingness of Chinese brands to become international, and I really believe we are now in that mode." He names two methods of expanding internationally. The first is the acquisition of international brands by Chinese brands. The second is the move of more Chinese conglomerates to acquire local fashion brands—especially in the luxury fashion subsector.

"It's a natural trend. The China market is saturated. So to take more market share, inevitably [Chinese companies] have to go out."

—**Hiroshi Takahashi,** Chairman & President, China, Sony

Among the China CEOs interviewed for this book, only those in highly technical fields, such as the top executives of ABB, Tata, and Maserati, said Chinese competitors were not yet ready to compete directly with them globally. Chenyuan Gu, ABB's China head, comments: "Of course, [expanding overseas] is their ambition, but they have a long way to go. You need to have the knowledge, the capabilities, the processes, and all these take some time. It's not just strategy—you can get a consultant for that. They don't have enough good people; this takes time to develop. You have to learn, you have to make mistakes. There are no shortcuts." He adds: "A Chinese utility company can do big projects in China, but to operate in a different country will take time. Some can set up branches in different countries, but to acquire the advantages of a multinational company takes time. How you leverage your global platform and how you achieve cultural integration takes time and leadership."

Strategies for Facing Chinese Competitors

Strategy 1: Empower Your Local Teams

One message that the China CEOs sent to the MNCs they lead is that competing in China requires empowerment of the local team. At IKEA, Freda Zhang advises her global leadership to "dare to utilize local intelligence and also dare to try the new things in this market." Not only IKEA, but many foreign brands should allow local teams to guide corporations in adapting to China's changes, she says. "Recently, all the foreign brands, including IKEA, are facing a huge challenge in operating in China. Because if you try to use 'one business model fits all,' your brand will not succeed in China. It will difficult to compete with Chinese local brands."

"Dare to utilize local intelligence and also dare to try the new things in this market."

—**Freda Zhang,**
Country Commercial VP, China, IKEA

Zhang warns that some aspects of Chinese culture—especially respect for hierarchy—may mislead some MNCs to not seek input from local teams: "Some traditional employees

Learning from Mistakes (Carrefour)

Retail is one industry that has been totally disrupted by China's digitization and the prevalence of shopping by mobile phone as an alternative to brick-and-mortar stores. Carrefour's top executive for China, Thierry Garnier, says a key learning point for retailers in China is humility. He explains the mindset shift in this way: "When everything is perfect, it's tempting to be arrogant. You say, 'Why change? I'm so perfect, and I am the leader.'" Garnier continues: "When everything is going well, that's when one needs to get ready for the future. When everything is fine, you cannot sleep—you need to prepare for the future. Otherwise you have to prepare for the future when you're in trouble."

Since Garnier became the top executive for this market in 2012, his China strategy has been to transform the domestic focus of Carrefour from growth to innovation. He describes China as the company's cutting-edge laboratory for retail. As one example, he explains the company's scan and go app that shoppers download via WeChat to digitize the check-out process. Shoppers with the app on their phones simply "scan all the product, pay by WeChat, then go—you don't need to go to the cashier."

The app is just part of a large-scale shift within Carrefour toward digital shopping. Garnier says: "In 2014, we created a very large Carrefour e-commerce operation and started cooperating with all major Chinese platforms: Jingdong, Meituan, and Eleme."

Another transformation is to reduce the supermarket's physical size to adapt to changing consumer needs. Garnier explains that "in today's world, and especially in China, stores need to be smaller." In China, he is now cutting the size of larger Carrefour stores by a third while also "re-allocating square meters" to the surrounding shopping mall to create "more restaurants, more cafes, more activities shoppers cannot do with their mobile." The goal is to turn shopping into part of entertainment experience. "For instance, you can have your haircut, go to a restaurant, or watch a movie."

Author's postscript: After this interview was conducted, news broke on June 23, 2019, that Carrefour China had sold 80% of its shares to the Chinese retailer Sunning. The announcement specified that Carrefour Group will retain a 20% stake in the business, as well as two seats on Carrefour China's supervisory board.[3]

will have a passive mindset of 'I take my boss exactly like I took my teacher. I expect him to give me all the instructions.'" Some Western executives, she says, wrongly welcome such

---

[3] AFP. https://www.languedocliving.com/carrefour-sells-to-suning-com/.

thinking: "Some foreign leaders, they enjoy this part: 'I tell you what you should do.' Or even, 'The head office tells us what we should do.'" But following this path, she says, will not allow MNCs to learn from the local team. "In that case, the strategy doesn't really involve the Chinese intelligence. And a lot of times, we see that it can lead to a totally wrong direction."

Chen Yudong of Bosch agrees that, among MNCs targeting the China market, localizing and empowering the local team is one key. "If you want to play the local market, then you want to localize the structure so that the team is effective." He explains that, as a Chinese citizen, he is often better equipped to face the challenges of his home country than are his international peers. "China is my home market, so we grow the market, and we fight local and international companies for this market." In his view, his company's mix of local to foreign employees, at roughly 1%, is correct. Other China CEOs expressed the importance of foreign headquarters giving autonomy to Chinese operations in order to ensure speed and market relevance (see Chapter 7).

"If you want to play the local market, then you want to localize the structure so that the team is effective."

—Chen Yudong,
President, China, Bosch

Strategy 2: Be an Innovation Leader

China CEOs also note that constant innovation is another must-have component in today's China strategy. Jonathan Woetzel of McKinsey & Co. advises: "In every segment, we see multinationals innovating. And innovation happens based on the level of local competitors and availability of local talent." In the business environment of today's China, Woetzel says any type of competitive strategy—such as beating Chinese competitors on cost or faster market response, or longer-term and closer customer relationships—relies on one central component. He explains: "No matter what the goal, you have to innovate to get there. You may have to rethink the supply chain, or redefine the product and features, or change the product definition itself to meet local customers' expectations."

Andy Ho, the top executive for China of Philips, explains the need for his company to innovate: "Every single day, you see a new, powerful local company in China. There are some very good companies in China now." The way to compete, he says, is constant innovation. "MNCs need to stay at the forefront of the technology curve. You need to invest in R&D: innovation is very important; innovative design is so important. There are a lot more local competitors in China now. They launch very vigorously in the low-end segment and gradually move up. You are starting to see some local enterprises becoming strong in the high-end [segment] as well." Sony's Takahashi expresses a similar view, stating that his company's future success in China will depend mainly on "how well we can adapt our products to Chinese customer taste."

Bosch's Chen Yudong says one advantage MNCs still enjoy over domestic companies is that the long-term investment in innovation from local companies is "still not matching international benchmarks." This allows Bosch to enjoy an advantage, especially in the B2B sector, as most local players there still focus on price as their competitive advantage. In the B2C space, such as home appliances, Chen faces "stronger and stronger local competition." He says: "Honestly speaking, the level of quality and technology is not much different. If we can keep our market-share, it's good enough." For products such as refrigerators and other white goods, Chen says local players "do a really good job" in quality and "are turning over products quicker." Bosch's only clear advantage, he says, is innovation. "For new stuff, maybe we still have an advantage. And for branding, we still have an advantage. But overall, for multinationals in the consumer side: If you can hold your position in China, it's good already."

In the education sector, Udacity's China CEO Robert Hsiung explains his company's innovation strategy for China in this way: "We have to continue moving fast, staying on the leading edge in business model innovation. We have to continue innovating our products to stay ahead of the market and maintain growth. This is a daily challenge, a daily war." He continues: "The competition moves a lot faster here in China. To keep up, we have to continually evolve our business model, continually evolve the products we sell. That's the only way we've been able to grow the business in China—by continually evolving our business over the past three years. We have completely revolutionized the way we sell our products several times."

> "MNCs need to stay at the forefront of the technology curve. You need to invest in R&D."
>
> —Andy Ho,
> Leader, Greater China, Philips

> "We have to continue innovating our products to stay ahead of the market and maintain growth. This is a daily challenge, a daily war."
>
> —Robert Hsiung,
> Managing Director, China, Udacity

> "We have completely revolutionized the way we sell our products several times."
>
> —Robert Hsiung,
> Managing Director, China, Udacity

At Victoria's Secret, Arun Bhardwaj agrees that the secret to surviving in China now is constant innovation to stay ahead of local competitors. "We see a lot of competitors coming out with similar products to ours—even the names are similar. That is the finest form of flattery but in order to succeed in the China market it's super, super important that you are continually innovating." The speed of China, he says, is faster than that of the US—a difference that is allowing his China team to "deliver China innovations to the rest of the company."

Strategy 3: Digitize with China

When asked what MNCs should do to survive in the China market, Mary Boyd, Director of Economist Corporate Network (Shanghai), says one strategy many foreign firms have undertaken is to digitize their sales channel. "It's interesting to see the tie-ups between big MNCs with sales platforms of Taobao and Jingdong, for example. Obviously, MNCs are diversifying the points of sale. And in other cases, they might be trying to acquire local companies, or trying to adapt their products to local markets, fine-tuning their approach. Lots of companies are doing all sorts of different things and pursuing different strategies. But the overall sense is that the MNCs have certainly not been complacent. They are facing a new wave of competition and they are trying to adapt to it to retain their competitive factor."

"The MNCs have certainly not been complacent. They are facing a new wave of competition and they are trying to adapt to it to retain their competitive factor."

—Mary Boyd,
Director, Shanghai,
Economist Corporate
Network

IKEA's Freda Zhang advises MNCs in China to learn from domestic startups about using digital channels to track customer needs. "All the small Chinese brands selling via Tmall, they can talk with customers directly. In the past, it was difficult for them to gain customers; they needed to invest in a big shop like us [IKEA]. But nowadays, you can meet customers anywhere. And the customer has become lazier. The more technology provided to empower them, the lazier the customer will be to come to us with our traditional business model." The answer, Zhang says, is for MNCs to operate in smaller and more entrepreneurial ways by also using digital channels. "If we don't change, we will lose market-share. It will not be possible to grow."

Strategy 4: Partner with Chinese Companies

At Standard Chartered, collaboration with domestic banks as they head overseas is part of the strategy described by China CEO Jerry Zhang. Zhang explains that one recent collaboration involving her bank's support of the Chinese government's Belt & Road Initiative. In support of the comprehensive initiative, local banks, including China Development Bank, ICBC, Pudong Development Bank, China Merchants Bank, and the Export-Import Bank of China, have signed MoUs with Standard Chartered to "deepen cooperation in Belt & Road countries."

China's technological revolution is transforming the business environment in another way: In the midst of furious growth, experimentation, and change, the lines between competition and collaboration have blurred. Microsoft's Crozier says that in today's China, his competitors can also become collaborators. "We cannot just compete in the old ways, where you had a black-and-white situation—I compete with you and I have nothing to do with you. Today, our main competitors are very often also our partners. . . . In the morning, you compete; in the afternoon, you partner. You need to be very clear, but also very flexible."

Crozier says such competitors/partners can be any digital Chinese company: "It can be Alibaba; It can be Tencent. It can be the big ones or the next generation that aspire to be very big in the future." He says China is fostering technology startups in all sectors of the industry. Chinese companies are now "doing a lot of things that we are doing—they are doing pure technology, such as cloud, IoT, machine learning, AI. But also, they are coming up with great solutions and new business models. And this is also very interesting; you see a proliferation of new business models. Some of them may not really work. But a lot will work."

For Microsoft, another aspect of partnering with Chinese clients is to assist them in expanding internationally. Alain Crozier says: "A lot of those Chinese companies are going global. They don't stay in China." He names ByteDance's expansion into Europe and the US and Xiaomi's spread into South Asia, India, and the US as examples. Crozier says: "Because these companies are built on pure technology, they can go abroad

"Today, our main competitors are very often also our partners."

—Alain Crozier,
CEO, Greater China Region, Microsoft

"[In China] you see a proliferation of new business models. Some of them may not really work. But a lot will work."

—Alain Crozier,
CEO, Greater China Region, Microsoft

very fast—especially with partners like Microsoft. We have a network of infrastructure; we have the resources and capabilities around the world to serve them."

One challenge for Microsoft is the strain on HR in terms of demanding a high level of internationalization among employees: "We need our people to have a global mindset. You cannot just serve the country you are based in—serving only your country doesn't exist anymore. . . . If I come to China as a manager, as a leader, my job is not to take care only of China. I need to take care of my customers who are going abroad. So I need to be totally global and I need the team to be totally global." Crozier says this transformation has been occurring since 2015 but has sped up in recent years. "The acceleration has been tremendous. Five years ago, none of the nontraditional [Chinese] companies were global. None. Zero. It started very very, recently. And today, you start to see more and more of it."

"Five years ago, none of the nontraditional [Chinese] companies were global. None. Zero. It started very very, recently. And today, you start to see more and more of it."

—**Alain Crozier,**
CEO, Greater China Region, Microsoft

Strategy 5: Use China as a Testing Ground

Mango's David Sancho notes that more global companies are using the strategy of Chinese competitors by piloting new concepts and products (many of them digital concepts) in China first, then taking them global. This makes sense, he claims, because Chinese digital systems are often the most advanced worldwide. As an example, he points to Alibaba's totally digital Hema supermarkets, which are far more advanced than Amazon Go. "In the US, everyone's talking about Amazon Go, but then you go to Hema [in China], and you already have proof of concept." The Hema operating model, he emphasizes, is more advanced than Amazon Go in that in-store payments are made by facial recognition, sales staff have virtually disappeared, and most sales are placed by mobile phone for local delivery within 30 minutes to the consumer's home or office—levels of convenience that the Amazon model has not yet reached. Another example is that Nike and Starbucks have both opened new, state-of-the-art flagship stores in Shanghai that offer such innovations as onsite virtual clothing design (via computer stations for customers) and onsite custom coffee roasting, respectively. Sancho notes: "These amazing concept stores were launched in China first, not abroad." Sancho points out that "the China market is really becoming a place where you can test new concepts and then become global."

Microsoft's Alain Crozier also advises MNCs to do as Chinese competitors do in terms of innovating domestically, then bringing those new solutions to their global markets. He explains: "Now, with the innovation you have in China—with the 'speed to market' of a lot of solutions—many MNCs are now giving some freedom and independence to their China operations to come up with new way of working, leveraging new technology and new business models." Crozier advocates this strategy. "And with some of them, their CEO is looking at what's being done in China and the day they feel that this is exportable, they are going to deploy it worldwide. You see this dynamic happening."

Strategy 6: Leverage Global CSR Initiatives for Competitive Advantage

Another strategy in use by Coca-Cola to maintain an edge over domestic competition is to upgrade environmental protection capabilities in its operations. This allows Coca-Cola to improve government relations and consumer image, as well as to attract future employees. The company's top executive in China, Curt Ferguson, explains that Coca-Cola has located its "most environmentally green plant ever created" in Kunming, China. The plant is not only LEED certified but also massive. When fully operational, it will boast an annual production capacity equal to the amount Coca-Cola sells in Germany per year. "One plant! It's massive. It's a fantastic plant—solar, hydro, the best efficiencies in the world." Such facilities located in China's underdeveloped areas solidify Coca-Cola's reputation as a company committed to sustainability, thus offering another method of competing against local players. Other CEOs also mentioned leveraging their global sustainability practices or international CSR programs to offer more extensive or more effective initiatives than could local competitors.

Strategy 7: Strengthen Responsible Supply Chains

Many MNCs still maintain an advantage over many domestic competitors in China because they have well-developed, well-maintained, and responsible supply chains. IKEA's Freda Zhang says that in this one area, foreign companies can maintain an advantage and even gain domestic market-share in the short term. "The next step is to create a responsible, complete supply-chain, with products that are really good quality. Because, at the end of the day, for retailing, it is all about the products. The customer comes to you because . . . they want to buy something. So, the products need to have good quality and good design, created via a well-managed supply chain. And this is where the older, traditional brands are strong." She expects that during the period until 2025, this will be an area of focus for both MNCs and domestic companies as consumers begin to care more about, for example, ethical supply chains. In fact, emerging uses of technology—such as bitcoin systems—are now being widely employed in China to improve reporting on supply chains, thus ensuring quality in terms of food safety and ISO certification, as well as monitoring for social factors, such as protecting against child labor and guaranteeing basic labor rights. IKEA's Zhang adds that while ethical supply chains are now an area of advantage for many MNCs vis-à-vis Chinese competitors, she expects this topic to become an area of focus and improvement among domestic companies. Other China CEOs echoed this sentiment, indicating that retailers and consumers in China and worldwide are beginning to value proof that companies operate ethically while guaranteeing environmental and social protections across their supply chains.

Summary of Tips

1. **Empower your local teams**
   Use your local talent and domestic intelligence to dare to try new things in the China market. Give voice to your local team and listen to them.

2. **Be a leader in innovation**
   Innovation is the key to survival when you are competing against Chinese companies. To stay relevant in the China market, innovate regularly. Invest in quality, design, and new features.

3. **Digitize with China**
   Learn from Chinese competitors by fully embracing the digital revolution. Chinese consumers expect easy access to your products. Convenience and speed of delivery are becoming the norm.

4. **Partner with Chinese companies**
   Your competitors can also become your partners. Look for areas where you can collaborate with the Chinese digital giants, not only in China but also abroad. Cooperate with domestic startups as well. They are developing interesting technologies and business models.

5. **Use China as a testing ground**
   Observe your China-based competitors closely. You may identify interesting ideas that you can adopt first in China and then roll out globally. Use the dynamic China market as a place to test and refine new offerings.

6. **Leverage global CSR practices for a competitive advantage**
   For an MNC, following global social responsibility practices can offer a competitive advantage over local competitors. Effective sustainability or CSR initiatives can reinforce your brand image and strengthen relationships with local authorities.

7. **Leverage responsible supply chain**

   One advantage MNCs may have over Chinese competitors is a responsible, ethical supply chain. As technology (such as block chain) improves, companies can guarantee the quality of their supply chains—ensuring that they meet international standards for environmental and social welfare protection.

Chapter 7
Managing Relations with the Chinese Government and Foreign Headquarters

Without a doubt, the Chinese government touches everything a company does in China. . . . It is important that all departments and functions, including senior managers, are educated in how to deal with government agencies. It is a crucial part of doing business.
—**China CEO** from a high-profile MNC

Local Chinese companies have a big advantage on us because foreign companies have to be very careful in following the rule of law in all aspects—the way you pay tax, social welfare, employees. And it's not the case for our local competition. If you have a local relationship, it can make a huge difference on the profit.
—**China CEO** from a high-profile MNC

China has its own issues and requires its own solutions. This makes them [executives at HQ] frustrated because they are used to running other markets from HQ. They believe the same action can be applied in Barcelona, Paris, London, and Shanghai. They say, "Why not? We do the same worldwide. Why should China be different?"
—**David Sancho**, CEO, East Asia & India, Mango

INSIDE CHAPTER 7

Part I: Managing with the Chinese Government

Government Relations Challenges

Government Relations Strategies and Solutions

Part II: Managing Relations with Headquarters

Success Factors for China Leadership's HQ Relations

Communicating with Headquarters

Summary of Tips: Strategies for Government Relations

Summary of Tips: Strategies for HQ Relations

This chapter covers two prevalent and important but distinct types of challenges expressed by the China CEOs interviewed for this book: managing relations with the Chinese government and managing relations with headquarters for the MNCs they represent. In the pages that follow, we share the insights, advice, and strategies from CEOs on both topics, in turn.

Part I: Managing with the Chinese Government

Introduction: Recognition for Government Accomplishments

As a starting point for outlining their government relations strategy and advice, many of the China CEOs interviewed in this book expressed recognition of and respect for the strong role of the Chinese government in the nation's economic transformation over the past 40 years of reform and opening. Korn Ferry's top executive for China, Charles Tseng, is representative of other China CEOs when he comments on the government's role in fostering the nation's economic boom: "The government didn't get in the way; they encouraged enterprises to grow." One key contribution, he emphasizes, is the Chinese government's role in providing "stability and the framework of a large, uniform single market," two factors which allowed companies to enjoy "the scale to expand." Like the US, Tseng says, China is now benefitting from a level of nationwide conformity in terms of business operating conditions. "In the US, you can fly from Boston in the morning and land in Nevada in the afternoon, and you can conduct business using the same format, same system," he says. "And in China, you can fly from Shanghai in the morning to Kunming in the afternoon, and you can operate using the same basic principles. We have scale—and that scale is very advantageous for businesses."

Tseng also commends the Chinese government for the high priority given to both speed and progress in its economic development, despite the size and scope of the country. He says, "The need and desire to improve and succeed is so great in China, in part because we started from a very low position and we were prepared to take [the] risk. We were prepared to move very fast and with great flexibility to get things done."

Chinese nationals were not the only group of CEOs praising the central government for its influential role in the nation's economic development. L'Oréal's top executive for China, Stéphane Rinderknech, is also representative of most of the China top executives interviewed when he praised governmental efforts to drive economic development. "If you look at mortality rate, education, literacy . . . all of it has improved. And that creates what we have today." He commends Beijing for dramatically reducing the percentage of Chinese citizens living below the poverty line—which has shrunk from more than 66% of the population in 1990[1] to less than 1% by 2018[2] (see Chapter 5). Calling China's economic growth "the most amazing economic development in the world," he stresses that China has developed as fast as other Asian nations, but on a far grander scale: "Here, it's the scale of 1.4 billion people. Let's never forget the scale."

The government's track record in fueling economic development, he says, has left him "super confident" that China is "moving in the right direction." He adds that there are "many areas that we expect to move further in opening up—deregulation, stimulating the domestic consumption, protecting IP—but the government is aware of it. We're confident that it will happen because it's part of the government's overall development frame." As an example of governmental ability to instigate rapid change, he points to recent reforms in China's one-child policy, introduced since 2016. "Take the second birth per family policy . . . They did it! It's 15 or 20 million additional births per year, which requires hospitals, maternity care, kindergarten, social

"The need and desire to improve and succeed is so great in China, in part because we started from a very low position and we were prepared to take [the] risk. We were prepared to move very fast and with great flexibility to get things done."

—**Charles Tseng,**
Chairman, Asia Pacific,
Korn Ferry

"If you look at mortality rate, education, literacy... all of it has improved. And that creates what we have today."

—**Stéphane Rinderknech,**
CEO, China, L'Oreal

[1] China Daily. http://www.chinadaily.com.cn/a/201903/14/WS5c89b8dea 3106c65c34ee93a.html.
[2] World Bank. https://data.worldbank.org/topic/poverty?locations=CN.

security, medical coverage, schools, et cetera. The scale is huge. . . . So, in China you take a step, let it be digested by the population, then take another step. I love the Chinese expression *yi bu, yi bu*— 'one step by one step.' That's how they meet goals."

Mixed Welcome Toward MNCs

Many MNCs included in this book noted a general improvement in the reception from the Chinese government since 2000, albeit while avoiding noncompetitive or heavily polluting operations. Tata Group's top China executive James Zhan is one CEO who has generally seen improved receptivity from government officials. "Unlike in the past, at the time of your first book [*China CEO*, 2006], you had to push government—sometimes begging government officials, sometimes fighting government officials. But today, for the most part, the Chinese government system is getting more mature, streamlined." Zhan notes, however, that potentially sensitive procedures such as approving environmental impact assessments or awarding land-use permits still require complex government processes.

ABB's head of China, Chunyuan Gu, has also found the Chinese government to more strongly follow market-driven principles over the past decade. "The good news is that Beijing is different from 10 or 15 years ago when you had large projects and you needed licenses from central government. Today, the government gives directions and guidance, and it is market driven. The focus is more to give you advice and support. . . . The relationship is very different compared to 10 years ago because the government is less involved in individual project approvals. It is more focused on larger goals like smart cities, smart manufacturing . . . this kind of industrial initiative."

"The relationship is very different compared to 10 years ago because the government is less involved in individual project approvals. It is more focused on larger goals like smart cities, smart manufacturing ...this kind of industrial initiative."

—Chunyuan Gu, Chairman & CEO, China, ABB

Central versus Local Governments

China CEOs also expressed that the business friendliness of China's central government has generally cascaded into the provincial and local government levels. For example, AB

InBev's China CEO, Frederico Freire, claims that working with local provincial government officials has been eased by the fact that they face pressure to meet specific economic KPIs which are similar to corporate targets. In fact, he notes that China's Five-Year Plans, released by the central government every year since 1952, set over-riding guidelines and national economic and social targets into which the provincial and local governments contribute.

At Coca-Cola, the 35-year career path of Curt Ferguson includes 30 years outside of the US. Ferguson, who was based in Cairo before taking the top role for China and Korea in 2016, describes Chinese government officials as generally giving a warmer welcome to his company than was the case elsewhere. He comments, "I've never seen more business-friendly provincial governments in my 35 years. I mean: turnkey, here's the land, here's what you have to do, here's the permit process. Boom, boom, boom!" He adds that many officials he works with have a "switched on" attitude because "they know they're in a competitive race." He also acknowledges that the scope of scale of Coca-Cola, as well as the company's long history in China (since re-opening domestic operations in 1978) has helped to warm the welcome from many local governments. He comments, "Nobody turns down a Coca-Cola plant. They know we're going to be a good citizen—provide jobs, pay taxes, give training. And we're going to boost a lot of other industries: for the packaging, for the glass, the distribution trucks. . . . We've had great cooperation with the government."

In the education sector, Udacity's Robert Hsiung has also been impressed by the speed of local government cooperation in establishing new ventures. "We've been in active discussions with city governments in Guizhou and Sanya, to work with them to train talent. In those conversations, I can see very clearly that, when you have something that Chinese government officials want or that benefits them, they can move very fast to support you."

China CEOs agreed that business friendliness varies across provinces but that, in general, second- and third-tier areas tend to more rigorously seek investment—especially in sectors

"I've never seen more business-friendly provincial governments in my 35 years. I mean: turnkey, here's the land, here's what you have to do, here's the permit process. Boom, boom, boom!"

—Curt Ferguson,
President, Greater China & Korea, Coca-Cola

matching the central government's overall plan to steer China away from low-end, polluting industries and toward value-added, high-tech, and green sectors. NIIT top executive for China Kamal Dhuper (who has worked in China since 2004), also notes a positive change in governmental attitude, overall: "There are some provinces which are not as progressive, not so open to creating a favorable environment and favorable policies. It depends on the leadership style. But by and large, the government is taking a much more open and much more friendly approach towards most businesses."

Dhuper finds that China's first-tier cities are already mature economies, and thus less eager for investment than those which are still developing. "Shanghai and Beijing and Guangzhou—they have already arrived. There are less flexibilities in these cities versus more inland cities which are still to catch up. These are much faster and more flexible in terms of creation of policies and a favorable environment." He points to the ambitious plans of Guizhou Province, one of China's poorest regions (with a 2017 per capita GDP of US\$6,000[3]), as an example. "That province has grown so fast! They came to us in 2015, saying 'We want to make Guizhou the capital for Big Data in China and the world.'" Backed by central government support, the Guizhou government approached NIIT to develop IT education and training programs within their software industrial parks. Dhuper says, "The kind of speed and openness which they have demonstrated is something which you'll not see in Shanghai or a Beijing. They want to catch up. They have this incentive to grow fast and they get support from the central government." He also names Ningxia Province as another ambitious and fast-developing inland province. "In the first phase of economic development, these inland provinces were not part of the growth story of China. They were not focused on by the government. But now, they are much more open, faster, and more flexible in terms of how they promote and grow industries. I see that more in the smaller provinces."

"By and large, the [Chinese] government is taking a much more open and much more friendly approach towards most businesses."

—**Kamal Dhuper,** President, China, NIIT

"The kind of speed and openness which [Guizhou's government has] demonstrated is something which you'll not see in Shanghai or Beijing. They want to catch up."

—**Kamal Dhuper,** President, China, NIIT

[3] Forbes. https://www.forbes.com/sites/salvatorebabones/2018/02/12/china-quietly-releases-2017-provincial-gdp-figures/#b4f0a3c20dc0.

Rule of Law: General Praise

Another area of general praise from China CEOs for the Chinese government in recent years has been an overall improvement in rule of law, although with some exceptions. Mango's head of China, David Sancho, represents the viewpoint of many CEOs interviewed when he describes the change he has witnessed. "When I arrived here [in 2010], rule of law was a bit in the gray area. When we signed some contracts, it didn't mean a lot when you had a dispute—especially being an international company against a Chinese company. But things are much more transparent now. People are mainly willing to comply—and if you do have any issue, you can rely on the court system to protect your rights." Bayer's top executive for China, Celina Chew, who served as a corporate lawyer before taking on her current role, says she has witnessed "massive amounts of progress regarding rule-of-law" during her 23 years in China.

Another positive comment from interviewees focuses on the evolution of rule-of-law in China over the past decade. In particular, China CEOs generally praised the efforts of President Xi Jinping (who has served as the nation's paramount leader since 2012) to crack down on corruption. AB InBev's head of China, Frederico Freire, comments on the change: "Everything the government has been doing against corruption, I see as very positive and with good intentions to really make things right. This impressed me." Bosch's top executive for China, Chen Yudong, echoes those thoughts: "China has improved a lot. Especially since Xi Jinping took over, most of the under-the-table deals are almost gone. You need to put everything on the table. Overall, its better."

"Everything the government has been doing against corruption, I see as very positive and with good intentions to really make things right."

—**Frederico Freire,** BU President, China, AB InBev

Regarding China's legal and court systems, China CEOs also noted an overall improvement over the past two decades. The comments of Tata's head of China, James Zhan, are representative: "In the past, legal issues went through the government—the executive branch. But now, the court system is getting more mature." He does add that rule-of-law can still falter in the lower levels of the court system, commenting that MNCs "still run into some sticky issues with the provincial high court, the medium court, or at the city level."

Another China CEO explains the extra effort which companies need to invest in order to maneuver and operate within China's regulatory environment. He says, "China is not like in Germany or other countries, in which you have the right to get something, and so you get it." He adds that, because China's regulations can be less clear or less complete, the best way to ensure understanding is through actively nurturing relations with relevant government bodies. "In Beijing, we have a relationship with those ministers who are relevant for us in terms of policy-making." He explains that, for his company, relations with the Ministry of Information Technology are critically important because this ministry not only "drives very important laws" but also manages "the interpretation of the law, which directly impacts our business." For many MNCs, the interpretation of China laws—which can be vague or opaque—is crucial to business success.

Another positive development regarding rule-of-law in China is the now well-established system in which the government allows private companies to provide feedback on not-yet-promulgated new regulations during a "comment period." SAP's top executive for China, Clas Neumann, is among the China CEOs who appreciate this system, even though the company's views are not always considered in the final regulation. "We offer feedback on the law and how the law impacts our business. And of course, sometimes we escalate some problems." He also mentions that strong government connections and clear understanding of policies also allow SAP to help customers to ensure they are compliant with the laws.

Government Relations Challenges

Despite the consensus that business friendliness has increased (for industries matching the central government's overall shift toward higher end, technology driven, less polluting industries) and that rule-of-law has more solidly taken root since

2000, China CEOs also noted a number of ongoing challenges related to government relations. One of the most-expressed difficulties for MNCs was simply the high level of government involvement in many aspects of doing business in China, relative to other countries worldwide. As one China CEO puts it, "Without a doubt, the Chinese government touches everything a company does in China. Therefore, to have an effective way of addressing government relations topics, it is not sufficient to have a specialized Government Relations Department. It is important that all departments and functions, including senior managers, are educated in how to deal with government agencies. It is a crucial part of doing business."

Speaking in his capacity of representing 1,500 multinational companies operating in China, American Chamber of Commerce Shanghai President Kenneth Jarrett has seen the government's role in the business operations for MNCs swinging back toward more involvement since 2012 or so. "For CEOs, it has gone in a bit of a cycle. When companies first came here (mainly in the 1980s and 1990s), all MNCs had their offices in Beijing. The State, or the party, ran the economy and everybody understood that the country was operated as 'China, Inc.'" Then, during the 2000s, he says, government restrictions eased across many fronts. "Now, we are at 40 years of reform and opening, and the economy has substantially changed to become more market driven. Probably for much of the 2000s, with the exception of certain sectors in which government remains important as a regulator, there was the sense that you didn't have to work so much with the government." However, since Xi Jinping took position as the Chinese President, the pendulum began swinging again. Jarrett says, "Now, the party is reintroducing itself into the economy in a major way. And it's not clear, frankly, which way this is headed. The momentum of reform and opening isn't as strong as it was. Even within China, there are plenty of Chinese academics and economists who feel that things have gotten stuck and are no longer moving fast enough to open up."

What this means for CEOs, Jarrett says, is placing a higher priority on government relations: "I sense that executives are quite focused on the government piece again." Jarrett explains

"It is important that all departments and functions, including senior managers, are educated in how to deal with government agencies. It is a crucial part of doing business."

—China CEO
of a high-profile MNC

"Now, the [Chinese Communist] party is reintroducing itself into the economy in a major way....I sense that executives are quite focused on the government piece again."

—Kenneth Jarrett,
President, American Chamber of Commerce, Shanghai

that, for many CEOs of MNCs, government relations can be a frustrating aspect of the job. "Most CEOs don't like to do it. . . . In China, government interaction is very formulaic, protocol heavy. Everyone is speaking in pat phrases which might be viewed as quite empty. It's all about having the meeting as opposed to the content. So, CEOs might feel: 'You had me come all the way out here for that 30-minute meeting? With no content?' It's hard for local people to convince senior people to spend time doing that, but it's actually important for a company's success here." Jarrett concludes by advising top managers of China operations that government relation remains a critically important aspect of the job. "In terms of the skillset executives here need, that is special about China. Here, senior executives need to wear a government relations cap to some degree. It's not about purely working with your customers."

"Here, senior executives need to wear a government relations cap to some degree. It's not about purely working with your customers."

—**Kenneth Jarrett,**
President, American
Chamber of Commerce,
Shanghai

Speaking in his capacity as President of the 1,600-member European Chamber of Commerce in China, Mat Harborn summarizes Xi Jinping's contribution to the business environment in this way: "There is a clear wish from the leadership under Mr. Xi to create a rule-based society—not a rule of law society in our sense of the term, but a rule-based society." For example, Harborn praises the Chinese government's stricter and more universal enforcement of environmental protection regulations as of 2017 as "a very open and clear ambition to create level playing fields."

But while President Xi's government has altered the business operating environment for MNCs in China in mostly positive ways, it has also introduced some new frustrations for China CEOS—such as increased government monitoring and new regulations for certain industries. One example named by MNCs, beginning around 2017, has been increasingly stringent regulations on work permits for international staff.

Comments from individual China CEOs regarding the degree of regulation they face tended to vary widely by industry. For MNCs in the automobile sector, for example, regulations have generally eased. Bosch China CEO Chen Yudong explains: "All our business—even in China—is a free competition market for the automotive components." For example, the battery cell sector formerly required a 50-50 joint venture, but not now.

In other industries, however, China CEOs expressed that a degree of over-regulation continues to exist in China. One representative view comes from Manulife's top executive for China, Kai Zhang, who comments that, due to the planned economic system, China's banking and insurance regulations are "even stronger" than those of the post–financial crisis in the US. Zhang, who spent 12 years working in the US, then 8 years for other MNCs in China before taking on the role of CEO and General Manager for Manulife-Sinochem in 2015, believes "China's central planning components are too heavy." She explains that new policy changes and regulations are issued very frequently, even on a monthly basis. In addition, banks and insurance companies sometimes experience micro-management of their operations by related government agencies—such as monitoring the amount of loans they issue, or managing their non-performing loan ratio. Zhang says, "When you get these directives, you feel that the financial institutions are just instruments for the government."

Another industry-specific issue for the banking and insurance sector, she says, is a relatively short experience and low maturity among regulators. Zhang comments, "They want to do the right thing but sometimes they go to extremes—either over-relaxing or over-tightening. They can be too relaxed for one segment; then suddenly, when they have a problem, they choke the innovation to death. The pendulum tends to swing." Overall, however, she comments that the regulatory environment for her industry is improving: "Although it's very painful for us to go through so many policy changes, overall, we are still encouraged by the positive direction along with further market opening."

Such over-monitoring can be experienced at the company or even the project level, other top executives at China-based MNCs explain. One interviewee says, "The Chinese government is business friendly, but it's really important to make sure that they like and support you but they don't love you." Asked to elaborate on this advice, Gu explains, "If they love you, they come to us with a lot of business proposals. They try to help too much in your daily operations. That is something to avoid because they don't understand that we have different governance regarding the process. . . . They have very good intentions, but we have a different process."

Another oft-cited reason for the complexity of working with the Chinese government, said China CEOs, is the necessity for companies to interact successfully with various levels of government simultaneously—from the central government to the provincial, city, district or local levels. Another reason for greater government intervention in China is that, under the nation's unique form of market socialism or socialism with Chinese characteristics, MNCs feel the influence of the government not only directly (i.e., via government agencies) but also indirectly, through interactions with state-owned enterprises, former SOEs, or quasi-government organizations such as trade associations. They also emphasize China's unique hybrid organizations, such as government-owned non-government organizations, which add complexity to business operations.

Addressing this challenge, ABB's Chunyuan Gu comments, "China requires being more proactive regarding government relationships . . . because China is not just one place. If you are very successful in Shanghai, that does not mean you are successful in another province. You have to make a lot of effort in China." He goes on to explain that, for MNCs, connections with local government can be more important than those with central government. Other China CEOs who manage large operations across the nation also noted that the business friendliness of provincial and local governments varies widely from government to government. Comments Coca-Cola's China head Curt Ferguson, "A lot of governments say they are business friendly and then you've got to stand in line for 27 permits, right? Some are impossible; some are great."

"A lot of [China's local] governments say they are business friendly and then you've got to stand in line for 27 permits, right? Some are impossible; some are great."

—Curt Ferguson,
President, Greater China & Korea, Coca-Cola

Challenge 1: Uneven Playing Field

One problem which has not disappeared in the past decade or two, long-time China CEOs said, is an "uneven playing field" upon which MNCs compete with local companies. In fact, in some respects, this problem has worsened, since around 2000. One top executive for China from a high profile MNC explains why the shift has taken place during the past two decades: While in the past, he says, multinationals were welcomed because local governments wanted to learn from them, today, this special status has diminished. "Now, if you want to come, it's OK, it's fine but you have to compete like everybody else." He also adds that, as a foreign company, "You may have a disadvantage due to the fact that local companies get more local government support than foreign companies."

Other companies also experienced quite clear favoritism for local companies or even other foreign companies with stronger *guanxi*. Among foreign enterprises polled in CEIBS' 2019 *China Business Survey*, 41% named "government and legal environment" as among the "greatest external challenges facing your company in China," a slight increase over the 39% giving this answer in 2015.[4] One China CEO with a negative experience says his company has, at times, been "the target of some unscrupulous government officials." Specifically, the company has been "reported for some obscure rule violations" and then "basically extorted," in the view of the CEO. "From what I see, our local competitors don't face the same scrutiny because the things that we were reported as violating, they do it in spades." As one example, the company was threatened with steep fines of over RMB1 million for posting client testimonials and certain marketing wording on their site—practices they see their competitors doing online. The CEO says the issue is related to *guanxi*, or the lack of it. The top executive says, "Other companies have better connections with the government. We do not." Another related issue: Chinese regulations may include "gray" or "obscure" wording, making unclear what is and is not allowed. The result can be arbitrary punishment for the offending behavior among MNCs, but less so for domestic competitors. The China CEO says, "If they want to catch you, they will. We have to deal with it."

> *"...[L]ocal companies get more local government support than foreign companies."*
>
> **—China CEO**
> of a high-profile MNC

---

[4] CEIBS. *China Business Survey,* 2019.

On the positive side, European Chamber of Commerce in China President Mats Harborn notes an overall shift away from preferential treatment for local companies vis-à-vis international companies in recent years. "The problem of [the] uneven playing field was very clear before 2016. From the following year, the government has been attempting to enforce rules equally to both sides. It's not 100% equal, but it's becoming more equal and I think this is a trend that will continue." In the Chamber's *Business Confidence Survey* 2019, when asked to name the top three "most significant regulatory obstacles for your company when doing business in Mainland China," polltakers named "ambiguous rules and regulations," "unpredictable legislative environment," and "administrative issues" as their biggest challenges.[5]

"Rule of law in China has improved, but not completely."

—**China CEO**
of a high-profile MNC

"Rule of law in China has improved, but not completely. This is still an area for improvement," comments one of the China CEO interviewees. The head of China points to difficulties his company has faced given that his suppliers often enjoy strong *guanxi* with local government. For example, during difficulties arising from market volatility, local suppliers may use their close relationships with local government to win disputes. The CEO clarifies, "The issues we run into in certain areas are: when there's a market downturn, with partners and suppliers. Like in the steel industry, when your suppliers are in a downturn, you have to be very careful. Many of the local courts are very close to local business—they all know each other." Other CEOs concurred regarding the uneven playing field, with one expressing, "Local Chinese companies have a big advantage over us because foreign companies have to be very careful in following the rule of law in all aspects—the way you pay tax, social welfare, employees. And it's not the case for our local competition. If you have local relationships, this can make a huge difference in the profit."

One aspect which China CEOs named as helpful when experiencing an unfair playing field is a recognized corporate

---

[5] European Chamber of Commerce in China. *European Business in China Business Confidence Survey 2019.*

name and a proven investment track record in China. Tata's James Zhan explains, "There are occasions when we have to intervene. Because we are Tata, we are relatively well known, so when we approach the party secretary or governor or mayor, most of the time, they help out."

Challenge 2: Opaque Regulations, Sudden Policy Changes

Another oft-named government-related challenge for China CEOs is the frequent policy changes which can be released unexpectedly as the central government refines its overall economic strategy or strengthens its targets. Philips' Andy Ho explains, "Besides maintaining government relationships, you also need a deep understanding of certain policies—to be able to respond to the new policies quite quickly. That may be a difference between inside China and outside of China." Especially in the healthcare sector, Ho says, the Chinese government can frequently issue new policies, such as changing the requirements for new types of permits. "If you don't tell your organization to take advantage of policy changes, you will miss an opportunity. You need to change very quickly. That means you have to be super sensitive."

"Besides maintaining government relationships, you also need a deep understanding of certain policies—to be able to respond to the new policies quite quickly."

—Andy Ho,
Leader, Greater China, Philips

Mary Boyd, Economist Corporate Network (Shanghai) Director, clarifies the frustration which MNCs can face as they scramble to stay abreast of policy changes, "Every country has an industrial template but China, with its legacy, has a much more muscular approach to this." She explains that, while MNCs working in or with China are generally "well used to reading the fine print of the Five-Year Plans (FYP) for clues as to which areas of the economy are moving, which sectors are likely to grow faster than others," companies still struggle to adapt to the policy changes which can be announced in an ad hoc way as the FYP is implemented. She points to the late 2017 announcement from Beijing requiring all vehicle manufacturers producing or importing more than 30,000 cars in China per year to ensure that 10% of these vehicles are categorized as zero- or low-emission (i.e., all-electric, plug-in hybrid, or hydrogen powered) by 2019. The percentage increased to 12% in 2020, with penalties for non-compliance—an announcement which left auto-makers in China scrambling to comply. Boyd says, "It's that kind of policy change that is more difficult to cope with because it's not tied to market demand." In such cases, she adds that the market forecasts that strategy teams would have created prior to the new policy would then suddenly need to be scrapped as the companies scramble to "re-order the strategic priorities." In addition, such unexpected top-down decrees must be "communicated back to headquarters" because top executives in headquarters must realize that "when these industrial directives are articulated by the government, everybody has to adjust to them, to change their practices to be compliant."

Another aspect of the regulatory environment in China which adds complexity to the role of China CEO, says Boyd, is the process, in China, of issuing laws which (at least initially) lack clarity. She explains, "The overall issue of the various iterations a law can pass through, and of waiting for the fine print, the implementing regulations—this is still a sequence that companies have to go through." For example, she points to China's new Foreign Investment Law (issued in March 2019) which left companies "waiting for the fine print" due to "vagueness of terminology." On the positive side, she notes that the Chinese government has solidified its practice of giving a preview of coming policy changes, thus allowing companies a "consultancy period" during which professional associations from related sectors can voice concerns. Boyd says, "That way, hopefully, by the time the fine print is issued, there will be some accommodation if industry feels that there is something that needs to be improved in the broader framework of the law—a clarification or perhaps an extension."

Challenge 3: Intellectual Property Rights Violations

One area of long-running concern for MNCs in China, and where improvements have been made, is in the protection of intellectual property rights. In fact, only 16% of WFOEs polled in the CEIBS' 2019 *China Business Survey* deemed IP infringements as among the 'greatest external challenge facing your company," a drop from 20% answering a similar question in 2012.[6] McKinsey & Company Senior Partner Jonathan Woetzel (who has worked 33 years in China) explains that China's IPR protections have evolved alongside the shift in technology transfer from international companies investing in China. Initially, during the 1970s and 1980s, he says, many MNCs brought to China technologies that were not considered modern in their home countries. "Obviously, that's no longer the case. The expectations and the competitiveness of the Chinese marketplace now require technologies that are current and commercial globally. The stakes have gone up." He adds, "The expectations from both sides have risen. Both in terms of the Chinese company's expectation of the quality of technology from a foreign company, to gain a competitive advantage in the marketplace, and in terms of the foreign company's expectation that that technology will receive the benefit of the laws and regulations which have allowed it to develop outside China. That's why we are in a different place from 10 or 15 years ago."

What has changed? One China CEO names China's improved track record in terms of courts protecting IP rights as one significant shift: "We can see that China has been investing more in intellectual property protection, creating many courts to arbitrate." In fact, he notes that legal studies have shown that an average of 80% of court decisions on IPR now favor foreign companies.

> "We can see that China has been investing more in intellectual property protection, creating many courts to arbitrate."
>
> —Jonathan Woetzel,
> Senior Partner, McKinsey & Company

As to the reasons for the shift, the CEO says China's own emerging IP is a key factor. He points out that, in recent years, one of the China-based companies most often suing for patent infringement in China has been Huawei—typically against its own former employees. Other China top executives also find that China's treatment of IP infringements in changing, including at Microsoft. Alain Crozier also believes improvements to China's IP enforcement in recent years has been fueled by reasons of self-protection:

---

[6] CEIBS. *2019 China Business Survey, 2012 China Business Survey.*

"Because China is now a technology powerhouse, [domestic companies] have also designed and developed a fair amount of IP—IP that they also want to sell. So, they understand that if they want to keep growing in this space, then IP has to be protected."

Another China CEO adds two reasons for the shift toward strengthened protections for IP. First, more Chinese brands are going abroad and seeking the same protections internationally. Second, the Chinese government appreciates that IP holding companies pay taxes while copyright infringers operating in China don't pay taxes.

Microsoft's Alain Crozier is among China CEOs who have witnessed "big changes" in improved IP protections even though the company previously struggled in a high-profile way to address the sale of counterfeit product. In years past, wide-scale use of fake copies of Microsoft's Windows operating system and other software was well-known by Microsoft. The problem did have a silver lining in that rampant use of bootlegged copies resulted in Chinese users migrating en masse to Microsoft platforms rather than those of its competitors. In recent years, the company has offered free upgrades to legitimate copies of Windows 10 to every consumer willing to upgrade, worldwide, which has reduced the rate of piracy. In addition, Microsoft has worked to develop customized software for various levels and departments of the Chinese government as well as corporate clients, creating a compelling value proposition for them to migrate to the latest software. Today, Crozier says, China has shown "progress in terms of how IP is treated today."

Looking ahead, Crozier expects IP to continue improving as Chinese tech companies expand abroad. He says, "Maybe it was not the case 5 or 10 years ago, but today you have some very interesting solutions, very interesting software programs developed by Chinese companies. And they want to make it happen not only in China but outside of China. They're going to have to transform all their approach to IP." He adds, "Is this overnight? No. This is going to take some time, definitively. But we see definitive progress there, and some of their IP is very high value. Transformation is underway, and we see some enforcement happening, which didn't really happen in the past."

IKEA's top executive for China, Freda Zhang, explains the evolution of IPR in China by remembering her shock, during the 2010 Canton Fair, at seeing multiple booths displaying exact copies of her company's furniture models. "I come in, and I see our 'mammal' stools for children and our 'lava' plastic chair. . . . They were everywhere in the Canton Fair." She later realized that these local companies were not actually selling IKEA copies, but sought a way to show their manufacturing abilities. "When I talked with them, actually they just wanted to show buyers they can match IKEA's quality level. But they did not understand that this is not OK—from the copyrights, this is not okay." Today, she says this type of false advertising as a sales lure still exists but mainly on e-commerce platforms. "Even today, if you search in Taobao for IKEA furniture, you can see a lot [of copies]. But most of them just try to use IKEA photos to attract visitors, like a search engine. When you click in, they are not really selling IKEA furniture."

Among those actually copying and selling fake IKEA products, Zhang says the most challenging to stop have been the company's own suppliers. She says, "If others copy our toys, no matter what they do, it still looks different because they don't know the manufacturing details. But if our supplier copies our product, that's another thing." In recent years, the company did discover a few suppliers taking the risk, including one case in which the supplier was selling fake IKEA products via B&Q (a main competitor). In that case, says Zhang, "We had to talk to them."

Since 2010, Zhang says IPR protections in China have improved for two reasons. First, because China's furnishings sector has matured, resulting in a growing pool of Chinese designers. "Nowadays, the [domestic] manufacturers can find Chinese designers to design for them. So, they don't need to copy from others anymore." Second, the rise of e-commerce now allows Chinese manufacturers to develop their own sales platforms rather than attracting buyers only via copying. Zhang says, "In the past, the Chinese manufacturers needed to prove that they were capable of copying IKEA products in order to promote themselves." But today, Chinese companies can market themselves directly to Chinese consumers via e-commerce platforms.

Another company which has faced serious infringement issues, both for its toys and for its education centers, is LEGO. The company's top executive for China, Jacob Kragh, explains that while the original patent on the famous LEGO brick has expired worldwide, the company still holds rights to protect its logo and brand. "Many companies are going a step beyond copying the LEGO brick, by copying our designs and confusing consumers to believe it's LEGO. We call them copycats. In that sense, we are struggling in China." In recent years, however, Kragh has seen a positive change: "The big change we are seeing now is that [China] has a much more structured judicial system to deal with these cases." In fact, in 2018, LEGO achieved "a great win" regarding one legal case against a copycat. "In the toy industry, like in many others, China has historically had the reputation of producing a lot of copycats. It is still the case but at least we've been able to take the most aggressive copycats to court and win."

Equally problematic, for LEGO, have been Chinese companies copying the company's education centers. Kragh says, "We're running 150 official centers in China and I think there are hundreds, if not thousands of centers that are trying to imitate the concept." While some are "legitimate competitors" which are not trying to confuse consumers, others are clearly misusing the LEGO brand to sell their services. And while Kragh claims that "a lot of local people are trying to take advantage of the LEGO brand," in the case of education services, the company has so far had only "partial success" in protecting its IP in China. Kragh's strategy has been to be "very present" in China, and to use "a strong local team of IP lawyers who really go out and take down what we believe are illegal products on websites. They are working with the judicial system in terms of putting forward claims against copycats." The result? "We were seeing a little less copycat activity in China. . . . When we engage in dialogues with the big e-commerce platforms about these illegal activities, we have a certain degree of success in terms of creating less and less appetite for local companies to enter into this space. But the problem is not gone."

AB InBev has also faced IP infringement in China fairly regularly, selling either fake or copy-cat beverages. The company's top China executive, Frederic Freire, says when he returned to

"When we engage in dialogues with the big e-commerce platforms about these illegal activities, we have a certain degree of success....But the [IP infrigement] problem is not gone."

—Jacob Kragh,
General Manager, China, LEGO

China in 2018 (after three years working in Korea), he noted "better engagement from local authorities" in cracking down on IPR infringements.

Giving the perspective of member MNCs in the European Chamber of Commerce in China, Chamber President Mats Harborn comments that both Chinese legislation and enforcement have improved since 2000, "but there is still much left to do." Today, he says, the main problem is "not the lack of interest," but rather "a lack of the resources and competence." Certain industries, such as auto parts and components, still see widespread copying. And fake luxury products are a problem that persists, even in surprising places such as airport terminals. "We see copious infringements. . . . You see shops that have chosen domestic brands that are almost like the foreign brand—same font, the same colors. It surprises me that this exists at all. It's just obvious and flagrant."

Still, Harborn has noted an overall mindset change within the government during his 40-year career here. "We need to move away from saying that China is, per definition, out to steal our IPR. The leadership fully understands and supports IPR protection now because intellectual property is a cornerstone of a modern economy." The best strategy now, he says, is to "recognize that the system is not complete" and to "support rigorous betterment."

ABB's Chunyuan Gu says China's system for reporting infringements has improved in recent years. "They have started to establish intellectual property framework. . . . You have a place you can go to file a complaint. There is a process." Still, other China CEOs express that, while IPR protections have improved, the result is still "not to the extent that we don't have that problem in China."

One company with a positive experience, but after committing seriously to the issue, is Bosch. The company's top executive for China Chen Yudong says, "In my personal experience, a lot of people still try to copy our products, steal our intellectual property in China, and then they do some variation of the copyright." However, Chen adds that the Chinese the court system has proven effective for Bosch in recent years: "If we raise this to the court or the business commerce bureau, they will help us

"In my personal experience, a lot of people still try to copy our products, steal our intellectual property in China, and then they do some variation of the copyright."

—Chen Yudong,
President, China, Bosch

to close down the shop selling our fake products. We have had some good experiences, if we raise complaints." In fact, Bosch recently has won several cases against IP infringers. Chen says, "We see a big improvement. . . . If you go to the system to complain, they will enforce it." Although many domestic infringers still do not understand the issues, Chen says, relevant officials do: "If you want to enforce the law, use the legal way—go to the department of commerce. They do support foreign companies in protecting their rights. They won't be pushed around." Finally, a large part of Bosch's success in protecting IP, Chen says, stems from the substantial investment the company has made toward resolving this issue. "We do have teams to do this work. One is for counterfeit parts and one for IP rights."

Another source of positive change in IP protection has come from the changing mindset of Chinese consumers. Sony's top executive in China, Hiroshi Takahashi, says the company has seen "huge improvement" compared with a decade ago when "nobody paid for content." For an entertainment company like Sony, "we consider the protection of copyright as one of the most important aspects in our business—it is crucial." The change, he says, has been triggered by two forces: "Now the Chinese government is managing the education of the public. And also, businesspeople in China are more and more in line with the rest of the world. The peoples' minds have changed because they became richer. Their living standard is now good enough to buy original things. They feel: 'I do not buy copies because that degrades me. I am a very successful businessperson, so I buy the original product.'" The result of the government's efforts, coupled with China's social transformation and public mindset, is improved IP protections, he says, "Sometimes we still see some gaps, but they are getting smaller."

Another MNC which has witnessed significant IP improvements is Bayer. The company's top executive for China Celina Chew says, "Looking at the basic IPR enforcement situation, for Bayer, we have seen huge improvements. In the IPR courts, we have had some successes in taking action against people counterfeiting our products or trying to use our trademarks illegally." While these wins did not result in "the big payouts that

"The peoples' minds have changed because they became richer. Their living standard is now good enough to buy original things. They feel: 'I do not buy copies because that degrades me."

—**Hiroshi Takahashi,**
Chairman & President, China, Sony

we might see in other jurisdictions," Chew says it was more valuable for her company to succeed within the court system. "The more important point is that the [Chinese] courts have stood by us, enforced our IPR and required the defendant to issue apology letters that are published." In recent years, she has seen an increasing number of court wins for Bayer. "We see the efforts of the Chinese government in setting up IPR courts around the country for better handling of IPR disputes." Although problems persist—especially in that "the further you get from the big cities, the less international the court system may be"—still, the court systems are moving toward greater internationalization and standardization.

Chew also notes that the evolution of China's own companies is spurring the development of IP protections. "Companies in China also rely on IPR to protect their innovations and brands. As Chinese companies increasingly engage with global companies—in global supply chains and global markets—they become more familiar with international systems and practices." One suggestion Chew offers to fellow MNCs is to find creative ways to leverage China's growing culture of IP protection by contributing positively to the change. As an example, she points to Bayer's ongoing program with Tongji University (in Shanghai) in which the company sponsors a Chair in Intellectual Property Rights. Bayer and Tongji jointly hold an annual IPR Forum which brings together more than 100 students, professionals, and academics from China and Germany to discuss IP. "The range of the discussions over more than a decade has been amazing and gratifying—spanning traditional trademark and patent topics, to protections for plant varieties, or algorithms, or digital IPR. It's a great forum to raise awareness and learn about new issues, exchange ideas and share best practices."

Looking to the education sector, Udacity's Hsiung also agrees that IP challenges have evolved. Today, traditional copying is "certainly reducing" due mainly to the fact that "Chinese companies are now able to innovate and develop products." He clarifies that while domestic competitors may still "get inspiration, ideas from somewhere," they are now adapting them and creating something new, rather than copying. The bigger problem for

"...[T]he further you get from the big cities, the less international the court system may be."

—Celina Chew, President, Greater China, Bayer

his company, Hsiung says, is the growing number of Chinese companies who are innovating in their own right, creating new competition for Udacity and other MNCs. "The bigger threat will be from companies that actually take innovation seriously, companies that actually listen to the customer and evolve their product. Those are the ones we need to focus on."

Even in the fashion sector, which has long been one of the industries hardest hit by domestic IP infringements, China CEOs say progress has been made. Mango's top China executive, David Sancho, comments on the shift during his time as head of China for his company. "In terms of brand copying, over the last eight years, I have seen an amazing and enormous improvement from the Chinese government—starting with actions like closing many fake markets, and really following up every time we discover someone faking our brand or selling our brand in places we never agreed to."

"The bigger threat will be from companies that actually take innovation seriously, companies that actually listen to the customer and evolve their product."

—**Robert Hsiung,**
Managing Director, China,
Udacity

Government Relations Strategies and Solutions

Strategy 1: Invest Time and Energy

The most-named strategy for China CEOs to successfully cultivate and manage government relations was simple: to invest a large percentage of their professional time and energy (including personal time) in this aspect of their role. Microsoft's Alain Crozier, who estimates spending 20% of his time on government-relations work, says the task of government meetings "cannot be delegated." Because Chinese protocol calls for the direct involvement of the top executive in order to show sincerity, he himself must participate in many of the government meetings. Crozier says, "You need to be at the core and center of things." Regarding projects involving a local government—whether the project focuses on establishing an incubator or selling Windows in China—Crozier himself attends the related meetings. "I don't have one trip outside of Beijing where I don't meet someone from the local government one way or another. None." He says his time is divided between three focus areas—commercial issues, public sector, and partners—each of which require his presence as a matter of protocol. In sum, he advises other China CEOs, "You need to show up, you need to show up, you need to show up."

Sony's top executive for China, Hiroshi Takahashi, who worked in Japan, the US, and Mexico before taking on his current post, also finds himself spending more time on government-related work in China than he did elsewhere. "The China government is more influential to business activities than the government in other countries," he comments, adding that this difference requires a significant amount of his professional focus. "Every month, I have a few events which include interaction with the government officials. In other countries, like the US or Mexico, I seldom have contact with the government. I think it's unique to China." Philips' Andy Ho expresses a similar viewpoint: "Government relations are very important. China is a highly regulated country, so you need to maintain the connection and also stay close to regulation changes."

[Regarding government relations strategies for China CEOs] "You need to show up, you need to show up, you need to show up."

—Alain Crozier,
CEO, Greater China Region, Microsoft

Strategy 2: Experienced Government Relations Team

Another essential part of the government relations strategy, China CEOs expressed, is an excellent, highly experienced government relations team. As one top executive from a high profile MNC explains, "The government in China is extremely strong. So, it's very important to have good advice—from good consultants and good lawyers—to make sure you always comply with Chinese laws, especially with consumer laws." Microsoft China's Alain Crozier agrees: "You also need to have a dedicated team on government relations. It's not a part-time job. It's not a temporary job. It's not a job you can delegate to external companies."

Strategy 3: Partner with Local Companies

Another method China CEOs have learned to use to better manage government relations is to form partnerships with local companies that can more easily navigate through official processes. Coca-Cola China's Curt Ferguson explains, "The other thing that works very well for us is that we have local partners—our bottlers. And they do a lot of the heavy lifting with the local government. They have the relationships."

For newcomers to China or those lacking local connections, hiring and maintaining the right team for government relations can be difficult. Mats Harborn of the European Chamber of Commerce in China says: "Government relations is extremely important but it's very difficult for us foreigners to maintain all the relationships we need. To get someone to manage this for us, we need to be very selective, to ensure that they manage for us in our way. This is key. Creating the trust and developing the relationships requires a lot of time, and as leaders, we don't have the time. On the other hand, if you have someone on your [government relations] team with the wrong values or wrong understanding, it won't help you."

Strategy 4: Align Your Goals with Those of the Government

The fourth government-relations strategy named by China CEOs was: ensuring that your company's goals are fully aligned with those of the relevant government entities. Top China executives stressed that understanding these goals may take time. For this reason, Microsoft's Crozier explains how critical it is to be patient when working with government. "You may say: 'I want to get it done!' If you have this mindset, stay home. Because it's not gonna happen. When you are in a job like mine, you're not here for one year or two. You better sign on for a long time. You need to be long-term and resilient." He adds that building government relationships takes time and persistence. "One discussion? Nothing is going to happen. Two discussions? Nothing is gonna happen. You need to be here three, four, five, six times. . . . You need to show them, you need to demonstrate. Is it taking more energy than maybe in many other countries? Yes, definitively."

At L'Oréal, a primary key to success has been in aligning carefully with the central government's overall "frame" so that the company's goals support the government's larger missions and goals. The company's head of China, Stéphane Rinderknech, shares his strategy on aligning with the government: "We see the concrete actions of the government and then we follow three steps: witness, benefit, and contribute. The government has its frame and we fit into it. We just expand and augment the frame." In addition, Rinderknech emphasizes that the company seeks ways to support government initiatives. For example, L'Oréal was among 1,700 companies which rushed to support the central government's massive China International Import Exhibition in 2018, officially hosted by President Xi. Rinderknech says, "We were first to say: 'We'll be present.' We bought a nearly 600-square-meter booth. We sent a very strong message that 'L'Oréal is here for you.'"

Another top China executive for a high profile MNC also comments that complex government relations is one of the most challenging aspects of his role. "There are two levels here. One is with local government; the other is with central government officials who are responsible for taxes, safety, and so on." Both levels of government are driven by a specific set of goals. He adds, "You need to understand how you help them to achieve their goals. Because they also have goals in terms of a certain amount of tax they need to achieve or certain amount of innovation and so on. It is important to keep these officials in the loop and to make sure you have good connections because when you have a problem, you need these people to back you up."

"You need to understand how you help [local government officials] to achieve their goals."

—**China CEO**
from a high-profile MNC

230 CHINA CEO II

Part II: Managing Relations with Headquarters

A separate but equally important type of struggle experienced widely by China CEOs relates to dealing with headquarters on China operations. AmCham Shanghai President Kenneth Jarrett says for most MNCs this issue has improved over the past decade—simply because China's "strategic importance is much greater than before." For that reason, at most companies, "the level of attention from CEOs and from Boards is very high."

The view of Sony's Hiroshi Takahashi is representative of China CEOs enjoying a high level of China knowledge and support from their headquarters: "In terms of what is going on in China, in this regard, I am very comfortable because Sony's global CEO, Mr. Oshido Shida, and the previous CEO both understood China very well." The reason for the high importance given to the nation, says Takahashi, stems largely from the share of global sales China now represents within Sony: "The US and China are the most important markets for Sony. Of course, Europe and Japan are also important, but the importance of China is getting higher and higher—not only as a market but also as the original innovation of new services like PlayStation." He emphasizes that China has shifted from mainly representing a consumer market to also representing an important research and development center. "There are so many publishers, so many creators of games, and there is a new culture of animation cartoons in China now. Our top management now knows that China offers a great opportunity to develop the entertainment business."

Bayer's Celina Chew also praises her global board for its China savvy: "There's quite a lot of China understanding in our global board. Several of the board members have had direct experience of living or working in China. They don't find China mysterious or strange." One reason for the high level of understanding is the abundant information on China from the world's leading consultancies as well as the steady stream of China reports from international media. Still, she says, keeping the global board up-to-date on new developments in China across important industry sectors is a key part of her job and that of her team.

Relations with HQ (Volvo Cars)

On October 28, 2009, Ford Motor Co. created news headlines around the world by announcing what many analysts considered a surprising choice as the buyer for its subsidiary, Volvo Cars. After considering several buyers, Ford decided on Zhejiang Geely Holding Group, the parent of Chinese motor manufacturer Geely Automobile. When the terms of the deal were finalized in 2010, Western news media called the new acquisition an "unlikely marriage" of Swedish technology and Chinese manufacturing, with some analysts publicly worrying about the future of the iconic brand and the quality of Chinese-made Volvo cars.

Almost a decade later, Volvo Cars sales are consistently strong. As one example, after record sales of 642,000 cars in 2018, the company declared a dividend of more than US$310 million to its shareholders. In another example, the China-based parent company has been widely acknowledged for not only maintaining the Volvo name but also its raising brand value. In fact, Volvo's website famously promises that "around 50% of the cars we produce and sell will be electric by 2025" and that "No one should be seriously injured or killed in a new Volvo car by 2020."[7]

Volvo Cars' top China executive, Xiaolin Yuan, stresses that the management structure did not change after the acquisition: "We are very much the same structure. Our headquarters are in Sweden, where we have all the functions—R&D, procurement, design and manufacturing of plants, and other functions." The company's commercial operations are divided into three regions: EMEA, the Americas, and APAC.

Yuan credits the smooth acquisition and the following successful first 10 years, including Volvo's "heroic turn-around" financially, to the vision of Geely chairman Li Shufu in treating Volvo Cars as "an independent case." Yuan says, "The biggest change and the biggest success factor—on top of all the proper governance—is that Volvo Cars has truly been transformed from a company very much headquartered and centered in Europe, with cars produced in Europe and sold worldwide, into a truly global company which is headquartered in Europe but having full operations around the world, a full value chain."

Li also gained respect worldwide with his "daring" 2017 announcement that Volvo Cars would cease producing pure internal-combustion-engine cars by 2019—a promise which led Fortune magazine to include Volvo on its 2018 list of 50 Change the World companies. Overall, Yuan describes Geely's post-merger strategy for Volvo in this way: "The strategy is to make sure that Volvo Cars remains premium, and to secure its stronghold in Europe and the Americas, as well as developing the world's fast-growing markets, particularly China." Following this "very straightforward" strategy, Volvo Cars operations expanded from

(continued)

---

[7] Volvo Cars. https://www.volvocars.com/en-om/about/our-stories/vision-2020.

Relations with HQ (Volvo Cars) (*continued*)

only operating a sales company in China after the acquisition to running an 8,000-strong organization with three vehicle manufacturing plants and one engine plant, which sold more than 130,000 cars in 2018 in China alone.

Today, Yuan says China is a "second home market" for Volvo Cars, providing all functions from R&D to manufacturing, procurement, and distribution. The system works well, Yuan says, because Geely Auto enjoys a "sister-brother" relationship with Volvo Cars rather than "father-son" relations. Since the two companies share the same owner (Zhejiang Geely), they both benefit from close collaboration via joint ventures that allow them to share existing and future technology, deepen industrial synergies, and provide economies of scale. However, Yuan adds that the relationship is still "very much independent and at arms' length."

Success Factors for China Leadership's HQ Relations

Factor 1: Recognition of China's Importance

One example of proof of the growing recognition of China among the global boards of many MNCs, says Kenneth Jarrett, is that more China CEOs now report directly to the global CEO rather than to a regional Vice President. Jarrett says, "Today, even in cases where the company has APAC operations, China has sometimes been broken off from APAC as a separate reporting line and that reflects the significance of China."

More proof of growing awareness of China's importance among global boards, Jarrett notes, is a new trend toward recognizing the role of China CEO at the board level. "There is also a growing awareness that those with aspirations to become global CEO may need to come to China for a few years—to get some understanding of this market." One such China CEO being recognized by his company is L'Oréal's Stéphane Rinderknech; in 2018, he became the group's first executive committee member in a role based outside France

"There is also a growing awareness that those with aspirations to become global CEO may need to come to China for a few years—to get some understanding of this market."

—**Kenneth Jarrett**,
President, American
Chamber of Commerce,
Shanghai

or the US. Rinderknech says the move shows the growing importance of the China market for the L'Oréal Group: "I'm there because they understand that China needs to speak its own voice, and that we need agility when it comes to China. We need to react with speed—we need the direct voice and direct presence of China." LEGO is another example of an MNC which recently raised the profile of its head of China by increasing the status of China to report directly to the top global team.

Rinderknech also explains the autonomy he enjoys, as China CEO, this way: "I love the company because I am free to operate within a modus operandi, within an aspirational frame. Once we [in China] understand the strategic frame of L'Oréal, we are free to operate in the way we think is best." He adds that, because of the long connection with China of the group's global CEO, Jean-Paul Agon, the domestic management team enjoys "tremendous trust" from the top. In turn, this trust allows the China team to react with "agility and speed."

Factor 2: Open Communication with HQ

But not all China CEOs described such smooth connections with headquarters. As AmCham Shanghai's Kenneth Jarrett explains, some top executives at MNCs in China face tension stemming from the fact that the China market is "so strategic." In those cases, the high importance of China "works against [the CEOs] because the corporate headquarters want to have some control over the decisions that are being made here since they have such an impact."

The bottom line for many China CEOs is that communicating on China remains a critically important aspect of the role. Many top executives expressed that, while the top management now understand China better, the layer of understanding remains thin. The views of Bosch's Chen Yudong sum up the situation described by many top executives of China-based MNCs: "In the beginning, we needed to lobby [headquarters] to do more in China. But now, 20% of our business is coming from China, so they are supporting China quite a lot."

Chen says his problem now lies in a lack of understanding, not within the group's top-tier management, but among middle managers at corporate headquarters: "That's where we need more work to win their 100% support." Tata's James Zhan echoes this concern, explaining that while his most senior management team know China well, those reporting to that team may not: "I find it is very amazing—many parts of the Western world, they are still thinking China is as it was 10 or 20 years ago. And even in India, many people have not been to China. Not everybody is current with China; their mindset is outdated. When they arrive in China, they say: 'This is China?'"

Microsoft's Crozier expresses a similar concern. Because the situation in China is changing so fast and has such deep implications globally, the commitment to support China from headquarters must run deeper than the very top layers of the executive team. "You need to do more than educate. You need to make sure that your corporation is with you on China, is working for you. And that takes some time. Everybody understands that the China market is an opportunity, because you have 1.4 billion people. But the question is: how make that opportunity a reality? That's a different story." Crozier's advice is to win support for China operations among the middle layers of the organization. He explains that the top tier typically already understands the importance of the Chinese market. "You need to present China to the rest of the organization. You need to make sure that [the whole management team] stays with you in thinking for the longer term. Not Satya Nadella, he understands; not the people who have been working with China for the past 15 years. But the newcomers—those who work on programs, on activities. They also need to have a long-term mindset for China."

AB InBev's Frederico Freire also finds that China understanding does not extend into all areas of his company: "My regional headquarters for APAC is China. So my line manager, the Zone President for ABI in APAC, sits in China. He lives here, so he

"I find it is very amazing—many parts of the Western world, they are still thinking China is as it was 10 or 20 years ago."

—James Zhan,
President, China, Tata Sons

understands. But you need to make the guys from New York understand the context." Lack of connection and understanding, he says, can lead to misunderstandings and frustration, especially regarding the speed of change in China. "China is extremely volatile, and US-based colleagues are probably not used to this volatility—up and down, up and down. . . . They want to see steady growth. But in China, one year, it may grow 10%, and another year, you grow only 2%. . . . I cannot change the volatility of China, so I need to change their mindset to understand what happens in China."

And even among executives who know China well, Tata's James Zhan says both the physical distance and the time difference take a toll. "The further away, the slower the response. Therefore, you have to manage that." Another issue, he says, is that teams located outside China tend to have unrealistic expectations regarding the business opportunities here. "When the China business is hot, people start to focus on it and to expect more. You have a nice problem, but people expect more. And when everything is not going fast, they have other priorities. Then people's attention tends to be somewhere else." Either way, he struggles to maintain realistic and constructive support for China. Manulife's China CEO, Kai Zhang, also "struggles" with this issue. "I spend a significant amount of time communicating with global and regional headquarters," she says. Because the company's senior management team is based in Canada, she adds, "it is naturally that much more difficult for them to grasp changes on the ground in China."

Another China CEO expresses that because "China has its own issues and requires own solutions," he often meets with push-back from executives at headquarters. "This make them frustrated because they are used to running other markets from HQ. They believe the same action can be applied in Barcelona, Paris, London, and Shanghai. They say 'Why not? We do it the same worldwide. Why should China be different?'" He names as one clear example of difference the fact that Facebook, Twitter, YouTube, and Google are blocked in China. "I can see there is a resistance, from a Western level, to embrace that difference. But I really believe that only those companies which

"China is extremely volatile, and US-based colleagues are probably not used to this volatility."

—**Frederico Freire,**
BU President, China,
AB InBev

"The further away [from headquarters], the slower the response. Therefore, you have to manage that."

—**James Zhan,**
President, China, Tata Sons

understand that China is different—that you must really local-ize your product, your strategy, your teams in China—can re-ally succeed in this market."

For Bayer's Celina Chew, the hot spots causing misun-derstanding with HQ often lie in the speed of doing busi-ness in China as well as the complexities of operating there. On the positive side, her company has given a large amount of autonomy to the China operations: "The level of certainty that they needed in the past—like needing a written docu-ment from the authorities for clarification of topics—as well as the level of understanding headquarters has regarding China, has changed a lot. Today, our global headquarters accept that we are able to make judgments locally about a range of issues, risks, or directions." Today, although there still may be misperceptions about the risks of doing business in China within HQ, these have diminished. Indeed, Chew says she now sometimes encounters overly rosy perceptions of China from some of her overseas colleagues, for example, that everything is possible, especially in the realm of digitalization. She says, "Of course there are a lot of amazing developments in digital in China. . . . But it's not like I can get into a flying taxi to get from one place to another in Shanghai." She has to explain, for example, that monetizing AI applications in healthcare is not yet as widespread and accepted in China as may be imagined. "So, it's a matter of managing understanding on both sides."

Communicating with Headquarters

Strategy 1: Bring Influential HQ Executives to China

The primary strategy used by nearly all CEO interviewees in communicating with headquarters is to increase awareness of China by bringing influential home-country executives here regularly. Maserati's China CEO Alberto Cavaggioni explains that the visits he arranges for the top management team cover a wide spectrum of topics and include personnel from a range of functions "including people from IT, from quality control, from the plants." His goal is to ensure a full understanding of the key issues he faces in China, including "how the authorities work, and which rules need to be respected." The approach, he says, "has paid off tremendously" mainly because the China team is then in direct contact with counterparts in headquarters. Says Cavaggioni, "It's a process of education for both sides."

Strategy 2: Digital Immersion Tours to China

Economist Corporate Network's Director for Shanghai, Mary Boyd, says the understanding gap between China-based operations and headquarters has in some cases worsened in the past decade, due to digitization. "I think MNCs probably struggle even more because not only is China now at a different pace, but . . . we have this split between the China ecosystem, when it comes to digital, and what is going on in the rest of the world. It's actually probably become even more difficult for headquarters to grasp the exceptionalism of the China market."

"...MNCs probably struggle even more now because...we have this split between the China ecosystem, when it comes to digital, and what is going on in the rest of the world."

—Mary Boyd,
Director, Shanghai,
Economist Corporate
Network

To combat the digital divide between China and headquarters, one new method has been for China-based MNCs to arrange digital immersion tours of the nation. Boyd has noted more companies arranging such tours of China in which the board members spend a day or two experiencing first-hand the technology-enhanced life of most Chinese: making daily purchases entirely via WeChat and Alipay, testing face-recognition purchasing at Hema stores, riding the high-speed train. "Just to make people aware that these things have changed in China and there is a new sensibility about the use of mobile payments and definitely advanced transport. To take people through that physical experience, it does bring it home. All the talks and all of the reports brought back to headquarters, it does not have the same immediacy."

Another aspect of China that such visits can illustrate to management from headquarters is that employee pools are often significantly younger in China than in other countries—adding a generational layer to the digital divide. Thus, such trips can also offer a chance for the team from headquarters to better understand the mindset of the China team. Boyd gives an example: "Western executives would probably assume that employees in China drive to work in their own car. So, it's worth-while to show them that you've got all these share-bikes lined up outside and everyone is doing everything digitally." Such immersion visits, she says, provide an opportunity to realize first-hand the lifestyle experienced by their employees and consumers—such as spending a lengthy public transport commute focused on their phones. Boyd adds, "You are trying to show to the visitors that this ecosystem has developed and how it shapes people's sensibilities." By the end of the short visit, Boyd says, board members typically have gained "a clearer understanding of the mindset here."

AB InBev is one MNC arranging such digital immersion tours to China for its board. During such trips, Frederico Freire says his China team seeks to demonstrate "what's going on here; what's normal for us in terms of payment methods and social networks and fast delivery, high convenience. It's everything on this front." During his event, each board member received a rented phone, a WeChat account, an Alipay account, and a Hema supermarket account. "We went to each one of those points of contact that consumers have in China with this new digital world, and we gave them an immersion: How you pay, how you order food, how you order beer, how you take your photos and you use Photoshop to look good. This is what Chinese do." Lastly, the tour included a chat with consumers. The result? Freire says his board really understood the China situation. "They said to us: 'China's not different. China's first.'" He says his board left China understanding that "what's going on in China is probably going to happen around the world later. We are definitely in a digital revolution."

"They said to us: 'China's not different. China's first.' What's going on in China is probably going to happen around the world later. We are definitely in a digital revolution."

—**Frederico Freire,**
BU President, China,
AB InBev

Strategy 3: Localize Decision-Making

The third strategy for successful interactions with headquarters, according to China CEOs, is a certain level of autonomy for China operations. Celina Chew of Bayer explains that she and her team communicate frequently with HQ on China developments (laws, market changes, employee reactions to new campaigns), especially on the speed of the China market. In return, she says, she expects a high level of trust from headquarters: "Once headquarters understands that we're professional, we know what we're doing, we can deliver, and we are results-oriented—once they believe we are a 'safe pair of hands'—that makes a very big difference. Then the interactions are based on informing, collaborating, and creating as opposed to prescribing, and merely implementing without discussion."

Marriott International's top executive for China in luxury, Rainer Burkle, agrees that localized decision-making power is a key to successful China operations: "For China, we have a regional office in Shanghai—which is very important. We also have management teams in Hong Kong, Beijing, and Guangzhou. So, we are really local. If I need somebody to help me with a decision, I don't need to call the corporate headquarters in the US; I call within Asia or even within China or directly. Decisions are made here, whereas other companies don't have that privilege, that advantage. Somebody was very smart several years ago with making that decision. We are happy with this setup."

One company which has succeeded in securing both local autonomy and global support for its China operations is LEGO. The company's China CEO, Jacob Kragh, explains that in 2015, the company replaced its APAC region with an APC region (Asia Pacific & China)—a change which elevated China to "the same level as Asia Pacific, Europe, and the Americas." In the new structure, Kragh himself reports directly to LEGO's top leadership. As a result, Kragh says, "That means, virtually every department inside LEGO is now—in one way or another—trying its best to best support the business in China.

"[V]irtually every department inside LEGO is now—in one way or another—trying its best to best support the business in China."

—Jacob Kragh,
General Manager, China, LEGO

When you elevate a market to that level of corporate currency, it also means that a lot of people have an incentive to actually go after and support China's success. So we had, in many ways, a very privileged situation in China." For Kragh himself, his role is now "part of the top 12 of the company," and the role of China has become "quite significant." He adds, "It was a rather significant move in indicating the strategic importance of the Chinese market." The new direct reporting line helps secure success in China, and Kragh says, "This allows us to turn consumer insight into new ideas and efficiency. In that respect, it's been really easy to communicate with headquarters."

Carrefour's Thierry Garnier explains the autonomy he and his team enjoy, and why it is necessary in China. He says many MNCs in retail understand that decision-making must be localized in the fast-moving China market. "That's the beauty of retail—but that is not the case for every sector." He adds that the speed of decision-making helps not only to match the pace of change in the market, but also to retain younger employees. "Millennials like speed."

By contrast, for MNCs in which the headquarters remain out of touch with China, interviewees had harsh words. Speaking in his capacity as European Chamber of Commerce China President, Mats Harborn explains, "I increasingly think the headquarters are irrelevant for our business in China because they don't understand, and from many news articles, they get the wrong impression. When they have an opinion about China, they are often very wrong. What they should do is send somebody to run the China operations who is fully trusted in two ways. One: the person is completely dedicated to your corporate values and has a proven track record of always walking the talk. Second: the person also must understand your business model 110%. Then this person needs to be empowered to develop the China business without always having to get the consent from headquarters."

"I increasingly think the headquarters are irrelevant for our business in China because they don't understand..."

—Mats Harborn,
President, European
Chamber of Commerce
in China

Summary of Tips: Strategies for Government Relations

1. **Invest time and energy**
    The Chinese government is more involved in and more influential toward business activities than is the case in most other countries. Many interactions with the government cannot be delegated; the China CEO often must participate directly in key government meetings.
2. **Form an experienced government relations team**
    Trusted in-house advice regarding government relations is a critical success factor for MNCs. Hire and retain a skilled government-relations team.
3. **Partner with local companies**
    Some MNCs use the connections of their partners to navigate the government labyrinth. Local partners can complement your in-house government-relations team.
4. **Align your goals with those of the local government**
    The Chinese government is very complex. Successful MNCs align with the goals not only of the central government, but also of local government entities.

Summary of Tips: Strategies for HQ Relations

1. **Bring influential HQ executives to China**
    Bring influential executives to China frequently to expose them to domestic operations and to the complexities of the market. Such visits also help to educate your local team.
2. **Organize digital immersion tours**
    The gap between HQ understanding about China has grown bigger in recent years due to China's digital

revolution. Organize "digital immersion tours" to China which allow top executives to experience shopping, commuting, and socializing as Chinese consumers do.

3. **Localize decision-making**

Fast decision-making is essential to keeping pace with the speed of change in China today. China operations need a high level of autonomy in order to remain nimble and reactive. One method used by some MNCs is elevate the position of China and/or the China CEO to report directly to the top executive board. Other MNCs designate decision-making power for China within Asia or even within China, to save time.

Chapter 8
Living in China

Living in China today is so much easier than before. But the old advice is valid: You need to be a psychologically stable person because there are still a lot of frustrations. If you're not stable, problems will surface, and you will suffer.

—**Mats Harborn,** President, European Chamber of Commerce in China

The first thing you need is a positive mindset because it's not easy here—the language, the way of thinking, the cultural barrier, the food. . . . In my view, it is all about mindset. . . . With the right mindset, I think China is an amazing place to live.

—**Frederico Freire,** BU President, China, AB InBev

For me, China is a binary culture. Either you like it, or you don't like it. I don't see people staying in the gray area. It's such a different country that you either adapt and like it and stay, or you leave after a while.

—**David Sancho,** CEO, East Asia & India, Mango

INSIDE CHAPTER 8

Non-Work Challenges for the Foreign Manager

Potential Problems for the Foreign Family

"Next-Pats" in China

Positive Aspects of Life in China

Strategies for Adapting to China

Summary of Tips

One aspect which changed during the time period between the writing of *China CEO* and *China CEO II* is the analysis of our interviewees regarding living in China—both for themselves and for their families. In the first round of information gathering (in 2006), although the CEOs themselves overwhelmingly reported enjoying life in China, they still described several types of hardship or potential hardships for foreigners. These included cultural mismatch or maladaptation to China either from the foreign managers (some foreigners are simply not able to enjoy living abroad) or their family members. During the second round of China CEO interviews (in 2019), foreign top executives of MNCs said that while these cases still do exist, they are now quite rare, especially among foreigners relocating to China's first-tier cities. In addition, many CEOs commented that in Shanghai, Beijing, or other developed urban centers, quality of life is actually higher than in many large cities elsewhere. Frederico Freire, AB InBev's China CEO, offers a representative view when he describes Shanghai in these words: "It's very safe. It's a diverse environment. Even pollution is no longer a big issue."

"[China is] very safe. It's a diverse environment. Even pollution is no longer a big issue."

—Frederico Freire,
BU President, China,
AB InBev

We note that all 25 China CEOs interviewed for this book reside in either Shanghai or Beijing. Both are ultra-modern, highly internationalized cities in which foreigners can find most of the hardware needed to care well for their families (acclaimed international schools, world-class hospitals, supermarkets full of imported products)—albeit at a price. In fact, most foreign interviewees who had been in China for more than five years noted an improvement during that time period in the accessibility of home-country goods. Zhen Zeng, Executive Director of the Community Center in Shanghai, explains the shift: "I don't think there is any hardship analysis anymore for China assignment."

Many CEOs described a dramatic change in China's livability for foreigners in recent years. When Philips' head of China, Andy Ho, returned to China in 1994, after living abroad, he struggled in the beginning. Relocating to Guangzhou that time, he says, meant adjusting to a lifestyle with few other English speakers, limited imported food, and poorly running transportation systems. But not now, he says. "Today, foreigners adapt quite easily in China. Now, the living conditions are much better. People live in China very comfortably." For those working in China's less developed cities, however, challenges still exist. "If you don't speak the language and you move yourself to a third-tier city, there might be some issues. But even then, no major problems."

Sony's China CEO Hiroshi Takahashi, who is joined in Shanghai by his wife, makes a telling comment: "Of course, being a foreigner here, there is some inconvenience. But in Shanghai, everything is available—and in many cases, it's more convenient than in Tokyo. We can't order dinner by smartphone in Tokyo but here, you can. Here, you can live for a month without taking one step out of your house."

Among the 25 China CEOs interviewed, not one them (including 20 non-PRC passport holders) reported wanting to leave China, either for the sake of themselves or their families. However, all acknowledged that a smooth transition into living in China requires some preparation for incoming foreigners. Their advice is collected in the following sections.

> *"If you don't speak the language and you move yourself to a third-tier city, there might be some issues. But even then, no major problems."*
>
> **—Andy Ho,**
> Leader, Greater China, Philips

> *"We can't order dinner by smartphone in Tokyo but here, you can."*
>
> **—Hiroshi Takahashi,**
> Chairman & President, China, Sony

Non-Work Challenges for the Foreign Manager

Zhen Zeng, Executive Director of the Community Center in Shanghai, remembers her own "reverse culture shock" after returning to China in 2005. A PRC citizen, she had been studying and working in the US for more than a decade, first studying for her master's degree, then marrying and starting a family. Upon her return to China, she started a challenging new position as Global Strategic Marketing Manager for Dow Corning. As the mother of two young children, her relocation to China brought several challenges: "Definitely one of the issues was work—the non-stop working schedule. I was working in a global role, so my hours were crazy." Because of the time difference between China and the US, the role involved many evening video and phone calls on top of typically long working days in China.

"People expect you to work around the clock. And that's why it's very easy, if you don't draw a line, to get exhausted at work."

Alberto Cavaggioni, Maserati's China CEO, describes his pace of work-life with a typical description: "If I tell you how many hours I'm currently working, you will tell me that I'm nuts." Due to the intense workload during his initial months in Shanghai, he recalls having literally no time to explore the city for leisure: "I visited many Chinese cities, but going to dealers, going to PR events. My time has been fully dedicated to work."

AB InBev's Frederico Freire also remembers struggling a bit, during his first half-year in the role, because every workday brought with it a steep learning curve. "Coming to work—until you get all the cultural nuances and understand the way of managing—it's tough. I remember my first six months were tough—adapting my working style to the new environment." He says his family blended in more smoothly. "They adapted much faster than I did. Later, of course, I adapted as well. And I like and enjoy China."

Culture Clash

Although the China CEOs interviewed for this book reported adjusting to China themselves, they also agreed that a certain percentage of foreign professionals simply do not adapt successfully to Chinese culture. After spending eight years as Mango's top executive for China, David Sancho has seen many incoming foreigners either thrive or leave: "For me, China is a binary culture. Either you like it, or you don't like it. I don't see people staying in the gray area. It's such a different country that you either adapt and like it and stay or you leave after a while."

He adds, "I've been eight years here and there's not so many of us who have stayed that long. Most [foreigners], they come here for two years, three years and after that they go back to their homeland or they change countries. But in my case, I really embraced in China."

Among the Chinese and returnee CEOs interviewed, many commented that the most important factor regarding foreigners adapting to China is their attitude. Kai Zhang, Manulife's top executive for China, explains, "A lot of it really depends on their personality. There are some [foreigners] who are very uptight and can never integrate. Some of them are the smartest people, but they struggle." Disagreements can occur, she explains, if the foreign manager is unable to understand the issue from the perspective of the Chinese staff. She gives an example of an international foreigner complaining that the "quality of work" from the local team is "not up to his standards." In such an instance, she says, the foreign manager may be overlooking the language barrier, forgetting that the local team is working with English as a second language. "So of course, they don't express themselves as strongly as they would in Chinese. So that disconnect is there." And in some cases, she adds, if the international foreigner is too critical of the local team, a serious rift may occur. "If there's no praise and only criticism, [the foreigner] quickly loses the support of the team." Those foreigners who adapt well to China, she adds, are able to understand and adjust to the situation without alienating the team. "The [foreigners] who thrive the best in China are those who are willing to invest in relationships, who can pat people on the back and socialize. They appreciate the mix of work life and personal life."

> *"There are some [foreigners] who are very uptight and can never integrate. Some of them are the smartest people, but they struggle."*
>
> —**Kai Zhang,**
> President & CEO, China, Manulife-Sinochem

Potential Problems for the Foreign Family

Challenge 1: Concerns Regarding Health and Comfort

On top of the stresses typical to foreign executives learning to lead teams in China, incoming foreigners (or their spouses) can face a number of non-work issues. At the Community Center Shanghai (CCS), a not-for-profit organization "dedicated to serving the needs of the international community in Shanghai," the staff have front-line contact with incoming non-Chinese who are facing challenges adapting. CCS's Director, Zhen Zeng, understands first-hand the issues which new arrivals may face, having experienced the transition herself as a returnee in 2005. During the initial months in China, she found that tasks which were no-brainers in the US suddenly triggered anxiety. "I'm also a mom, so when I first came back to China, my first year, I really struggled. Even though I grew up in China, everything was so foreign to me." Suddenly, she faced uncertainties regarding how to guarantee food safety and clean air for her children. "I had to reverse adapt to the culture. There is still a very significant amount of cultural shock that everyone has to go through."

In his role in executive recruitment, Korn Ferry's top executive for China, Charles Tseng, says air pollution in China can leave some foreigners reluctant to relocate here. "It doesn't help when the pollution is high. For someone living in Brussels or Paris and moving to Shanghai, air pollution is a concern."

Regarding air pollution, most China CEOs who have been working in China for several years noted a significant improvement in the problem in recent years. Both Manulife's Kai Zhang and Maserati's Alberto Cavaggioni, for example, worried about this issue when relocating their children to Shanghai to start their current positions, but today, both commented that Shanghai's air quality has improved. The viewpoint of Cavaggioni is typical: "Being in Shanghai, I don't have any problem at all. It's a very safe place. In terms of noise, it is much less polluted than our European cities. Nobody's using their horn, for example. Pollution-wise, it's much better compared to when I used to come here a few years ago."

Still, the transition to life in a crowded Chinese megapolis requires guidance for most newcomers. Community Center's Zhen Zeng seeks to systematically address the concerns of incoming foreigners, especially parents. She names the most common worries for newcomers—whether foreigners or returning Chinese—as food and water safety, air pollution, hospitals, and healthcare. Hence, the Community Center Shanghai and other similar organizations offer introductory "living in China" workshops to address these issues—telling newcomers where to buy imported foods, how to find daily air quality reports, where to buy air purifiers, how to purify drinking water, where to find international hospitals. In fact, Zeng says her center

serves as a hub to connect foreigners or returnees to join informal social groups where information is constantly shared. Zeng
says, "Once the information is presented to them, they feel a
huge relief. You have a lot of resources and a lot of choices." In
contrast, tackling such issues on one's own can be daunting.
Zeng says that when she arrived, she did not know anyone in
Shanghai. "I wish I knew of this center when I came back to
China. It took me a year to really get comfortable."

Challenge 2: Isolation Among Trailing Spouses

Integration of the trailing spouse can be an issue, says Manulife's Kai Zhang, especially for foreigners living outside China's
first-tier cities: "In a city like Shanghai, it's not a problem. There
are big [foreign] communities, and wives would actually have
groups to learn Chinese or local culture. But in smaller cities,
I think there might be a problem." She explains that, in underdeveloped areas, trailing spouses may feel isolated or face
challenges making friends. "Psychologically, they may feel that
they don't have any roots here."

*"Psychologically,
[trailing spouses]
might feel that they
don't have any roots
here."*

—Kai Zhang,
President & CEO, China,
Manulife-Sinochem

Challenge 3: Relationship Issues

Aside from learning to ensure basic levels of safety and health
for one's family, other more complicated issues can and do arise
for foreigners in China. The most common serious issue faced
by international couples relocating to China is relationship
problems exacerbated by the stress of suddenly living and
working in a foreign culture—particularly when one spouse
is working and the other is not. Making the problems worse,
explains CCS's Zhen Zeng, is the fact that the types of stresses
faced by the working and the non-working spouse are often
radically different. The working spouse is typically surrounded
by a team of assistants and colleagues who offer an immediate
professional network; however, he or she also faces the stress
of difficult-to-meet professional targets as well as long working
hours and tiring business travel. The non-working spouse often

faces an opposite scenario: she or he typically is free to create her/his own focus and goals during the time in China but must do so without a ready-made team or professional network. This contrast can lead to conflicts within the couple. When non-working spouses, either trailing wives or trailing husbands, feel lost initially, Zhen advises them to link into existing networks and support systems. She says, "Many people ask me, 'What's your advice on helping spouses and children to adapt?' My advice is to get involved. Don't just lock yourself in, serving whole-heartedly only your family. Create a social life. You have to go out; you have to be involved." Community Center Shanghai, for example, focuses on a mission to "connect, support, and enable" all types of "internationals" living in Shanghai.

Among the most serious issues for incoming couples, Zeng says, are extra-marital affairs. A common scenario is that the working spouse, more often the husband, develops a relationship through a connection at work. Zeng explains that persisting differences in earning power between foreign executives and younger local team-members or professional contacts can trigger attempts to break up marriages. She says, "Obviously, there are more temptations when you come to China as a foreigner. Just the fact that you're a foreigner—it doesn't matter what is your real financial worth—some young girls think you are worth a lot." She continues, "If your family is strong, with a strong foundation, then you will be OK despite those temptations. But when you don't have a very strong relationship foundation, those things can start to creep in. There's never an isolated source of problems—it's always a combination of different factors."

"There are more temptations when you come to China as a foreigner. Just the fact that you're a foreigner—it doesn't matter what is your real financial worth—some young girls think you are worth a lot."

—**Zhen Zeng,**
Executive Director,
Community Center,
Shanghai

"Next-Pats" in China

One interesting change noted by interviewees is a shift among foreign professionals in China, away from older, senior foreigners on traditional, short-term assignment and toward younger, more junior foreigners who have come to China on their own initiative—a new group nicknamed "next-pats." Zhen Zeng has noted this change in the type of foreigners taking positions in

China: "We see the trends. We have data from immigration that shows that the number of foreign visas issued is pretty much the same as several years ago. But the conversation is different now. Before, it was mostly executives, more high-level managers. Now we are moving more into the young professional category."

As European Chamber of Commerce in China President, Mats Harborn also observes this trend: "Foreign companies are sending ambitious young people to China. Of course, these people do not need an expat salary and don't need help for children's schooling. This is very important."

The shift toward younger, more junior foreigners entering China to work has created a new population who typically lack the support system which accompanies older, more senior managers. Zhen Zeng explains, "This new group really doesn't have much support. Some come on their own initiative and find a job once they get to China. We do see a lot of those people now. Or they come here with a very basic job. They are hired by a local company and are treated as a local employee." In such cases, Zeng says, no assistant helps these newcomers with their daily life. "You have to figure out everything by yourself."

Despite the challenges and lack of resources for younger foreign professionals, Zeng says many are drawn to China for work opportunities. She says, "They either work for one of the English-teaching institutions or they work for a small startup company. There are tons of them now. . . . They really love Shanghai because there are so many opportunities." One key to success for this group, she emphasizes, is "better Chinese language skills."

At Marriott International, the company's top executive for luxury hotels, Rainer Burkle, also observes a trend toward incoming younger foreigners willing to work on local contracts. He says, "We are also seeing a tremendous change in the foreigners coming into China. When I first came, there were many senior executives—CEOs, presidents of companies. Now, many of them have left. But what we're seeing now from international is youngsters—aged 20, 25. They study here in China; they are learning the language, they're picking up Chinese in a totally different way. They're going from the inside out—which is great to see." Celina Chew, Bayer's head of China, also observes—and

"Before, [foreigners working in China were] mostly executives, more high-level managers. Now we are moving more into the young professional category."

—**Zhen Zeng,**
Executive Director,
Community Center,
Shanghai

"What we're seeing now from international is youngsters—aged 20, 25. They study here in China; they are learning the language....They're going from the inside out."

—**Rainer Burkle,**
Area Vice President, Luxury,
Greater China, Marriott
International

hires from—a growing population of younger non-Chinese who are willing to work here without a traditional "expat" package.

In summary, Zhen Zeng says that today, there are "two extremes" among the foreign population in China: "If your company sent you here, they really want you here. Then those people are really well taken care of. The other are the young professionals seeking jobs. They are totally on their own."

One emerging challenge for the so-called next-pats in China, that is, those hired locally and without an expat contract, is job security. For this group of foreign employees, if they lose their position in China or if their contract is not renewed, they also often do not have a secure position in their home country. Even those expats sent to China on assignment may no longer have a secure position to return to back home. As Manulife's Kai Zhang explains, "For a lot of [foreigners] now, they don't have the sense of job security. They don't consider China their home. And they might want to return home, but their position [back home] probably was taken by an equally capable person. They cannot return to their original position anymore. So that's a challenge."

Finally, Mats Harborn of the European Chamber of Commerce China advises MNCs to maximize the valuable China experience of the foreigners they send on assignment in China, rather than returning them home too quickly. "Companies need to be very proactive and really looking at the assets that the experience has been created by working in China. It may be a good idea to send this person on to another posting where skills learned in China can help."

Positive Aspects of Life in China

Benefit 1: Exciting Career Opportunities

Because the job scopes tend to be broader and the pace of change tends to be faster in China, many foreigners working here list exciting career opportunities as a top reason for coming to

China and for staying in China. The Community Center in Shanghai's Zhen Zeng explains, "There are so many opportunities in China; you are allowed more responsibility. So, the excitement of the job and the career growth—for the career driven, this is one reason." In fact, she says many foreign families even try to stay in China after their assignment. "A lot of them want to stay here in China. People start to really love living here."

Frederico Freire of AB InBev expresses a similar view, showing the contrast between working in China and returning home: "Here, you are like an entrepreneur. Even if you are part of the big corporation. You go back to head office, you're back to the routine."

"Here, you are like an entrepreneur. Even if you are part of the big corporation. You go back to head office, you're back to the routine."

—**Frederico Freire,** BU President, China, AB InBev

Maserati's Alberto Cavaggioni explains the sense of excitement he feels in being in the right place at the right time during his posting in China: "I have, in China today, the same feeling that people who experienced the US in the 1960s had." He explains that people who witnessed the emergence of the US onto the world stage 50 years ago had a front-row seat to experiencing the emergence of that country taking its position as a new world leader nation across industries and sectors. "Today, you can see that China can become the biggest country in the world both in terms of economic power and industrial power. It doesn't matter which sector." He adds, "This makes me very excited to be working and living in China right now."

Benefit 2: Quality Education for Children

One of the most positive aspects of living in China for foreign executives who are parents is the educational opportunities for their children. Rainer Burkle of Marriott International strongly endorses the international school system in Chinese first-tier cities, stating, "The international schools in China are probably among the best in the world."[1]

---

[1] Author's Note: International school fees in China are among the highest in the world, with tuition and related fees reaching to US$40,000 per year—a significant hardship for those foreign professionals not offered a contract including children's school fees.

Burkle says both of his sons have benefitted from their years in China. His youngest, a high-schooler still living with Burkle in Shanghai at the time of this interview, gained not just Chinese language skills but also a deep understanding of Chinese culture. Burkle says, "My young son learned Chinese with the *ayi* [nanny], which is perfect. . . . He is probably, in many ways, more Chinese than even the Chinese when it comes to negotiation, and communication, and relationships versus just to fix something. He is very adapted to the culture." Burkle is confident that his son will benefit from his experiences in China even after he leaves for university. "It will help him when he moves around in the world."

Benefit 3: Cosmopolitan Lifestyle (in Tier 1 Cities)

Another commonly voiced benefit of life in China, said the CEOs, is a generally high quality of life and a lively, urban lifestyle. Zhen Zeng lists several positive attributes which her clients appreciate. First, China is safe. Second, it is "very dynamic" in first-tier cities. She explains that developed cities such as Shanghai and Beijing offer a diverse "after-work life" that is hard to find elsewhere: "That's also one of the things that attract a lot of people to stay. There are so many options here. You can choose to be a couch potato and watch international movies sold from the street vendor. Or you can go out clubbing all night. Or you can go to really high-quality concerts or theater. A lot of leading artists come into Shanghai. And the restaurants—now we have many Michelin-starred restaurants. It's just so diverse, with so many options."

Alberto Cavaggioni agrees that dining in China's first-tier cities is at a world-class level. "They do serve amazing food in the big cities. For food, it doesn't matter which cuisine you like—you can find everything in Shanghai." He adds, "You also have a lot of online food ordering also. This makes things much easier."

In fact, given the fast pace and diversity of life in China's most international cities, Zhen Zeng says moving back to one's home country can be a disappointment, especially for younger generations. In her own case, her children, who grew up in Shanghai but are now attending college in the US, faced a degree of culture shock with the relocation. "My kids are back in the US. They all live in major cities, but they all say that the US is not so exciting anymore because they have seen what's available in Shanghai. In the US, you can only find this kind of life in the major cities."

> "My kids are back in the US. They all live in major cities, but they all say that the US is not so exciting anymore because they have seen what's available in Shanghai."
>
> —Zhen Zeng,
> Executive Director,
> Community Center,
> Shanghai

Strategies for Adapting to China

Advice 1: Positive Attitude, Exploring Mindset

Overwhelmingly, the China CEOs interviewed gave positive assessments of living in China, both for themselves and for their families—with the right attitude. European Chamber's Mats Harborn offered this typical assessment: "Living in China today is so much easier than before. But the old advice is valid: You need to be a psychologically stable person because there are still a lot of frustrations. If you're not stable, problems will surface, and you will suffer."

AB InBev's Frederico Freire echoes these comments. He says his wife and kids "enjoy China lot," but mainly because of adopting "the right mindset." He clarifies, "The first thing you need is a positive mindset because it's not easy here—the language, the way of thinking, the cultural barrier, the food." He adds that finding international food—even Brazilian food—has grown much easier now than it was when he arrived in 2010. "In my view, it is all about mindset. If you have a positive mindset, then a problem or a challenge doesn't become a hurdle. It becomes a learning process, a learning curve. With the right mindset, I think China is an amazing place to live."

Overall, he describes living in Shanghai in very positive terms. "Shanghai is a city where I feel welcome. I don't have the feeling that because you are a foreigner, you're not well

> "If you have a positive mindset, then a problem or a challenge doesn't become a hurdle. It becomes a learning process."
>
> —Frederico Freire,
> BU President, China,
> AB InBev

received. If you come here saying, 'I am missing my friends, missing the food,' then you miss a lot of things. But if you come with the mindset to explore, it's an amazing place to live." He adds that newcomers must invest time into patiently learning to understand Chinse culture. Freire says, "China is not easy: It's a different culture, a different language, a different way of thinking. Chinese have a different rationale, a different mindset. It's cultural. But if you have an exploring mindset, a learning mindset, you will be happy here."

Rainer Burkle of Marriott International has similar advice for newcomers adapting to the fast pace of life in China, both at work and after hours: "I use the term 'fast and furious' to describe China. Not just for the pace professionally, but also in your personal life—for your family, for your kids." Burkle gives this advice to incoming foreigners in order to adapt: "You have to truly embrace the different culture and the constant changes. You have to embrace all this." He adds this advice: "If you fall in love with the environment and with the people and the culture—what you see and feel and touch—then for you, China will be a great country." He adds, "I will never be Chinese, but I respect the culture and I love certain behavior patterns in China. If life is all about experiences, then China is a great part of my life, definitely."

David Sancho of Mango has this advice for newcomers: "Basically, you have to be very open minded, very respectful with the culture. We are here as guests, not to teach something to Chinese people." Most important, he says, is to maintain an "attitude of respect" for Chinese culture. Secondly, he advises embracing the speed of life and work in China as a make or break factor. "I have to say that the speed here is so amazing. If you don't fit the environment, it's better to leave." Sancho adds that, among those foreigners who do not adapt to China well, they usually know when the relocation is not working out. "When a [foreigner] doesn't belong here, they are usually the first ones saying, 'I want to go back.'"

After three years in China, Microsoft's Alain Crozier advises incoming foreign managers in this way: "You have to come with an open mind. You need to say, 'I'm here to learn. I'm not here to provide guidance.' And if you come to China with your partner, your partner must also be curious. We are here to discover, and we have to embrace this discovery and learning mindset."

Advice 2: Use the Resources and Support Systems

One piece of advice offered by Mats Harborn of the European Chamber is for newcomers to fully leverage existing communities and resources. He says simply, "You need to have your social networks." China CEOs pointed out that organizations like the Community Center Shanghai have been established specifically to help internationals to integrate into life in China.

AB InBev's Frederico Freire concurs, saying his family's fast adaptation to life in China was helped by reaching out to and joining local community groups for internationals. "Shanghai has great international schools. My kids adapted really fast to the schools. And we have this expat community which supports each other. The wives help each other with tasks like going to supermarkets—because at first, you cannot find the products you are used to. They get along very easily."

Advice 3: Be Willing to Learn and Travel

One factor which China CEOs say contributed to the adaptability of their spouses and families was the decision to use their time in China to develop and learn. Frederico Freire of AB InBev explains, "It's a matter of being open to learn. Doing all the courses you can. My wife, she speaks Chinese now. She managed her time in order to study. And my kids too. My wife started learning Chinese and took a lot of courses—from Chinese medicine to photography. You need to get your mind occupied." He adds that learning happens not only in formal study programs, but through living abroad. "Living abroad, it opens your mind in a way that you will never be the same. It transforms you, big time."

Traveling is another important way to learn, emphasized the China CEOs. Mats Harborn of the European Chamber says,

"You should always take advantage of living in China and explore the China local environment. Then travel in China extensively because there's so much to see and do in this country."

L'Oréal's top China executive, Stéphane Rinderknech, says this of his family's time in China: "It's been a fascinating, fascinating ride. Traveling really educates you about China—how much it has grown, how much the lives of people have changed, how much their lives have improved. It's very fascinating because there's not just one China. There are so many different Chinas: Harbin, Guangzhou, Chengdu, Xian, Urimuqi, Gansu Province. There's just no similarity of one to another." His advice to incoming foreigners: "You have to understand the diversity of China. It's a great life. The kids really loved it. My wife really loved it."

Microsoft's Alain Crozier advises trailing spouses, "Try to be occupied by something. It's not always easy to work; it's complex. My wife went for painting and calligraphy, and she's studying Chinese. She's really into it. But she doesn't wait for things to happen. You have to go and get it—get moving."

> *"Traveling really educates you about China—how much it has grown, how much the lives of people have changed....There are so many different Chinas: Harbin, Guangzhou, Chengdu, Xian, Urimuqi, Gansu Province. There's just no similarity of one to another."*
>
> **—Stéphane Rinderknech,** CEO, China, L'Oreal

Advice 4: Make Local Friends

The most difficult obstacle to overcome for international executives can be in making local friends. Mats Harborn of the European Chamber says, "If you don't get a social context, life becomes very difficult. There has to be a meaningful social context." AB InBev's Frederico Freire has witnessed a similar phenomenon: "We saw sometimes that some foreigners only have friends from their own nationality." He advises, "Use this opportunity to meet people from all over the world."

Alberto Cavaggioni of Maserati agrees, stating that making local friends has been his biggest challenge to integrating into Chinese life: "My only weakness has been in making friends—in the sense that the relationships which I have today are with my colleagues and with my business partners, like dealers or people that I met in my business life. So, a challenge and a test

> *"Use this opportunity to meet people from all over the world."*
>
> **—Frederico Freire,** BU President, China, AB InBev

I gave myself is to integrate a little bit more with the locals and doing maybe something that will allow me to get to know more people."

Microsoft's Alain Crozier explains the benefits of making true friendships with Chinese people: "You need to make efforts to meet Chinese people because it's important to really learn and to understand the culture. You won't learn the culture—or you'll only get 30%—if you stay in the international community. You need to go in and really learn the depths of the culture because it's quite fascinating."

"You won't learn the culture—or you'll only get 30%—if you stay in the international community."

—**Alain Crozier,**
CEO, Greater China Region, Microsoft

One of the best ways to enter into the Chinese friendships, said other CEOs, is to study in China. Mango's David Sancho, who conducted his MBA at China Europe International Business School (CEIBS) in Shanghai, graduating in 2013, explains the benefits of studying with Chinese classmates: "Studying here definitely helps you to know more people and to know more about China. Definitely, definitely. From the government relations side, to the market—everything." Sancho adds, "It's one of the reasons I have stayed in China so long. We alumni form part of a family. It's very easy for me to connect not only with my own classmates, but with anyone from CEIBS. People really open their doors and their hearts because you have all been part of this journey, which has been so important for all of them."

"Studying here definitely helps you to know more people and to know more about China."

—**David Sancho,**
CEO, East Asia & India, Mango

Coca-Cola's top executive for China, Curt Ferguson, also advises fellow foreigners to leave their social comfort zone. He says, "I would encourage the [foreign] manager, instead of doing all the things you should do—which is to join the councils and the AmChams, these organizations—I kind of forced myself to meet local friends."

But for those foreigners who lack fluent Mandarin skills, such a goal is difficult to meet. Ferguson shares his strategy for making Chinese friends outside of work, even with limited Chinese skills: "What was the secret to meet a lot of Chinese friends? Wine clubs! I'm enrolled in every single wine club there is! I get a good meal, I get good wine, and the Chinese are fantastic in knowing about wines." Through the wine-tasting events, he has also found Chinese friends who share his interest in international travel. "Chinese love a story from someplace. They all said, 'Tell me about Egypt. Where should I go? What about Morocco?'" Ferguson says making Chinese friends outside of work "gives you a whole different perspective." In fact, he recently achieved his personal goal to meet 1,000 Chinese friends: "I hit 1,060 contacts on WeChat." Ferguson says, "I don't run with them every day, but I certainly keep up with them and we have fun."

"I hit 1,060 [Chinese] contacts on WeChat."

—Curt Ferguson,
President, Greater China & Korea, Coca-Cola

Summary of Tips

1. **Positive attitude, exploring mindset**
   Relocating to China will require adaptation. Bring a positive mindset and enjoy discovering the differences.
2. **Use existing "expat" resources and support systems**
   Build your social network. Make full use of existing channels that help incoming internationals to adapt.
3. **Be willing to learn and travel**
   Be curious about China and its culture. Use your time in China to learn Mandarin and to explore this diverse and fascinating country. Spouses who are not working can also find many opportunities to volunteer, study the language, or learn about Chinese culture.
4. **Make local friends**
   Seek out opportunities to make friends with Chinese professionals who are not connected to your work. Studying together is one way to connect. Other strategies include joining clubs, sports teams or classes, or other hobbies that also interest Chinese.

Chapter 9
The Future of MNCs in China

*The good times are coming; the future is ahead of us, definitely. . . .
There are opportunities everywhere, everywhere. . . . But, foreign
companies must look at what value you bring to the market; do
your homework.*

—**Mats Harborn,** President, European Chamber of Commerce in China

*In China, thanks to the large population, even a very small niche
market can be big enough for us to make business. I am confident
that we'll find segments to chase after.*

—**Hiroshi Takahashi,** Chairman & President, China, Sony

*Every sector in China has an opportunity, simply because of the
growth of China's consumer class. There's always going to be an
upside in every category of consumer product or service. . . . The
main thing is to be focused on the needs of emerging consumers,
then being able to respond quickly to the very intense local competitive environment.*

—**Jonathan Woetzel,** Senior Partner, McKinsey & Company

INSIDE CHAPTER 9

China's Economic Outlook

**The Changing Role of International Companies
in China**

Predicting the future of China is a tricky task. As we printed the first edition of *China CEO* in 2006, it was impossible to foresee the changes which have created the China which exists as we finalize *China CEO II* in 2020. No one could have guessed the phenomenal changes brought about by digitization, pummeling China into position as a world leader in fin-tech and placing Chinese consumers as the world's most linked-in, always-on, e-commerce-using society. No one could have predicted that domestic tech players would zoom ahead, taking advantage of the nation's alternative digital ecosystems to create some of the world's largest and most comprehensive e-commerce and social media platforms, then expand globally. Nor could we have foreseen that the Chinese entrepreneurs founding these companies would rise to national hero status, inspiring an entire generation of young Chinese. And lastly, no one could have predicted the stark generational differences that would arise as the nation's millennials and post-millennials came of working age, bringing new values into the workplace and turning the traditional Chinese dream on its head.

These changes have been particularly disruptive for MNCs operating in China. As the comments from China CEOs in the preceding chapters have shown, the position of foreign companies here has been deeply shaken over the past 15 or so years. Many foreign companies have lost their advantage in terms of offering superior technology, international best practices, and a strong brand image. In short, domestic competitors have gained ground across all three fronts while keeping prices lower. Couple these societal changes with the Chinese central government's Made in China 2025 initiative, which aims to solidify the nation's position as a global leader in high tech industries (see "Mini-Case: Made in China 2025 Initiative" later in this chapter),[1] and the competitive arena in China becomes extremely challenging for many foreign companies.

---

[1] Institute for Security and Development Policy. "Made in China 2025" Backgrounder, June 2018. www.isde.eu.

Given all of these factors, an underlying question begs to be asked: Just what is the role for multinational companies in China going forward? How can MNCs prepare to compete in the China of tomorrow? This is the focus of the final chapter.

China's Economic Outlook

As a starting point: What is the outlook for China's expected economic development over the medium and long term? In fact, business confidence survey results show that both MNCs and Chinese companies are less optimistic now than they were in years past. One of the largest such annual surveys, CEIBS's *China Business Survey* (collecting more than 1,000 responses) for 2019 shows that the outlook from both categories of companies became less rosy in 2019, but was still generally cautiously optimistic. Asked "How confident are you that your operations in China will be successful in the next five years?" foreign companies gave an average rating of 6.6 out of 10 (with 10 being "extremely optimistic")—a drop from 6.8 in 2018 and 7.7 in 2011.[2] Meanwhile, Chinese companies polled gave a rating of 6.5, a drop from 7.2 in 2018 and 7.0 in 2011.[3]

Jonathan Woetzel, McKinsey's & Company senior partner, gives his expert take on the near-term future of China's economic development in this way: "Napoleon said, 'When China wakes, it will shake the world.' I think we are in for a little bit more of world-shaking, some more volatility all around." During this period of China disrupting the economic world order, foreign companies operating in China will naturally feel the upheaval, he says. Woetzel points out that, when purchasing power parity (PPP) is factored in, China overtook the US as the world's largest economy in 2014, while without PPP, China is expected by some analysts (including HSBC) to surpass the US as the world's number one economy by 2030.

"Napoleon said, 'When China wakes, it will shake the world.' I think we are in for a little bit more of world-shaking, some more volatility all around."

—**Jonathan Woetzel,** Senior Partner, McKinsey & Company

---

[2] CEIBS. *China Business Survey*, 2019.
[3] CEIBS. *China Business Survey*, 2019.

What are the implications for MNCs of China's continued economic rise? Woetzel advises foreign companies to take a realistic view: "All of a sudden, the world's second-largest economy is becoming the first-largest economy. But at the same time, China is very early in its development. China does not have the consumption or infrastructure or technology base of the United States or Western Europe." Catching up to the West, in the above-mentioned aspects, he predicts, "is going to take quite a few decades . . . assuming things go well," predicts Woetzel.

"All of a sudden, the world's second-largest economy is becoming the first-largest economy. But at the same time, China is very early in its development."

—Jonathan Woetzel, Senior Partner, McKinsey & Company

Woetzel's hope for China's mid-term economic development is that the nation "stays the course and continues with economic reform as its guiding principle." If so, he expects China to rise into position as "a great contributor to the global economy, creating many great companies, and creating many great opportunities for companies in China." He warns, however, that the short-term transition period will inevitably also include "some mistakes along the way."

Other experts and China CEOs also voiced general optimism regarding the outlook for China's economic growth and the role of MNCs in that growth. China remains a "safe bet," in the view of Kenneth Yu, former China CEO of 3M. He explains, "The Chinese economy is growing way beyond the point of no return. It cannot go back. That's a given. Now, as the GDP base becomes bigger, it would be naive to expect that the country can keep on growing at 6 or 7%—it just won't happen." Yu is confident that China's growth trajectory, while slowing, will continue to rise: "Depending on which prediction you look at, it's only a matter of years before the Chinese economy—even at current prices—will catch up with that of the US. And quite frankly, I don't think that's a big deal. The US has less than 400 million people; China has 1.4 billion—over three times the population—and the track record of building the economy at this breakneck rate. So, what is the big surprise? It should happen. I wouldn't worry about it."

"The Chinese economy is growing way beyond the point of no return. It cannot go back. That's a given....Depending on which prediction you look at, it's only a matter of years before the Chinese economy—even at current prices—will catch up with that of the US."

—Kenneth Yu, advisor, CCF & MTS

Kamal Dhuper, NIIT's top executive for China, is also cautiously optimistic on China's future economic development: "Everyone is rightly saying China's economy will slow down. With such a big base, you can't continue to grow at 8 or 9%. But even the forecasts the Chinese government has shared—to grow at 6 or 6.5% for the next few years—is very, very good growth on a huge base." However, Dhuper does expect a change in the type of growth China will experience: "As we all know, China is moving toward importing more and developing more consumption-driven growth." He adds that the new forms of growth offer many viable opportunities for MNCs: "I have been here for almost 15 years, and I've seen so much development happening in front of my eyes. Whether it's buildings or other infrastructure, it's amazing, amazing. I've not seen that kind of development so fast in any other country."

At ABB, Chunyuan Gu, the company's top China executive, says periods of slow economic growth-rate actually can spur some industries (including his) upward. "For us, [China's recent economic slowdown] is actually very positive because China needs to improve its productivity and we offer good automation solutions. When the economy gets tough, governments tend to release infrastructure projects—such as transmission lines, subways. They need more electrification products—so for us, it's not too bad. The main concern is exports, the external environment. For those focused-on exports, they need to watch out."

Gu also reminds us that, while China's overall growth-rate is slowing and is susceptible to ups and downs caused by fluctuating relations with key trading partners, the "pie has been getting bigger." One factor boosting the economy is the government's focus on developing the domestic services sector and on keeping unemployment rates low. Gu says, "If they can create enough jobs, they don't mind the growth-rate. The pressure is creating new jobs."

At IKEA, China CEO Freda Zhang says her optimism on China is sometimes viewed by global executives as nationalistic. "There are different views on China. Some [colleagues] say, 'Oh, you're Chinese. You believe this about yourself.'" She emphasizes, however, that confidence in China's future is strong not only within China but throughout Asia. Through her frequent business travels across Asia Pacific, and because her husband is Taiwanese, Zhang has gained insight into the high view of China held by neighboring geographies. One telling trend that illustrates the high degree of confidence in China is the shift toward more parents across the region encouraging their children to study in mainland China. "Nowadays I see my friends from surrounding places—especially Taiwanese—starting to even send their children to China for education. The reason is not because Chinese education is so good; it's because of the need to get used to the competition, the network, and to let the kids adapt to the future economic game." She adds that her husband's generation of Taiwanese sought to send their children to Japan and the US for an education because "they thought the world belonged to these two countries." Today, she says, the focus has shifted to China.

Another factor strengthening China's economy, Zhang says, is the growing pool of successful Chinese companies, from tech giants Alibaba and Tencent to Baidu, Jingdong, and Huawei to runaway startups such as DJI, Sensetime, and ByteDance. She continues, "The reason they will influence the world is because of the spirit. Because of the Chinese entrepreneurs, we see a lot of intelligent people with super strong spirit. That is important for any economy to grow. . . . Many years ago, it was the US dream. Now it is very much about the China dream."

For Chen Yudong, Bosch's China CEO, confidence in China's continued economic development is tied to the culture and strong values of the nation. "No matter what, China will grow. For Chinese people, there is an underlying motivation in the society to move up. This pressure comes from the family. Everyone wants to do better in society because they want to give face to their parents, their family. The Chinese people's drive for improvement is much stronger than in other countries. So, that's why nobody can stop the motivation of Chinese people to improve themselves." Chen says the traditionally high value placed on education in Chinese culture is another factor fueling the nation's drive to improve. "The reason education is so important to Chinese people is that they believe education will bring a bright future. Education will help you perform better later on, in society. . . . That's why China will grow, in my opinion, long-term." Chen believes that, while China's economy may slow in the near term, it will continue to show positive growth.

At Philips, Andy Ho, the company's China head, also expresses optimism concerning China's future economic growth: "For sure, China will be more and more important in the world

"The Chinese people's drive for improvement is much stronger than in other countries. So, that's why nobody can stop the motivation of Chinese people to improve themselves."

—Chen Yudong,
President, China, Bosch

THE FUTURE OF MNCs IN CHINA 267

simply because of the transformation now underway: local enterprises popping up, local talent educated with degrees from the best universities in the world—aggressive, mobile. China will be more and more competitive."

But what about the role of MNCs in tomorrow's China?

The Changing Role of International Companies in China

McKinsey's Jonathan Woetzel expresses a representative view when he offers this advice to MNCs operating in China: "Every sector in China has an opportunity simply because of the growth of China's consumer class. There's always going to be an upside in every category of consumer product or service. There's always new growth—even in categories like milk or beer where Chinese brands hold the majority share." For MNCs, he adds that there is "no shortage of opportunities" but advises MNCs serving the China market to focus on response time to the fast-evolving needs of domestic consumers. "The main thing is to be focused on the needs of emerging consumers, then being able to respond quickly to the very intense local competitive environment."

Woetzel is not put off by such developments as bilateral trade disputes or the potential for a Chinese government backlash against MNCs due to the protectionist actions of some nations against Chinese companies. He says, "I try not to take my cues from newspapers." Looking at the world market, he believes MNCs can continue taking advantage of "what is clearly a massive demand-side shock" in the China market. He explains, "You have trillions and trillions of dollars of demand showing up. If you can respond effectively, it could make a good result for your company and for your country. Most of the rest of the world is looking at China and saying, 'Can we participate in this tremendous market you have created? We helped to create it and now we'd like to be an even bigger part of it going forward.'"

"You have trillions and trillions of dollars of demand showing up. If you can respond effectively, it could make a good result for your company and for your country."

—Jonathan Woetzel, Senior Partner, McKinsey & Company

He adds that China now faces a series of critical challenges. "China has to defend intellectual property, China has to improve the environment, and China must guarantee public safety and help with public health." In grappling with these difficult issues, he encourages MNCs operating here to present themselves as collaborative partners helping the government to develop solutions. "Along the way, it's quite possible that some mistakes will be made, and some misunderstandings will occur. That's normal. What's important is that we continue the dialogue. That we realize what happened and then come up with better solutions."

Asked for his input on whether the future looks dark or bright for Western companies in China, European Chamber of Commerce in China President Mats Harborn also remains positive. "I tell them the good times are coming; the future is ahead of us, definitely. . . . There are opportunities everywhere, everywhere . . . But foreign companies must look at what value you bring to the market, do your homework." Most important, he says, "If you decide to invest in China, never make an investment decision based on where you get the best incentives from local governments. If that is your main criteria for making decisions, you will not make an optimal decision."

China CEO for Sony, Hiroshi Takahashi, explains the continued optimism among MNCs is related to China's continued strong economic growth-rates relative to the rest of the world. He says, "A 6% annual economic growth-rate [like China's] is a combination of higher numbers and lower numbers by sector. So, there will always be customer segments in the market who desire to spend money, to improve their lives, who seek a high quality of life. In China, thanks to the large population, even a very small niche market can be big enough for us to make business. I am confident that we'll find segments to chase after." He adds, "Of course, it depends on how well we can adapt our products to Chinese customer tastes."

"There will always be customer segments in the [China] market who desire to spend money, to improve their lives, who seek a high quality of life."

—Hiroshi Takahashi,
Chairman & President,
China, Sony

Echoing those thoughts, Alberto Cavaggioni, Maserati's China CEO, says China's consumer market will remain important for his company, simply based on scale. "China will be the most sizeable consumer market, and largest industrial market, in the world." His car brand is particularly encouraged by the young generation. "China has 450 million millennials—by far the highest number of millennials in the world—and there are 8 million university graduates per year in China. That's a sizeable number of young people coming into the market. Think of the potential of this." Another shift bringing potential to the China market, he says, is the continued development of China's under-developed regions—in the west, north west, south, and southwest. Cavaggioni also cites China's advancements toward reducing poverty as positive signs: "China has lifted 700 million people out of poverty. 700 million! No other country has gotten near to that." Today, the Chinese central government's promotion of creating a "moderately wealthy society," mentioned as a goal of the 13th Five-Year Plan (2016–2020) is also bringing high potential to foreign companies in that every Chinese family will aspire to acquire the items fitting for a moderately wealthy family. Cavaggioni says, "The consumer market, just by itself, is going to be very significant."

"China has 450 million millennials—by far the highest number of millennials in the world....Think of the potential of this."

—Alberto Cavaggioni,
Managing Director, China, Maserati

"China has lifted 700 million people out of poverty. 700 million! No other country has gotten near to that."

—Alberto Cavaggioni,
Managing Director, China, Maserati

MINI-CASE

Made in China 2025 Initiative

One of the survival strategies expressed to us by China CEOs is to keep well informed on changes in the policies, initiatives, and targets of the Chinese government. One much-discussed government initiative now making waves is Made in China 2025 (MIC2025) which directly addresses foreign companies operating domestically. The policy was introduced by Prime Minister Li Keqiang in 2015 but came back into prominence in 2018 following the launch of the US-China trade war. The goal of the campaign is to build China's position as a world leader in emerging tech fields such as new energy vehicles and robotics. The policy is widely seen by analysts as superseding the 2006 Strategic Emerging Industries initiative (although the SEI Catalogue continues to be used to identify those industries now favored by the Chinese government). In contrast, MIC2025 is seen as broader in focus and seeks a more ambitious goal: to end the nation's reliance on international technology by developing domestic capabilities in smart manufacturing, innovation, and product quality across a wide spectrum of industries. The Chinese government has announced the following goals for supplying the domestic market via local sources by 2025: new energy vehicles (80%), new and renewable energy equipment (80%), industrial robots (70%), high performance medical devices (70%), mobile phone chips (40%), and wide-body aircraft (10%).[4]

---

[4] Institute for Security and Development Policy. http://isdp.eu/content/uploads/2018/06/Made-in-China-Backgrounder.pdf/.

About the Authors

Juan Antonio Fernandez is Professor of Management, Associate Dean, and Director of MBA Programme China Europe International Business School (CEIBS), which ranks fifth worldwide among MBA programs on the *Financial Times* index of 2019. Prior to joining CEIBS, he was a professor at the School of International Business (ESCI) in Barcelona, Spain. He has taught at the Korean Development Institute (Korea), Asian Pacific University (Japan), IESE (Spain), John Cabot University (Italy), and EADA (Spain).

He has coauthored six books, including *China CEO*, *China Entrepreneur*, *China CEO: A Case Guide for Business Leaders in China*, *America Latina en China*, and *China's State-Owned Enterprise Reforms*, and has given presentations about his Chinese research in the UK, India, Japan, South Korea, France, Italy, Chile, Peru, Mexico, Mongolia, Ghana, Zambia, and Spain.

Juan received his PhD and MBA from IESE, Spain. He received a diploma in economics from the Economic Institute, University of Colorado, US, and a Master of Liberal Arts (ALM) degree in psychology from Harvard University and has been a Fellow of the Kennedy School, Harvard University.

* * *

Laurie Ann Underwood is a Senior Associate Professor of Management (adjunct) with the Xi'an Jiaotong–Liverpool University's International Business School Suzhou and a senior consultant with Sino Associates. Her current areas of research, consulting, and teaching expertise include intercultural business communications, corporate communications, relationship marketing, and technology-assisted communications.

She worked as a journalist covering business, politics, and social issues in Greater China and Taiwan for 11 years before shifting to corporate communications and consulting. She has given numerous talks on doing business in China to business associations in the US, China, and Southeast Asia and has co-authored three books, including *China Entrepreneur* and the first volume of *China CEO*.

A native of Alaska, US, Laurie is proud to have raised her two children in Taipei and Shanghai and is grateful to continue her adventure, together with her partner, in exciting and ever-changing China. She holds an MBA and CMO Certificate from CEIBS and a DBA from the Grenoble Ecole de Management.